12

HUMAN ERROR

CARY WOLFE, SERIES EDITOR

(continued on page 319)

HUMAN ERROR
Species-Being and
Media Machines

Dominic Pettman

posthumanities 14

University of Minnesota Press
Minneapolis
London

Parts of chapter 1 appeared previously as "Bear Life: Tracing an Opening in Werner Herzog's *Grizzly Man*," in *Mind the Screen: Media Concepts According to Thomas Elsaesser,* ed. Jaap Kooijman, Patricia Pisters, and Wanda Strauven, 153–65 (Amsterdam: Amsterdam University Press, 2008), and "*Grizzly Man:* Werner Herzog's Anthropological Machine," *Theory and Event* 12, no. 2 (2009). Chapter 3 first appeared in "After the Beep: Answering Machines and Creaturely Life," *boundary 2* 37, no. 2 (Summer 2010): 133–53.

Published by the University of Minnesota Press
111 Third Avenue South, Suite 290
Minneapolis, MN 55401–2520
http://www.upress.umn.edu

Library of Congress Cataloging-in-Publication Data

Pettman, Dominic.
   Human error : species-being and media machines / Dominic Pettman.
   p. cm. — (Posthumanities ; v. 14)
   Includes bibliographical references (p.) and index.
   ISBN 978-0-8166-7298-1 (hc : alk. paper) — ISBN 978-0-8166-7299-8 (pb : alk. paper)
1. Philosophical anthropology. 2. Animals (Philosophy). 3. Technology—Philosophy. I. Title.
   BD450.P467 2011
   128—dc22
                    2010032723

Printed in the United States of America on acid-free paper

The University of Minnesota is an equal-opportunity educator and employer.

17 16 15 14 13 12 11   10 9 8 7 6 5 4 3 2 1

For Merritt. The most marvelous of creatures.

... the human being, this wonderful, terrible and yet
miraculous entity of atomic being, of language, of
expression, of perception and imperception, of dull
drowsing, of calculations in sesterces, of desires, of
enigmas, this creature indivisible yet divided into
an infinite number of individual parts, individual
abilities, individual spheres, divided into organs and
living-zones, into substances, into atoms, multiplied
over and over again; all this multiplicity of being, this
maze of human particles, not even well composed,
this creaturely thicket, as earthly in its reality as earth's
stony ribs, earthly as death's skeleton, this underbrush
of bodies, limbs, eyes, and voices, this thicket of the
half-created and the unfinished which issues from
chance lust and is forever sprouting out, one from the
other, indiscriminately coupled in constantly renewed
lust, carelessly commingled, copulated, interwoven,
ramified, continuing to branch out and renew itself
while constantly withering, so that what was withered,
dried-up and faded might fall back to the earth.
—Hermann Broch, *The Death of Virgil*

The humans are dead.
—*The Flight of the Conchords*

Contents

Acknowledgments

Sometimes it takes a village. To come to fruition, however, this book took something closer to a mid-size metropolis. Paul Bové, Patricia Pisters, Wanda Strauven, and Jaap Kooijman supported earlier versions of chapters, for which I am exceedingly grateful. Vigilant readers of the work in progress, as well as influential interlocutors on related topics, include Rey Chow, Jodi Dean, Thomas Elsaesser, Alexander Galloway, Wlad Godzich, Pierre Grosjean, Jeffrey Kastner, Deborah Levitt, Cynthia Lugo, Sylvère Lotringer, Edward Maloney, Robin Mookerjee, David Odell, Hugh Raffles, Eugene Thacker, and McKenzie Wark. A special thank-you goes to Steven Shaviro for his invaluable parsing of the entire project. Carla Freccero, Aras Özgün, Ahmet Gürata, Andreas Treske, and Ben Peters all gave me the opportunity to explore some of my semiformed notions in the ideal conditions of consummate hospitality and attentive critical engagement. My gratitude also goes to Sumita Chakravarty and Jonathan Veitch for arranging a full-year sabbatical, without which I would no doubt still be tinkering with the opening paragraphs. Kali Handelman deserves particular mention for her research assistance, her constant stream of fascinating links, and her default role as cultural translator–navigator for what Bernard Stiegler simply calls *les jeunes*. For their exceptional (inter)-collegial and moral support, I'd like to thank Emily Apter, Simon During, Laura Frost, Peter Haratonik, Noah Isenberg, Jim Miller, and Silvia Vega-Llona.

Ultimately, this book would not be what it is without the generous support and sanguine feedback of Cary Wolfe, Douglas Armato, and the excellent staff at the University of Minnesota Press. Finally, my family is a constant source of intellectual and emotional nourishment, so a special and enduring thank-you goes to Jindy, Tasha, Mike, Chris, Kerrin, David, Jen, Ralph, and Setsuko.

Introduction

The Human Element

Wherever life thrives, trouble soon follows.
—BBC's *Planet Earth*

Where better to rediscover our sense of species-being than on the Discovery Channel? This staple of basic cable television in the United States has recently become a cultural magnet for explicit explorations of what it means to be a human, at a time when new technologies are making such a sovereign category seem increasingly arbitrary and precarious. One television event in particular stands out as worthy of our attention, for it betrays a general anxiety about not only our role in an increasingly automated and algorithmic world but our very existential mandate. For while the historical transition from sacred to secular left *Homo sapiens* on top of the great chain of sublunary beings, those new machines meshing with our thoughts, bodies, and habits are obliging us to see the world less as a Darwinian pecking order and more as a cybernetic web of distributed dependencies.

The symptomatic event to consider is the U.S. debut of the celebrated BBC series *Planet Earth*. This program is indeed a quantum leap in our visual experience of "nature" in all its complex, fragile, and ingenious glory. Filmed over several years with an army of high-definition cameras, *Planet Earth* is both beautiful and melancholy: like the portrait a family commissions when it knows that one of its members has a terminal illness. In this case, however, the whole family

1

is facing extinction due to the reckless behavior of its formerly most promising child. Much of the popular fascination with this series, no doubt, arose from a genuine interest in the "otherness" embodied by the exotic creatures that we simply do not encounter in twenty-first-century urban existence: sharks, jellyfish, condors, chimps, giraffes, and so on.[1] However, two different advertising campaigns, aired during the breaks, suggest that something else was also at play, namely, the "narcissus trance" that Marshall McLuhan insisted accompanies the introduction of all new technologies.

These two campaigns were authorized by Dow Chemical and Cisco Systems, valorizing the "human element" and the "human network," respectively. Both employ the kind of visual rhetoric associated with what can be called the corporate sublime: variable-speed vignettes weaving the micro and the macro in such a way as to suggest profound global connections between people of all colors and creeds. The emphasis is not on the conflicts that can arise from difference but on that aspect we all presumably share: an intangible human essence. This essence may be difficult to define, yet it can be evoked or gestured toward through the reified poetry of television commercials: representations of celebrations, smiling, exercising, dancing, performing, conversing, commuting, and computing.[2] These ads are prime examples of that ideological primal scene described by Louis Althusser known as interpellation, only in this case, it is not a policeman hailing an individual into a sociopolitically enmeshed subjectivity but rather a siren song designed to make the entire human population turn its hydra-head collectively. The interpellation is not a commanding tone ("Hey, you, halt!") but a seductive and inspiring one ("Hey, you. Yes, *you*. Come here."). These campaigns discursively create (or at the very least, assume) an abstract "we" of all people. They are thus both the cause and the effect of our ability even to conceive of an "our" in the first place. And they do this in a similar manner to the waking dream work of "narrating the nation," only this time on a planetary scale. *Humanity* thus becomes the ultimate imagined community, erected on the permanent building site of many previous attempts to engineer the same, all toward different ends, but according to the same species-based notions of progress and purpose.

In the case of Dow, the human element is inserted into the same periodic table that has been so profitable for them. The adult male voice-over reassuringly coos:

For each of us there's a moment of discovery. We turn a page. We raise a hand. And just then in a flash of a synapse, we learn that life is elemental. And this knowledge changes everything. We look around and see the grandness of the scheme. Sodium bonding with chlorine. Carbon bonding with oxygen. Hydrogen bonding with oxygen. We see all things connected. We see life unfolded. And in the dazzling brilliance of this knowledge we may overlook the element not listed on the chart. Its importance so obvious—its presence is simply understood. The missing element is the human element. And when we add it to the equation, the chemistry changes. Every reaction is different. Potassium looks to bond with potential. Metals behave with hardened resolve. And hydrogen and oxygen form desire. The human element is the element of change. It gives us our footing to stand fearlessly and face the future. It is a way of seeing. It gives us a way of touching issues, ambitions, lives. The human element. Nothing is more fundamental. Nothing more elemental.

I quote the entire commercial because it provides a succinct synopsis of the contemporary search for, and understanding of, the elusive X-factor that resides somewhere in our material and spiritual makeup. As the voice of a global corporation with a less than exemplary environmental record, this narrative is a cut-and-dry case of so-called greenwashing: the cynical commercial use of environmentally friendly rhetoric to camouflage continuing toxic policies (reinforced by pristine *National Geographic*–style landscapes). And it seeks to achieve this goal by way of self-contradictory, self-congratulatory pandering to the species that buys its products. All at once, the human represents change, unpredictability, the overlooked, the obvious, the understood, firm footing, and fundament.

The grammatically challenged copy on Dow's Web site notes that "the Human Element advertising creative was developed featuring real people rather than professional actors and includes dramatic environmental and human imagery (a blacksmith in Mexico, children at an orphanage in Namibia, an artist at his studio in Prague) gathered on location on four continents." For Dow's vice president of global communications and reputation, "this is more than an ad campaign to our company. It is a statement to the world and, more importantly, to ourselves about the future direction of our business. It will be our calling card to people around the world who care about the future relationship between businesses, society and the environment. It reflects our intention as a company to prioritize the things we do to advance innovation and focus the people and resources of Dow on solving human problems."[3]

For its part, Cisco Systems takes a slightly different route, highlighting its own networking technologies as civilization's nervous system, encouraging citizen–consumers to feel connected and empowered through its fiber optic infrastructure.[4] Another voice-over, this time by a young girl, states chirpily:

> Welcome to a brand new day! A new way of getting things done. Welcome to a place where maps are rewritten and remote villages are included. A place where body language is business language. Where people subscribe to people not magazines. And the team you follow, now follows you. Welcome to a place where books rewrite themselves. Where you can drag and drop people wherever they want to go. And your phone doubles as a train ticket, plane ticket or lift ticket. Welcome to a place where a wedding is captured and recaptured again and again. Where home video is experienced everywhere at once. Where a library travels across the world. Where businesses are born, countries are transformed. And we're more powerful together than we ever could be apart. Welcome to the human network.[5]

In this case, the human is not an isolated atomic principle but is rather manifested in its collectivity and connection. The human node only counts by virtue of the people to whom it subscribes (presumably a reference to blogs or social networking streams). Indeed, it is possible to detect a sinister subtext to all this relentless, vectorized motion. Who, for example, could truly relish "a place where body language is business language"?—a stark admission of the Benjaminian belief that authentic human gestures have been eradicated through the reifications of capitalism.[6] Similarly, the prospect of being "dragged and dropped" from place to place does not appeal, at least, to *this* consumer (although, admittedly, it is an accurate description of air travel these days). Likewise, the eternal-return wedding could also have its ominous side, "captured and recaptured" over and over, until the moment itself has been rubbed smooth of all mnemonic traction. "If Descartes lived today," notes the official Cisco blog, "and wrote about Mobility and the Human network, he might say: 'I am there, connected, even when I move, therefore I am.'"[7]

As with the Dow commercials, the corporate sublime is deployed to suggest that "we" can create a new Babel—successful this time because of our advanced communication technologies—along the lines of McLuhan's global village. Of course, cultural difference is reduced to stereotypes and clichés, lacquered over by the assumed universal desire to experience seamless business transactions, travel arrangements, entertainment, and/or sporting triumphs. Indeed, these campaigns seem to be selling us (on) ourselves, as if our species has reached the point where it needs venture capitalist cheerleaders to sponsor our ontological status as well as to counter a growing insecurity concerning its significance.[8] (As Geert Lovink notes, "*Dasein* is design.")[9]

Such an emphasis on the importance of humanity punctuating *Planet Earth,* a television event allegedly dedicated to our underrepresented animal cotenants, suggests a confusion or split sensibility about our future as the assumed überspecies of the planet. After all, Norbert Wiener delivered a devastating blow when he stated in 1950 that humans, animals, and machines can all be modeled and understood in the same manner and according to the same principles (the regulation of energy and information). "To me, personally," Wiener wrote, "the fact that the signal . . . has gone through a machine rather than through a person is irrelevant and does not in any case greatly change my relation to the signal. Thus the theory of control in engineering, whether human or animal or mechanical, is a chapter in the theory of messages" (Wiener 1988, 16–17).

Throughout this book, I will be referring to the "cybernetic triangle" to denote the unholy trinity of human, animal, and machine, including the various ways in which they have been figured, and reconfigured, conceptually over time: sometimes spliced together, other times branching off into different directions. In whatever context, the diagramming of this fundamental (yet flexible) discursive geometry will, by necessity, follow the historical habit of working with three poles or points.[10] Sometimes the triangle is conceived vertically, with humans at the top (i.e., Man) and animals and machines below (the Great Chain of Being).

Sometimes the triangle is horizontal, without an architectonic hierarchy (the Great Plain of Being). The challenge is thus being attuned to those occasions when it is expedient to maintain the distinctions embodied by the different words we have for these categories, while remaining sensitive to the situations in which these same distinctions are merely residues of obsolete (not to mention self-serving) taxonomic—and thus political—contrivances and conveniences.[11]

Wiener's understanding of cybernetics certainly qualifies as a dramatic ego bruise to the human sense of itself so that the separate points of the triangle collapse flat and indeed can be potentially considered the same abstract node. From the culturally disembodied perspective of signals, no matter the real-world context, we are dealing with a *humanimalchine.* Moreover, when viewed from this angle, the history of hominization[12] has been an ongoing waltz of repression and denial concerning the similarities between us and our nonhuman neighbors. "We are at our most insistent about boundaries," notes Adam Phillips, "when we sense their precariousness" (Bersani and Phillips 2008, 90).

And yet Wiener was not the first to make the faux pas of pointing out these affinities, so troubling to the species that considers itself the universe's favorite son. Leonardo da Vinci, for instance, saw living creatures as organic machines and machines as functioning according to the same mathematical principles as animals and humans (Mazlish 1993, 15). Indeed, as a race, we who so confidently call ourselves humans are yet to face fully the implications of that shock to the system that Bruce Mazlish calls the "fourth discontinuity": something that may better be described, for our purposes at least, as the "fourth displacement"—a violent philosophical jolt *away* from the center of things. Coming relatively close on the historical heels of Copernicus, Darwin, and Freud (the three previous ego bruises: cosmological, biological, and psychological), it is no wonder that humans today are spending billions of dollars on isolating, securing, and fortifying the increasingly elusive "human element."

But can this really be done? Is the metaphor of the chemical or atomic element misleading in its reliance on a pure and essential identifying quality?[13] Given that many of us are inoculated at birth, continue throughout our lives to take highly engineered pills, wear clothes,[14] sport spectacles, and chew our cooked, industrialized food with augmented and reinforced teeth, it is dubious at best to claim that humans can somehow return to a "natural" state, stripped of all prostheses and artifice. After all, the Paleolithic emergence of tools, which first externalized or fortified our organs and skeletal structure, itself disqualifies any neat division between the natural and the artificial.[15]

Indeed, it is the symbiotic relationship between humans, technology, and other animals that prompts the German philosopher Peter Sloterdijk (2005) to shift the traditional metaphysical question of what is the human to a more pragmatic one: where is the human?[16] In an interlinked biosphere and mediasphere, the task of locating a species that is increasingly hybrid—even parasitic—is both a challenge and an opportunity. Or rather, the opportunity is to *reject* this challenge as quixotic and instead focus on a collective attempt to retrofit our own self-understanding according to a less paranoid and fascistic logic of secured borders and pure typologies. It is to see differences in degree, where we hold fast to differences in kind. For while we like to think that the simple act of pointing can distinguish between, say, a dolphin, the camera affixed to its body, and the scientist who put it there, evolutionary overlaps between animals, machines, and humans do not allow us to use our index finger (a physical "index" of our linguistic technologies and the mental categories they enable) with any confidence.

Even before the era of genetically modified organisms, the properties assigned to each point of the cybernetic triangle were never stable. Supposedly exclusive human traits—such as reason, soul, language, empathy, or tool use—have been (against the cultural grain) attributed to animals or automatons in myth, literature, the humanities, the sciences, the social sciences, and the arts, and have now been deployed deep within the postcinematic Spectacle of digital life. "Humanity" is thus located in the eye of the beholder: a beholder who is beholden to ideas of his, her, or its own belonging—or exclusion—from this privileged set. (One need only ask the sick, the insane, the criminal, the child, the woman, the slave, the Jew, the homosexual, the primitive, the heathen, or the barbarian—among many other figures of proximous alterity—to see just how mobile the borderline between the human and its Others has been over the centuries, in many different domains.)[17]

For Giorgio Agamben, the primary motor in this autogenetic, narcissistic narrative of humanity is the "anthropological machine": an abstract apparatus comprising all those potent symbols, figures, and tropes of belonging and exclusion. In effect, the anthropological machine (henceforth simply the *anthro-machine,* for convenience) is a metaphoric instance of Maxwell's Demon, a hypothetical contraption that was designed to sort swift from slow molecules—only in this case, it sorts the human from the nonhuman, subhuman, inhuman, posthuman, and so on. For Agamben, the crucial component of the machine is the way in which its optics have been rigged (in both senses) to encourage self-reflection and nurture a sense of exceptionalism and superiority by virtue of one's proper humanness. The anthro-machine provides us with lenses and mirrors from before even our first word, compelling us to look for our own reflection, to recognize it.

In his book *Profanations,* Agamben (2007, 56–57) turns to etymology, noting that "the Latin term *species,* which means 'appearance,' 'aspect,' or 'vision,' derives from a root signifying 'to look, to see.' This root is also found in *speculum* (mirror), *spectrum* (image, ghost), *perspicuus* (transparent, clearly seen), *speciosus* (beautiful, giving itself to be seen), *specimen* (example, sign), and *spectaculum* (spectacle)." Thus, "*species* was first defined as that which makes visible and only later became the principle of classification and equivalence" (58). It is in his book *The Open: Man and Animal,* however, that Agamben (2004) gives his most thorough account of the anthro-machine, noting that Carl Linnaeus, "the father of modern taxonomy," was one of the device's most important engineers, working on both maintenance and upgrades. It was Linnaeus's ongoing, neo-Aristotelian "division of life into vegetal and relational, organic and animal, animal and human" elements that created a "mobile border" within vital humans, "and without this intimate caesura the very decision of what is human and what is not would probably not be possible" (15).

Historically, the anthro-machine fuses various incongruous or oxymoronic elements together: the soul and the body, the pulse and language, the natural and the supernatural, the terrestrial and the divine. It is a complex soldering operation that proceeds through capture and suspension. Agamben's vital task is to unhinge these rusting articulations and "ask in what way—within man—has man been separated from non-man, and the animal from the human?"[18] The public debates on so-called human rights do very little to sabotage the anthro-machine, which operates on a much more subliminal level than political policy or morality management. The United Nations and other guardians of the higher aspirations of the species assume we know what the human is, even if we can't define it with scientific certainty (a quality the human shares with pornography, ironically . . . or not).

Speaking as a "naturalist," Linnaeus concludes that he "hardly knows a single distinguishing mark which separates man from the apes, save for the fact that the latter have as empty space between their canines and their other teeth" (Agamben 2004, 24). In other words, even the inventor of the Dewey Decimal System for sentient creatures could find no "generic difference" between "us" and our evolutionary cousins. This leads to something of a paradox since the human sciences are usually credited with rationalizing and standardizing important differences and sweeping away the fanciful overlaps of more superstitious times, in which "the boundaries of man are much more uncertain and fluctuating than they will appear in the nineteenth century" (24). And so Linnaeus is obliged to class *Homo sapiens* as a "taxonomic anomaly, which assigns not a given, but rather an imperative *[know thyself]* as a specific discourse." According to Agamben, this results in a maxim: "man has no specific identity other than the *ability* to recognize himself" (26). In other words, "*man is the animal that must recognize itself as human to be human.*"

Depending on your ideological orientation, this is either earthshattering news or quite self-evident. The religious minded find the essence of our humanity in our proximity to God, the scientist in our double helix and pineal gland, the artist in our mortal coil, the philosopher in the monad's exceptional capacities, potentialities, and/or perversions (reason, language, ethics, art, technological mastery). None of these schematic caricatures, however, would go so far as Agamben does in rereading Linnaeus's legacy as a biopolitical operation that simultaneously recognizes, and then relentlessly *disavows,* the "default" at the origin of our species.[19] *Homo sapiens* "is neither a clearly defined species nor a substance; it is, rather, a machine or device for producing the recognition of the human" (Agamben 2004, 26). The human is a technospecies without qualities, according to Agamben, and the anthro-machine is designed to provide positive content to a creature that seemingly has none. Furthermore, "the anthropological machine is an optical one . . . constructed of a series of mirrors in which man, looking at himself, sees his own image always already deformed in the features of an ape" (Agamben 2004, 26–27). The underlying principle of the modern anthro-machine is that the human "resembles" man and must recognize itself in a nonman to fully identify with that resemblance.[20] This "transience and inhumanity of the human" traces a border "at once the separation and proximity—between animal and man" (Agamben 2004, 30, 59).[21]

According to this hypothesis, there are two major variations of the anthro-machine: the ancient and the modern. The first operates by humanizing the animal, whereas the latter animalizes the human.[22] Throughout this book, I shall be dealing with the postmodern version of the machine, in the sense that it has simultaneously enabled, and adapted to, the exponential extension and intensification of the Spectacle or Simulacrum of the last sixty years or so. In a case of meta-metamorphosis, this conceptual tool itself—described by Agamben but engineered by the trajectory of Western thought—mutates in the pages that follow, its soft metallic morphology shaped by the programming of the two preceding models of the anthro-machine but also pulled in new directions by the recent dominance of the digital.

In my previous book, *Love and Other Technologies* (Pettman 2006), I hijacked Agamben's notion of "whateverbeing" for my own purposes—in that case, to argue that "love is external" and thus best understood through a relinquishing of self-identification. On this occasion, I will be doing the same with the anthro-machine—appropriating it for myself as a revealing metaphor to approach the white noise of contemporary society and discover the secret coherences within it. As such, it is a metaphor that is literally crystallized in the interlocking technological exchanges that we refer to misleadingly in the singular as the Media.

I confess that in my less sophisticated moments (of which there are many), I visualize the anthro-machine as a kind of steam-punk functional sculpture, built by a mad neo-Victorian genius who has assembled a room-sized contraption of astrolabes, sextants, cogs, steam valves, keyboards, mirrors, cameras, screens, lenses, and ticker-tape printers. *Metropolis* meets *Brazil*. The reality, of course, is that the anthro-machine has no single inventor but is customized by all of us, according to the protocological limits of our conceptual inheritance.[23] Furthermore, it is diffused and distributed throughout our entire environment: from the books we read to the furniture to which we adapt to the emotions we endure or encourage. For the human, practically everything can be a mirror.

THE UNBEARABLE TRITENESS OF BEING:
FOUR PERSPECTIVES ON BEING HUMAN

> Error has made animals into men; might truth then be
> capable of making man back into an animal?
> —Friedrich Nietzsche

> But the life of a man is of no greater importance to the
> universe than that of an oyster.
> —David Hume, *Of Suicide*

The book you currently hold in your hands might not have existed
had it not been for Tom Brook, the mustachioed host of BBC World's
film review show *Talking Movies*. After repeated viewings, I became
so exasperated by his weekly reference to the "humanity" (or lack of)
purportedly displayed by whichever film he happened to be appraising
that I resolved to create a counterweight to the unthinking, undefined
abuse of our species-being, especially as a criterion against which the
worth of aesthetic objects are measured. Yet Brook hardly stands in
isolation. The expression of our *humanity* continues to be sacrosanct
for us bastard children of nineteenth-century high romanticism, religious humanism, and secular liberal humanism. Truly the human
love affair with its own abstract humanity does not show any sign of
waning. Indeed, consistent with other such relationships, perceived
threats from outside are sparking something of an umpteenth honey-
moon. In our case, the threat is technology in the form of machinic
efficiency, biological engineering, and artificial intelligence. The self-
preserving reflex that prompted the Council of Danzig to order the
death-by-strangling of the unfortunate inventor of a weaving machine
in 1597 extends into the present, although the hostility now is usually
expressed in less crude forms.

As already noted, the anthro-machine is produced by the feedback
loop between "our" objects, our environment, and ourselves. What is
more, it creates these poles in the same gesture with which it reinforces
the differences between them. Humans are thus the privileged processor
of the system. The anthro-machine is, to put it quite simply, present
everywhere a human happens to be or has been (although the explicit

force of its presence adjusts, depending on the scene).[24] Which is to say that I could pluck any random "text" out of the mediasphere and demonstrate the ways in which it both encodes and decodes messages circulating within the circuitry of the apparatus. The rationale for selection thus becomes—as with all examples and case studies—a combination of disciplinary training; serendipity; cultural bias; personal experience; research budget; elective affinity; and mysterious, stubborn attachments that only the most vigilant psychoanalyst might comprehend. In any case (and for the sake of getting this show on the road), I will rely on only four figures in this introductory section as singular distillations of the millions of voices who have profound stakes in valorizing "the human," even as they acknowledge the horrendous aspects of our species. Let us now go through them in turn.

For high-profile literary critic Harold Bloom, there is only one midwife of the human, and that is Shakespeare. This is not to say that there were not humans toiling away before the sixteenth century but rather to propose that these were not individuals in the modern sense that we consider them today, with internal, inscrutable lives, prompting conflicts of both conscience and consciousness. According to this reading, pre-Shakespearean personalities were not yet fully, authentically human, trapped as they were between the imperatives of existence and the external ideals bequeathed by religion and society (cf. the Hellenic Golden Age). The key difference comes in the emergence of a developed self-consciousness, which does not, in Bloom's account, evolve slowly over time but rather strides on to the world stage with one fell swoop of the Bard's quill.

Bloom (1998, xix) writes at the outset of his massive book, *Shakespeare: The Invention of the Human*:

> Literary character before Shakespeare is relatively unchanging; women and men are represented as aging and dying, but not as changing because their relationship to themselves, rather than to the gods or God, has changed. In Shakespeare, characters develop rather than unfold, and they develop because they reconceive themselves. Sometimes this comes about because they *overhear* themselves talking, whether to themselves or others. Self-overhearing is their royal road to individuation, and no other writer,

before or since Shakespeare, has accomplished so well the virtual miracle of creating utterly different yet self-consistent voices.

Furthermore,

> The idea of Western character, of the self as moral agent, has many sources: Homer and Plato, Aristotle and Sophocles, the Bible and St. Augustine, Dante and Kant, and all you might care to add. Personality, in our sense, is a Shakespearean invention, and is not only Shakespeare's greatest originality but also the authentic cause of his perpetual pervasiveness. Insofar as we ourselves value, and deplore our own personalities, we are the heirs of Falstaff and of Hamlet. (4)

Bloom is not timid in proclaiming several things at once: the "oceanic superiority" of the playwright, the awestruck extent of his own "Bardolatry," and the infinite effect of the plays themselves on the course of all human development. "The plays remain the outward limit of human achievement," he writes, "aesthetically, cognitively, in certain ways morally, even spiritually" (xix). One could well interject at this point and offer possible alternatives to the summit of human civilization: the Apollo moon landing, the Manhattan skyline, Chinese martial arts, or my breakfast crepes, to name only a few possibilities. But Bloom is deaf to anyone who would dare place Shakespeare anywhere other than on the transcendental apex of human endeavor.

For Bloom, Shakespeare is nothing less than "a mortal god" whose "total effect upon the world's culture is incalculable" (xxi). Moreover, his plays "will go on explaining us, in part because he invented us" (xx) (by virtue of "an excess beyond representation"). Thus the most memorable Shakespearean characters are "extraordinary instances not only of how meaning gets started, rather than repeated, but also of how new modes of consciousness come into being. . . . What Shakespeare invents are ways of representing human changes, alterations not only caused by flaws and by decay but effected by the will as well, and by the will's temporal vulnerabilities" (2).

The important point from our perspective is the ideological cargo smuggled into the discussion inside the clenched cheeks of this key protagonist: the human. And it is important despite—or rather because of—Bloom's insistence that his topic is beyond such pedantic, pejoratively political concerns.[25] The critic's unhidden agenda is thus most apparent in his confident claim that *"the representation of human character and personality remains always the supreme literary value"* (3–4; emphasis added). (Despite, we might note, the best efforts of Robbe-Grillet and friends.) Yet there are other angles available from which to view this epochal shift. For instance, John Lyons, in his book *The Invention of the Self,* looks to the medium itself rather than to the message: "The invention and spread of moveable type is probably the most important mechanical contributor to the idea of the unique self" (quoted in Deibert 1997, 98). Bloom (1998, 9–10), by contrast, believes it is possible—nay, desirable—to locate an essential, human nature, liberated from the contingent epiphenomena of social conditions. Quite simply, "Shakespeare teaches us how and what to perceive . . . [seeking] to enlarge us, not as citizens or as Christians but as consciousnesses."

Shakespeare thus offers his progeny many valuable gifts: the uncanny vitality of four-dimensional characters (6),[26] the preternatural capacity to externalize the mental workings of human inwardness (8, 5), "the inauguration of personality as we have come to recognize it" (4), and "a secular transcendence, a vision of the sublime" (13)—all reflected inside the supremely polished surface of "a mirror within a mirror" (15). Bloom thus spends the better part of 750 pages analyzing every one of the completed plays attributable to the Bard, demonstrating how the poetics embodied in the major characters melt humanity down to its essence before remolding "the representation of self in and by language" (726). As already noted, the primary device is "self-hearing": the autoreflexive process of ontological feedback, of which Hamlet is the ultimate example (which, ironically, could make the human seem increasingly machinic, at least to the observer of systems).

For Bloom (1998, 388–89), the Dane is himself both object and subject of a questioning and is thus a "perfected experiment"—"the demon-stration that meaning gets started not by repetition nor by fortunate accident nor error, but by a new transcendentalizing of the secular, an apotheosis that is also an annihilation of all the certainties of the cultural past." As both a "divided a consciousness" (387) and a "universal instance of our will-to-identity" (420), Hamlet dramatizes the enigmatic evolutionary gap between consciousness and *self*-consciousness, that is, between life and *human* life. (So whereas we may argue over whether a dog "knows" that it is hungry, few would claim that a dog *knows* that it "knows" that it is hungry.) As a consequence, figures such as Hamlet and Falstaff function in Bloom's account as something akin to highly complex Sims characters who have evolved to the degree that they become autonomous from their creator, continuing, however, to act as avatars of historical individuation (or of what Derrida might call "autoinfection" [47]).

Not surprisingly, then, Bloom answers the rhetorical question, can we conceive of ourselves without Shakespeare? with a resounding no. And in case the reader has not yet quite understood the message, he also asks, "Who besides Shakespeare can continue to inform an authentic idea of the human?" (Answer: no one!) Indeed, Bloom describes our reinvention at the hands of the playwright as "shocking" in degree. "Without mature Shakespeare," he ventures, "we would be very different, because we would think and feel and speak differently. Our ideas would be different, particularly our ideas of the human, since they were, more often than not, Shakespeare's ideas before they were ours" (Bloom 1998, 716). Bloom is aware that this is an extremely grand legacy to lay at the feet of one man, even one as enduring and celebrated as the Bard. Yet he is adamant in his conviction that the claim is not a hyperbolic indulgence. "To have invented our feelings is to have gone beyond psychologizing us," he notes. "Shakespeare made us theatrical, even if we never attend a performance" (13).[27]

All the world is a stage, on which our species-being is scripted, prompted, blocked, and performed. The "performativity" that Judith Butler sees as the sine qua non of human identity is indeed dappled by the symbolic shadow of the Globe. It emerges from a splitting of subjectivity, to be both actor and audience at the same time. One watches oneself acting, both in the sense of dissimulation and decisive behavior. But there is an unwitting cybernetic subtext to Bloom's paradigm whereby humans become most human when they reach the threshold of self-programming. What he calls "self-overhearing" is essentially an ability to reconfigure autopoieses—something that scientists working on artificial intelligence and virtual life most covet.[28] Many computer algorithms and viruses work on this principle, adapting their behavior both within one life span and from generation to generation. In other words, this ability is not necessarily the unique property of self-identified humans.

Beyond Homer, beyond Plato, beyond even the scriptures of East and West, the plays collected in the various Folia have represented, for Bloom, the blueprint for authentic humanity since the moment they were written. But can this still be the case today, in an age when lovers are more likely to exchange emoticons via text messages than compose sonnets to each other? Bloom (1998, 716) himself takes pause at this prospect to ask a similar question: "In the culture of virtual reality, partly prophesied by Aldous Huxley, and in another way by George Orwell, will Falstaff and Hamlet still seem paradigms of the human?" For the sake of his own sanity as well as the "secular salvation" of the species, he answers his own question in the affirmative, albeit not as confidently as in other sections of the book. Though the Internet will undoubtedly continue to expand and intensify, "and in time may constitute one vast computer . . . that will not quite be a culture" (718), a certain signature is still legible among the chaotic Babel. Moreover, the continuing hegemony of the English language is something that Bloom takes for granted, in contrast to demographic trends and forecasts to the contrary. But even allowing for imminent Chinese linguistic dominance of the planet, translated Shakespeare will continue to fuel the world with its universal energies. "Shakespeare is an international possession" (717).

Bloom is correct insofar as human nature is not fixed, not an ontological given. But he tries to compensate for this contingency by presenting it as something that appears on the scene, almost miraculously. Shakespeare plays the same role as the big bang in this logocentric etiology. "Before Hamlet taught us how *not* to have faith either in language or ourselves," writes Bloom (1998, 715), "being human was much simpler for us but also rather less interesting." So though there is not a timeless essence to humanity, there is a universal property or character, after a certain historical point. (Hence the claim that Hamlet is "a universal figure and not a picnic of selves.") The critic's hypothesis thus rests on Shakespeare's unprecedented ability to put a linear spin on human endeavor, which was previously considered cyclical. (Indeed, Shakespeare precedes Vico, one of the great inaugurators of "progress.") The

Bard's greatest invention, according to Bloom, is "the inner self that is not only ever-changing but also ever-augmenting" (741).[29] This vision is very different to Foucault's famous depiction of "Man" as a figure drawn in the sand, threatened by the incoming waves of history.[30] For while both date the birth of modern subjectivity to the same period (circa seventeenth century) and general location (Western Europe), Bloom sees Shakespeare's invention as eternal; Foucault, in contrast, sees him as fleeting.

Which is why, at the very end of his massive tome, Bloom (1998, 733) suggests that it is the quotidian and the terrestrial—the secular, in other words—that makes us most human:

> When we consider the human, we think first of parents and children, brothers and sisters, husbands and wives. We do not think of these relationships in terms of Homer and of Athenian tragedy, or even of the Hebrew Bible, because the gods and God are not primarily involved. Rather, we think of families as being alone with one another, whatever the social contexts, and that is to think in Shakespearean terms.

We are creatures of Shakespeare's creativity (both terms sharing the same etymological root).

In Bloom's (1998, 745) final analysis, "when we are wholly human, and know ourselves, we become most like either Hamlet or Falstaff." For his detested purveyors of "cultural studies"—of which, I suppose, I am one—this is a remarkably reductionist view of what it means to be human. For a start, the only two options are gendered as masculine and white. Moreover, the two modes on offer are radical, existential angst and the vainglorious consolations of the wise fool. I do not disagree with Bloom that Shakespeare had an immeasurable impact on our own identity and, by extension, our identity crises. He was without question one of the major engineers of the anthro-machine. However, the question must surely be asked whose identity is at issue. Certainly it is not the thousands of cultures and languages that have been eradicated since his plays were first performed, and the world-views that died with them. The human was not invented by one man but rather by a seemingly endless ad hoc committee (which probably explains a lot about humanity). To reduce the human to the bluster of two Shakespearean characters, no matter how sophisticated, is to ignore the entire anthropological record.

To put it a little differently, Bloom underestimates the power of reality TV and video games. Shakespeare does indeed have an incredible half-life; however, Bloom is preaching not only to the converted but also to the cloistered. Any resemblance that Generations X, Y, and Z might have to the Prince of Denmark is now so diluted that we would need sensitive scientific instruments to detect its traces. So Bloom has mistaken the justifiable enthusiasm of his own literate biography for absolute, universal, immediate significance. Then again, if Shakespeare did not exist, we would have to invent him. For humanity requires an impressively ornate mirror in which to contemplate itself, to judge the effects of time, and to reassure itself of its enduring beauty. (Who, but humanity, is the fairest of them all?) Of course, we should not blame Shakespeare for people like Tom Brook, who cannot see the world beyond their own noses and reflections. But we can blame, or at least point out the error, of people, such as Bloom, who have such an arch-humanist notion of the trickle-down effect of capital-C Culture. This cosmology responds to the challenge of nihilism by putting Man back in the center of things, as the Author of his own fate. This is a reassuring delusion. Shakespeare has merely rushed in to fill the vacuum left by the hasty departure of God. And as we shall soon see, this anthropocentric restoration frames humanity as the Audience so that the entire universe, in its infinite vastness and mystery, is tamed through our specular perspective on it.

Journalist and cultural commentator Michael Frayn may not be of the same stature as Bloom, but he writes books of similar physical heft. He also uses the royal "we" when discussing humanity, a sure sign that he is a direct descendent of Matthew Arnold, John Dewey, and the Humanist Manifesto.[31] From the title of his recent book, *The Human Touch: Our Part in the Creation of a Universe* (Frayn 2006), the reader already gets the sense that this is not a humbling exercise in self-effacing Zen minimalism. In fact, what we are presented with is a sometimes ingratiating, other times grating, pop-philosophical defense of the essential cosmic relevance of our species-being. Frayn seeks nothing less than to describe the profound consequence of the human condition *beyond ourselves,* to demonstrate that we are not irrelevant bystanders but significant eyewitnesses to the universe. As such, it is what Michelangelo's *Creation of Adam* would have looked like had it been a best-selling polemic on the history of science, art, and culture.

Frayn (2006, 411–12) cites the rendering of perspective in painting as "one of the most remarkable inventions of the Renaissance." And though he does not fetishize any single individual to the extent that Bloom does, the fifteenth-century painters Brunelleschi and Alberti play a similar role to Shakespeare in the book's narrative, returning Man to his rightful place at the head of the captain's table, after Copernicus and Galileo so rudely bumped Him to far-flung corners. We are masters of what we survey because the world prostrates itself visibly in front of us in measurable vectors, leading to a vanishing point in the distance. For the first time, representation truly resembles reality, as eye and ego happily align.

Leaping ahead several centuries, Frayn connects the invention of perspective to the uncanny power of the observer granted in popular accounts of quantum theory. Despite figures of such intimidating stature as Feynman, Popper, and Priogine, all working to eliminate "the anthropocentric features implicit in the traditional formulation of quantum theory" (Frayn 2006, 45), Frayn attempts to expose the contradictions in their account. For instance, Murray Gell-Mann, co-discoverer of the quark, writes that "the universe presumably couldn't care less whether human beings have evolved on some obscure planet to study its history; it goes on obeying the quantum-mechanical laws of physics irrespective of observation by physicists" (quoted in Frayn 2006, 44–45). Frayn parries with his response: "Having thrown the wretched observer out of the front door, most of the dissenters seem obliged to let him slip in again round the back to do the lawmaking itself" (45). In other words, while quantum *physics* may occur without the blessing, or even the knowledge, of humankind, quantum *theory* is *our* invention. For Frayn, the laws of time or space—whether Euclidean, Newtonian, or Einsteinian—would not exist without humans to measure them. Or rather, they may exist, but they would not *apply.* To his positivistic outlook, a tree may fall in the forest if there is no one there to see it—but who the hell cares?

Such a high estimation of humanity prompts Frayn's (2006, 484) own philosophy teacher to describe his ex-pupil's argument as "anthropocentrism run amok," something we can see clearly in the following extracts:

> This is what it comes down to in the end: the world has no form or substance without you and me to provide them, and you and I have no form or substance without the world to provide them in its turn. We are supporting the globe on our shoulders, like Atlas—and we are standing on the globe that we are supporting. (421)

But in that case,

> what will happen to the great mutual balancing act, as the last man on earth finally closes his eyes, and there is suddenly no here, no there, no anywhere? No is, no was, no will be?
> Nothing will happen. We . . . [all] know that the universe will go on exactly as before. It will be affected by our departure no more than it was by our presence. What were we, after all? Merely a few fleeting eddies on the surface of the ocean.
> The paradox remains. (422)

Here we see what I call the "double gesture" in its naked purity: we are conceived as part of the world, but we also transcend it (419–20). Bloom (1998, 724) himself makes the same gesture when he claims that "nature can achieve mind only by associating itself with Falstaff." The humanist assumption is that the universe only achieves actualization through our apprehension and comprehension of it, no matter how limited. Indeed, Frayn (2006, 47) states this explicitly: "So the universe is writing histories now? It's telling stories? The shameful truth about the universe, though, is that it's illiterate. . . . It can't even open its mouth to speak." One need not be Dersu Uzala, however, to see the rampant narcissism—even solipsism—in such comments.

Frayn is, of course, fully aware of the objective insignificance of his own individuality, when measured at the scale of the universe, but his coping mechanism is to inflate the subjective to cosmic proportions: "Humanism humanized all things, and made man the measure of them; it also humanized the man who was its measure" (Frayn 2006, 33). To paraphrase, we may only constitute a tiny fraction of the intergalactic show, but we are its sole attentive audience, and for that, we are its match—even its cocreator.

On the face of it, this is the prime human error to which my own title refers. It is to mistake the perception of our reflection for reality: a mistake all the more perplexing for coming from a secular world-view. It seems that humanity is far more robust than Freud thought and can withstand dozens of ego bruises before it admits to being an ex-centric being.[32] In the following chapters, I will explore how even the most sophisticated antihumanists—such as Heidegger and the poststructuralists who follow in his wake—still manifest a resistant strain (or should that be *stain*?) of anthropocentrism. Their errors are not so easily detected or accounted for. For now, however, it is sufficient to note that Frayn and Bloom both exhibit a hubristic melancholy concerning the place of the human in the contemporary moment. In doing so, they follow the logic of ideology in general; that is to say, the more it exposes itself, and the more ironic distance we feel from its force field, the greater the stranglehold it has on us in terms of ac-tual actions. Everybody knows that humans are froth on the ocean of eternity—but what sublime froth!

One telling statistic is found in Frayn's index, where only 5 pages of 484 mention animals. It is as if other creatures no longer illumi-nate anything about who we are, now that mass extinction is nearing completion. What is more, when he does condescend to use animals, they function as a semisentient part of the cybernetic triangle: subhu-man illustrations of why machines will never truly "choose" or "create." In that sense, Frayn feels an affinity with animals, considering them as more ontologically developed than computers, which he holds in modest contempt. For him, the computer is "bound absolutely" by the architectural laws of decision making:

> We have made its gait straight, and we have given it techniques for reducing the complexity of the world to a flow of digits that can pass through the strait gait only one by one. This is after all what a computer began as—a thought experiment for distinguishing between the decidable and the undecidable. . . . The computer that has developed from Turing's machine is able to decide because we ourselves have decided that it should be able to, and because

it obliges us to submit material to it in decidable form. All the decisions . . . have really already been made by human minds. (Frayn 2006, 215)

This line of reasoning echoes the vigorous rationalization that followed in the wake of Kasparov's defeat at the mechanical hands of the chess-playing computer Deep Blue in May 1997.[33] On that occasion, the Russian grand master was so perplexed that he implied that the computer must have benefited from human coaching.[34] Certainly we are a far cry here from McLuhan's hypothesis that humans are the sex organs of the machine world.

The common accusation against computers is that they are blindingly fast but numbingly dumb. They are glorified calculators, whereas we have imagination. Concerning the discrepancy, Frayn (2006, 336) writes, "If we imagine that, say, the Russian revolution never happened we don't imagine it being replaced by a packet of cornflakes, or the key of A minor," referring to the machinic limits of algorithmic randomness. Computers lack the organic wherewithal to truly understand the unexplainable architecture of the world beyond calculation—a capacity we absorb through social osmosis.[35]

In Frayn's (2006, 412–13) words:

In the case of human beings, consciousness is plainly inseparable from the body and its functions. We can give the computer ways of taking in information—cameras, microphones, etc., which have at any rate some plausible similarity to their human equivalents— and programs for processing the information. But why *should* it take in information, why *should* it process it, if it doesn't have a reason to, other than the instructions we have written into it? . . . We can give it a voice, and robot arms and the means of locomotion, but *why* should it talk, why should it think, why should it do *anything*?

The assumption here is that we human folk know why we assess and process information and thus why we operate in the world. But the preceding could be said equally of a depressed person as a robot (or of both, in the case of Marvin from Douglas Adams's *Restaurant at the*

End of the Universe). Frayn is thus isolating a kind of primal curiosity as the human element. As such, the desire to know is more important than any specific knowledge one might happen to acquire along the way. In Frayn's view, computers are not sentient enough to have an existential crisis. They may have Deep Blue as their cultural hero, but they will never have Hamlet (despite Kubrick's HAL). Artificial intelligence will thus always lack the human touch—that intangible quality that we instinctively grasp but cannot outsource to our objects, much as Bruno Latour would have us do so. (Let it be noted that the human element is almost always depicted as the baby rather than the bathwater.)

The issue of differences in kind or degree cannot be settled in any definitive, that is to say, metaphysical way. It depends on the context, situation, framing, and angle of appraisal. Thus it is necessary, in terms of the cybernetic triangle, to know when to slice as opposed to when to splice. Frayn neglects to recognize the red herring involved in his inert taxonomy, given that computers need humans to operate, and humans need machines to be human in any recognizable sense.[36] The mistake is to base one's species identity on the disavowal of an essential symbiosis, whereby computers are but the latest externalization of technics.

Ultimately, there is an inescapable naiveté in any attempt to allegorize the human condition. Whatever truly constitutes the "human touch" is assumed to be implicitly understood, despite the reams of evidence tailored to its presence. Nevertheless, some thinkers have been more convincing than others at creating a grand narrative on the scale of our species-being. One such is Hannah Arendt, who wrote extensively on the human condition.[37] Proclaiming her admiration of French existentialism immediately following the war, she paraphrased the basis of its philosophy in *The Nation* (Arendt 2007, 118):

> Man is the only "thing" in the world which obviously does not belong in it, for only man does not exist simply as a man among men in the way animals exist among animals and trees among trees—all of which necessarily exist, so to speak, in the plural. Man is basically alone with his "revolt" and his "clairvoyance," that is, with his reasoning, which makes him ridiculous because the gift of reason was bestowed upon him in a world "where everything is given and nothing ever explained."[38]

In the wake of Nietzsche's and Dostoevsky's deicide, humans have no one to whom to turn but themselves. The exhortation was to take humanity's collective, newly orphaned status and turn it into a type of secular, spiritual maturity. And the most profound and effective way to do this, goes the argument, is culture, in the most elevated sense. Life may very well be futile—as is action and speech—but a more modest meaning can be fabricated through art on a truly human scale, for the first time, since the Hellenic Golden Age.

But Arendt was not merely an existentialist. Influenced greatly by Heidegger, she was sensitive to the dangers awaiting us if we take the absence of God to be an opportunity to turn the world into a giant case of *Lord of the Flies*. In a piece originally published in *The Human Condition,* "The Permanence of the World and the Work of Art," she writes, "We need not . . . decide whether man or a god should be the measure of all things; what is certain is that the measure can be neither the driving necessity of biological life and labor nor the utilitarian instrumentalism of fabrication and usage" (Arendt 1998, 178). Her sophisticated strain of humanism is most obvious, however, in the following passage, which characterizes an entire school of thought from the mid-twentieth century to the present:

> The immediate source of the art work is the human capacity for thought. . . . These are capacities of man and not mere[39] attributes of the human animal like feelings, wants, and needs, to which they are related and which often constitute their content. Such human properties are as unrelated to the world which man creates as his home on earth as the corresponding properties of other animal species, and if they were to constitute a man-made environment for the human animal, this would be a non-world, the product of emanation rather than creation. . . . In each instance, a human capacity which *by its very nature* is world-open and communicative transcends and releases into the world a passionate intensity from its imprisonment within the self. (173; emphasis added)

Arendt here is offering a positive gloss on reification, in which the active and consequential human spirit can objectify itself, that is, become a tangible and enduring object whose sole purpose is not utility but beauty. The human does not merely emanate, as animals do, but

produces. (We shall see in subsequent chapters how more recent thinkers, such as Derrida, refuse to make such a self-flattering distinction
between traces—a critical statement Manzoni also made more directly
when selling his own canned feces as art.) So while at this juncture
we cannot go into the nuanced distinctions Arendt makes between
Hellenic and Roman notions of culture, and thus different branches
in historical consciousness, we can detect the implicit Heideggerian
hierarchy structuring her entire approach: the stone has no world, the
animal is poor in world, and only the human is world forming (i.e.,
capable of "transfiguration, a veritable metamorphosis").[40]

   "In this permanence," Arendt (1998, 172–73) writes, "in the very
stability of human artifice . . . does the sheer durability of the world of
things appear in such purity and clarity . . . [and as] the non-mortal
home for mortal beings." Moreover, "it is as though worldly stability had
become transparent in the permanence of art, so that a premonition of
immortality, not the immortality of the soul or of life but of something
immortal achieved by mortal hands, has become tangibly present, to
shine and to be seen, to sound and to be heard, to speak and to read"
(173). Arendt thus seeks to abandon the project of modernity, in which
"society" threatens to swamp "culture," to return to the "unparalled
dignity" of antiquity. The key word here, of course, is *dignity*: a load-
bearing word that has been obliged to do far more ideological work
over the centuries than its three syllables can withstand. Dignity is the
recto to shame's verso, both being an exclusive human trait, allegedly.
The mistake here, however, is to conflate the socialized with the human,
given the possibility that simians and dogs can quiver in "shame" (i.e.,
the recognition of transgressing the forbidden), while animals in general
can suffer from an attack on their (supposed, inherent) dignity. That
is to say, the dignity–shame complex emerges out of a social matrix
of power, respect, deference, and behavioral expectations that are not
necessarily confined to the sons and daughters of Adam.

   Arendt herself is consistently careful to signal her skepticism regarding traditional humanism. She is not a cheerleader for humanity,
as many others have been. But she is an earnest lobbyist. "The greatness of man," she writes (in a different piece[41]), " . . . on which the
whole question turns, is taken to consist in the human ability to do
things and to speak words that are deserving of immortality—that is,
worthy of eternal remembrance—despite the fact that human beings

are mortal. This exclusively human and purely earthly immortality to which greatness lays claim is called 'fame.'" The question must be asked, then: deserving to whom?

Yet despite her caveats and qualifications, like Frayn, Arendt believes the stakes to be too high to posit a continuum between ourselves and "our" machines:

> If it were true that man is an *animal rationale* in the sense in which the modern age understood the term, namely, an animal species which differs from other animals in that it is endowed with superior brain power, then the newly invented electronic machines, which, sometimes to the dismay and sometimes to the confusion of their inventors, are so spectacularly more "intelligent" than human beings, would indeed be *homunculi*. As it is, they are, like all machines, mere substitutes and artificial improvers of human labor power. (Arendt 2007, 176)

Arendt thus takes issue with Hobbes's belief that rationality is "the highest and most human of man's capacities" since rationality can indeed be mimicked more efficiently with machines. She thus locates the human elsewhere, in the capacity to produce an enduring and autoaffirming lifeworld—something reified "brain power" cannot do, for computers are worldless. "If one looks at objects in the world from the perspective of their durability," she writes, "it is clear that artworks are superior to all other objects. Even after millennia they have the ability to shine for us, as they did on the day that brought them into the world" (190).[42] The anthropocentrism here is manifest. Superiority is indexed to "the ability to shine for *us*." No doubt, the shine here is a reflection off the polished surface of a mirror. Then again, one creature's immortal relevance is another's toilet, as the statues in public parks eloquently remind us.

That someone as conceptually complex as Arendt can succumb to humanism—through the back door, as it were—says much about the subliminal sway of its agenda.[43] She notes that "it is well-known that the term humanity is of Roman origin, and that no word corresponding to the Latin *humanitas* could be found in Greek" (Arendt 1998, 201). The implication is that Greek philosophies of worldliness need not be quarantined in one species but may be the result of the dialogic encounter between enlightened animals and gods. The question for our time, then, is who—or what—takes the place of absconded deities? Bloom, Frayn, and Arendt—all in different ways, and for divergent purposes—delineate the silhouette of a figure that, in the information age, may or may not have left the building.

Thus far, I have been discussing figures who all congregate in the blue corner of the debate on humanity, that is, who are resolutely *for*. In the red corner, however, we need only introduce the English critic John Gray, whose slim volume *Straw Dogs* is full of heavyweight invective against his own kind. He represents the case *against*, as is immediately clear, when he describes humanism as a persistent "superstition," before placing it alongside "the moth-eaten brocade of progressive hope" (xi). For Gray, secularism is little more than "a pastiche of current scientific orthodoxy and pious hopes," and the human-centric discourse it produces an unfortunate mash-up of "evangelical Darwinism" (xii) and inverted Christianity.[44] All our most cherished grand narratives, he argues, are designed to disguise that we are really nothing more than *Homo rapiens*—an "exceptionally rapacious primate" (7), a "plague animal" (12).

With a combination of acid wit, pithy put-downs, and erudite petulance, Gray flips through the catalog of human atrocities in a polemic designed to slap the humanoid mask from our animal faces and thus to jolt us out of our smug moral complacency. His pessimism runs so deep, however, that one wonders why he would bother delivering the slap in the first place since we are clearly a creature that does not learn from its mistakes. Take, for instance, our faith in scientific progress. According to our misanthropic guide, science increases human power, but it also magnifies the flaws in human nature. "Humanity's worst crimes were made possible only by modern technology," he writes (14), not inaccurately. Moreover, our use of technology has created "a new geological era, the Eremozoic,[45] the Era of Solitude" (8), in which we are suspended in a prosthetic environment, removed from all the other vital creatures with which we once consorted: a fitting end for the solipsistic children of idealism. (For this author, *idealism* "is the belief that only humans exist" [Gray 2007, 53].)

Gray's jujitsu attacks on our collective ego would be more effective if he were a little more consistent. For instance, on one hand, he notes that "Darwinism has been used to put humanity back on its pedestal," via the notion that we can transcend our animal natures through co-evolution with machines and thus rule the earth.[46] On the other hand, he is happy to remind us that "Darwin teaches that species are only assemblies of genes, interacting at random with each other and their shifting environments. Species cannot control their fates. Species do not exist" (3). While the contradiction could be read as a symptom of that which he attacks (i.e., the willful denial and recuperation of our contingency), he is not above taking certain figures to task for being delusional and anthropocentric and then using their concepts to frame his own ex-centric arguments (as he does with Heidegger). Nevertheless, there is a certain self-reflexive schadenfreude to be had reading *Straw Dogs,* in which we are informed that "perhaps what distinguishes humans from other animals is that humans have learnt to cling more abjectly to life" (131).

Gray's most compelling point, however, is his realization that there is no "Humanity," as such, but rather only humans. What is more, these poor lowercase creatures are "subject to every kind of infirmity of will and judgement" (12). That our names are floating signifiers, and our categories expedient abstractions, is indeed an important reminder. In the grandiose singularity of humanity, we see a transcendent purpose, where there is only a highfalutin preening: "Philosophers from Plato to Hegel have interpreted the world as if it was a mirror of human thinking" (53). For Gray, channeling the cynicism of Schopenhauer, humanity is far too nebulous a concept to capture all the individual human errors that have been perpetuated in its name. "Free will," he writes, "is a trick of perspective" (67), and thus—quoting Pascal—"we must make no mistake about ourselves: we are as much automaton as mind" (29).

Returning to the issue of *Homo faber,* Gray asserts that "if globalization means anything, it is the chaotic drift of new technologies" (175). And yet "technology is not a human artifact: it is as old as life on Earth," embodied and utilized by other animals, from leaf-cutter ants who farm to semiaquatic rodents who erect dams to birds who construct architectural love nests. We should not, therefore, take pride in our technological achievements but rather indict ourselves for presuming to be masters of our advanced tools. Furthermore, our exceptionalism does not reside in the possession of language but in "the crystallization of language in writing" (56). Fleshing out his attack on the very notion of humanity, Gray continues:

Plato was what historians of philosophy call a realist—he believed that abstract terms designated spiritual or intellectual entities. In contrast, throughout its long history, Chinese thought has been nominalist—it has understood that even the most abstract terms are labels, names for the diversity of things in the world. As a result, Chinese thinkers have rarely mistaken ideas for facts.

Plato's legacy to European thought was a trio of capital letters—the Good, the Beautiful and the True. Wars have been fought and tyrannies established, cultures have been ravaged and peoples exterminated in the service of these abstractions. (57–58)

According to this line of reasoning, it is McLuhan's "typographical man" who has wrought so much havoc on the world: "Europe owes much of its murderous history to errors of thinking engendered by the alphabet" (58). So while one might look at China over the last half century and wonder if it has been any less tyrannical than the West, Gray would no doubt explain the recent aberration of the Cultural Revolution and its turbulent wake on Western influence (i.e., Marxist–Hegelian ideas). Indeed, it seems like one of his disingenuous moments to play the bipolar, Orientalist card here, given the contemporary moment in which he is writing, when—by his own admission—a global and postmodern logic is at work, a logic in which consumption, anarchocapitalism, and terrorism are inextricably linked. For Gray's polemic to have rhetorical momentum, however, some geophilosophical alternative to the Western *connerie* must be available, for the purposes of contrast. (For there is no blame to attribute if things could not have been otherwise.)

"Happily," writes Gray, "humans will never live in a world of their own making." For while "new technologies are steadily stripping away the functions of the labour force that the Industrial Revolution has created . . . we are approaching a time when . . . 'almost all humans work to amuse other humans'" (160).[47] This is indeed a horrifying scenario, anticipated with dread by Adorno, where salary represents the reverse ratio of need and responsibility, and where the encouragement of easy distraction is rewarded over all else. Such an all-encompassing mandate pulls the tablecloth of reason from beneath our bleary and debauched dinner party. "Financial markets are moved by contagion and hysteria," Gray writes. "New communication technologies magnify suggestibility. Mesmer and Charcot are better guides to the new economy than Hayek or Keynes" (171). That is to say, our media machines are playing havoc with our species-being, whose error was to have a much too inflated sense of itself in the first place.

Science is no answer because it is a false coherence, providing "the comforting illusion of a single established worldview" (19). Political activism is no answer because nothing straight will ever be made from the crooked timber of humanity. Art is no answer because it is the sycophantic entourage of the insufferable mortal subject. And mysticism is a false option because "mystics imagine that by seeking out empty places they can open themselves to something other than themselves. Nearly always they do the opposite. They carry the trash and litter of humanity wherever they go" (150).[48] For this reason, a "zoo is a better window from which to look out of the human world than a monastery" (151).[49]

Between Frayn, Arendt, and Bloom, on one hand, and Gray, on the other, we have the wire frame on which we can build the avatar of the human as a trope that functions across all sorts of conceptual platforms. Ultimately, however, one gets the sense that these thinkers are essentially on the same team since Gray would not bother writing such a book if he did not respect humans enough to respond to his message. True misanthropes don't attack humanity, they abandon it, whether to watch peregrines or live with bears or dissolve into the Matrix. It is embittered romantics or idealists who attack humanity. (Or perhaps I've revealed too much here.) Some may consider such targets—with the exception of the nuanced Arendt—to be too easy even to bother attacking. The combined force of their arguments, however, represents a rather pure version of the sensibility that has infused contemporary culture to such a degree so as to become the wallpaper or muzak of our subliminal complacency. And it is this *generalized* presumption of human exceptionalism that I seek to question and counter throughout the following pages rather than any specific philosophical instance of it. The bearers and amplifiers of this extremely pervasive ideological blindness do not deserve a critical pass by virtue of relative conceptual crudity. In any case, we now have a better sense of the discursive curvature that figures the human "race," both as a clearly delineated species and as a millennia-long marathon toward the Hegelian finishing line. It is to Marx, however, that we turn now for a brief crosshatching of humanity's silhouette.

THE ORIGIN OF SPECIOUSNESS

> *Man* is directly a *natural being*. As a natural being and as a
> living natural being he is on the one hand furnished with
> *natural powers of life*—he is an *active* natural being. These
> forces exist in him as tendencies and abilities—as *impulses*.
> On the other hand, as a natural, corporeal, sensuous,
> objective being he is a *suffering*, conditioned and limited
> creature, like animals and plants.
> —Karl Marx, *Economic and Philosophic*
> *Manuscripts of 1844*

On several occasions up to this point, I have used the term *species-being*:
a phrase associated most closely with Karl Marx, especially in his earlier
writings, up to and including *The German Ideology*. For the younger
Marx, the term *Gattungswesen* (which can also be translated as "species-
essence") is an important index of the alienation of an individual, a class,
or—as the name suggests—an entire subgenus. Marx's sophisticated
form of anthropocentrism is embodied in this phrase because for him,
only humans have species-being, owing to his belief that only we—of
all living creatures—have the degree of self-consciousness necessary
to grasp our own lives in true ontological perspective.

In *Manuscripts of 1844* (Marx 1988, 76), he writes:

> The animal is immediately identical with its life-activity. It does
> not distinguish itself from it. It is *its life-activity*. Man makes his
> life-activity itself the object of his will and of his consciousness.
> He has conscious life-activity. It is not a determination with which
> he directly merges. Conscious life-activity directly distinguishes
> man from animal life-activity. It is just because of this that he is
> a species being. Or it is only because he is a species being that he
> is a Conscious Being, i.e., that his own life is an object for him.
> Only because of that is his activity free activity.

It is the effects (and affects) of labor and capital that alienate us
from our true species-being, conceived not as an immutable and ahistorical essence of human nature but rather as a common potentiality

toward which to work, and eventually realize, an authentic existence (i.e., communism), liberated from both the exigencies of biology and the economic exploitation perpetuated by our fellow man. "Man is a species-being," writes Marx (1992b, 327), "not only because he practically and theoretically makes the species—both his own and those of other things—his object, but also—and this is simply another way of saying the same thing—because he looks upon himself as the present, living species, because he looks upon himself as a *universal* and therefore free being." We have already encountered this importance of *looking* for/through the anthro-machine, and Marx is one of the key members of the team of scientists who adapted the ancient model to the modern one. Recognition *of* humans *by* humans is paramount to its operation. Man is thus both subject and object of his own history, insofar as dialectical materialism is the road leading to a posthistorical plateau in production and profits.

In the sixth of his "Theses on Feuerbach" (published in English as a supplementary text of *The German Ideology*), Marx (1970, 122) notes that the philosopher in question is obliged to "abstract from the historical process" and thus "to presuppose an abstract—*isolated*—human individual," that is, an individual who self-perpetuates an essence and displays a legible human nature, despite the plethora of social and economic conditions in which he or she may find himself or herself. He continues, "Essence, therefore, can be comprehended only as 'genus,' as an internal, dumb generality which *naturally* unites the many individuals" (122). Marx's self-appointed task, therefore, is to rescue this notion of species-being from its "dumb" generality to demonstrate how class, among other cultural forces, shapes the human in ways that are anything but natural. Given the exegetical nature of Marx's legacy, the question and role of "human nature" in his *oeuvre* can be interpreted in many different ways. Norman Geras, for instance, argues against the orthodoxy that Marx follows Darwin in terms of relinquishing a fixed human nature altogether.[50] (In *Capital*, Marx [1992, 668] refers to "human nature in general," as opposed to "human nature as historically modified in each epoch.")[51]

For Marx, the gravest human error is to identify ideologically with inhumane or dehumanizing conditions, which block the full expression of our unalienated species-being. "In tearing away from man the object of his production, therefore, estranged labor tears him from

THE HUMAN ELEMENT 33

his *species life* . . . and transforms his advantage over animals into the disadvantage that his inorganic body, nature, is taken from him" (Marx 1988, 77). (For Freud, by contrast, the error is more primordial than that, having more to do with a misidentification with the authority of Old Father Phallus than an acquiescence to the dominant mode of production.) But as long as there is an understanding of such inhumane or dehumanizing conditions in Marx (which, for Eagleton and others, is present all the way to the end), then there is a structuring notion of human nature—or at least, *humanity*—at work. And though Marx's project may be to redefine what such a term might possibly mean freed from the tyranny of labor, it is still to describe a zone in which animals and machines are barred access.[52]

Thus the chapters that follow examine a tiny fraction of the ways in which species-being has been deployed in an age of intensified capitalism that Marx could not have foreseen in his wildest nightmares: a biopolitical age dominated by sign value, as much as, if not more than, use value and exchange value (hence my other emphasis on "media machines"—a more book title–friendly way of saying "the anthropological machine"). These machines, considered both in the abstract sense and in the particular medium of their material, create a great deal of friction in the effort to regulate the "us" from the "them" from the "it." Sparks fly and smoke billows out as the gears and circuits attempt to process the contradictions that emerge with each passing year, as technics evolves and distinctions between creatures dissolve, thanks to the pressures of extinction and the advances of biotechnology (of, if you prefer, the advances of extinction and the pressures of biotechnology). And yet the engineers continue to smile, mop their brows, and tow the company line. They talk of gains in efficiency, profits, and well-being, even as the smell of burning plastic permeates the room. But what if the engineers left the machine to its own "devices" for a while? What might happen if it were infected with a trojan virus that would question the logic of its calculations, to the depths of its own root directory?

Each example, figure, site, or text considered in this volume speaks directly to the ways in which we, as a conceived species, are constantly recommunicating—and thus re-creating—a relationship between ourselves, our others, and our environment. Whether focusing on the intensities of cross-species congress, the legitimacy of human dominion, the mechanics of interentity empathy, or the posthuman implications of chthonic politics, these various crystallizations of the topic at hand illustrate the ways that "we" humans sometimes seek to open ourselves—in sometimes frightening ways—to potentially liberating encounters with difference (considered locally and immanently). The focus on *technics*—as a dynamic form of technological relation that shapes us as much as we shape it—is key. As a result, these case studies are necessarily diverse since the stakes involved can be revealed in the most unexpected and joltingly different places. I have chosen especially suggestive glimpses and provocative moments when humans either acknowledge or refuse—and sometimes both simultaneously—the possibility of becoming-otherwise (whether this be animal, molecule, machine, or whatever). In the attempt to displace the human from center stage, I have also dedicated a great deal of space to the stage itself, that is, the "environment," whether figured as Nature or Culture, or a Frankensteinian hybrid of both. This is not simply a tale of entities or objects or subjects but also of the cultural processes that produce and regulate them (and are challenged by them in turn).

Human error is evident wherever human eyes care to look without the rose-tinted lenses bequeathed to us by our forebears. A critique of such, figured in the singular, understands that the subject under discussion is itself holographic. That is to say, the mythic, originary error is fractured and fractalized into an infinite number of micromistakes, which themselves comprehensively reflect the primal image, even as the conditions and context continue to change (e.g., the pendulum swings between the sacred and the secular). The *methodology of metonymy,* as this may be called, in which one isolated aspect of a complex problem or issue is analyzed as a surrogate for a nebulous whole—and then is fed back into the kinetic system from which it was artificially extracted—is, thankfully, increasingly appreciated in contemporary theoretical writings. This is itself a reflection of a greater interest in communicating across certain boundaries, primarily that of discipline. Indeed, there is nothing intrinsically suspect about boundaries per se, nor other sites or strategies of demarcation, provided these are not policed for reasons of paranoia, exclusion, or containment. The true traffic in ideas allows for the fact that grass will grow on both sides of the fence. Judging degrees of greenness can thus be a collective project.

Depending on one's accent, *human error* can also be heard as *human era*. In a sense, I would like to conflate these two concepts: not as a self-hating human necessarily but as a card-carrying inhabitant of all three segments of the cybernetic triangle.

The initial chapter is an exploration of the ambient mechanics of Agamben's anthropological machine, which, as we have seen, is the sociocultural apparatus designed to regulate and produce the subject through a complex interplay of recognitions. Here I read Werner Herzog's remarkable film *Grizzly Man* (2005) as a particularly revealing text concerning the mobile and permeable boundary between so-called Man and animal as well as the stakes involved in "playing out in the *open*." I argue that the gruesome fate of Timothy Treadwell and Amie Huguenard, torn to shreds by a hungry grizzly in the late Alaskan summer of 2003, is a complicated sacrifice to the three gods of the present age: the media, sexual identity, and species-being.

Chapter 2 is an extension of these concerns into questions of representation (both aesthetically and juridically), especially in relation to the symbolic commerce between humans and other species, whether figured as *theriophily* (the love of animals) or bestiality proper. The discussion begins with Nietzsche's famous breakdown after witnessing the thrashing of a horse in Turin and ends with the recent work of both Donna Haraway and Jacques Derrida, both of whom have been prompted to rethink the enigmatic encounter between themselves and companion animals. Between these bookends of an extended twentieth century, we explore Thomas Edison's film *Electrocuting an Elephant*; the series of prints titled "The Four Stages of Cruelty," by William Hogarth; the Sufi fable of the Ikhwān al-Ṣafā' titled *The Animals' Lawsuit against Humanity*; Robinson Devor's documentary on illicit animal congress, *Zoo*; and Ulrich Seidl's remarkable film *Animal Love*. Taken together, these mediated interventions shed some light on the culturally oscillating fear of—and attraction to—our ontological others. The guiding question is thus, what exactly is the relationship between the human and the inhuman(e) in terms of the evolution of the social Spectacle?

Chapter 3 explores the different ways in which the capacity to "respond" has been figured, and reconfigured, through different technologies over the past century and a half. Beginning with a rather harrowing telephone message, sampled by the Glaswegian band Aero-gramme, in which an anonymous woman pleas into the receiver for help, the discussion seeks both to locate and to complicate the "human element" captured in recordings of the voice. Using Eric Santner's notion of "creaturely life" as a conceptual lens, I argue that the melan-choly poetics that often accompany the subfield of media hauntology are still too anthropocentric, given the continued investment in hu-man exceptionalism (albeit of an abject kind); rather the cybernetic interdependence of humans, animals, and machines should be fully acknowledged and appreciated to avoid the conflation of pathos with the human, thereby perpetuating Descartes's (other) error: the assump-tion that animals and/or machines can *react* but not *respond*.

Chapter 4 widens the circle of our discussion to incorporate "the environment" in toto, comparing environmental concerns with economic ones (because both are understood to be in poor health). In doing so, it tests Bernard Stiegler's claim that "the program industries" of intensi-fied capitalism have led to a catastrophic destruction of libido, leaving only a ruthless collection of drives in its wake. As a consequence, we exhume some related Marcusian claims about the fate of Eros under hostile economic conditions to put them in dialogue with parallel contemporary critiques that are more sensitive to the importance of climate change (James Lovelock), alternative energy regimes (Alan Stoekl), and "ecology without [or after] nature" (Timothy Morton). What, in other words, does Stiegler's notion of "peak libido" have to tell us about the self-conception of the human in an age—and on a planet—that appears to be ushering in a drastic correction, not only in terms of the stock market, but in terms of the possibilities and limits of the species itself?

I conclude by noting that whether the human era ushered in the age of media, or vice versa, this pseudodialectical process has led to several tenacious human errors, including the existence of "humanity" as an autonomous, discrete, sovereign species.

1

Bear Life: Tracing an Opening in *Grizzly Man*

And we, spectators always, everywhere,
looking at, never out of, everything!
It fills us. We arrange it. It decays.
We re-arrange it, and decay ourselves.
            —Rainer Maria Rilke, *Eighth Duino Elegy*

The year 2006 was a big one for snuff movies. Not only did Australia's self-appointed "crocodile hunter" Steve Irwin find himself on the wrong end of a stingray barb, but Werner Herzog's remarkable film *Grizzly Man* debuted on the Discovery Channel.[1] In the first case, the footage of the fatal moment has been safeguarded by Irwin's widow and daughter, who, together, continue his dubious legacy in plucky showbiz style. In the second case, the footage of the murderous moment is absent in two senses: due to the lens cap over the camera during the attack and because of Herzog's decision not to include the audio itself in his own film (although, in a crucial scene, he does show himself *listening* to the gruesome sound track on headphones).

   This remarkable documentary explores the life and death of Timothy Treadwell, who styled himself as a "samurai" and "kind warrior": champion and friend of the grizzly bears of the Alaskan hinterland. Treadwell spent thirteen summers camping (mostly) alone in the Katmai National Park, during five of which he brought a video camera, capturing over one hundred hours of raw footage. After Treadwell's death (usually flagged as "tragic"), Herzog—who has always been drawn to people on the periphery of their species-being—then carefully edited this footage of the grizzly man interacting with the camera, with the local fauna, and with his own inner demons. These often manic monologues were then spliced with Herzog's own interviews and commentary from friends, family, and other people who crossed Treadwell's path.

Herzog's voice-over notes:

> Having myself filmed in the wilderness of jungle, I found that beyond a wildlife film, in his material lay dormant a story of astonishing beauty and depth. I discovered a story of human ecstasies and darkest inner turmoil. As if there was a desire in him to leave the confines of his humanness and bond with the bears, Treadwell reached out and sought a primordial encounter. But in doing so he crossed an invisible borderline.

Several critics noted the dramatic irony inherent to this project, namely, that Herzog functions as a kind of omnipotent, semivisible architect, shaping the material he has been given into a narrative with a particularly queasy and uncanny momentum. "I will die for them," says Treadwell, gesturing toward a group of bears early on in the film. "But I will not die at their claws and paws." And yet our protagonist is far from oblivious, as on other occasions, when he seems to relish flirting with his own possible violent end. "Love ya, Rowdy," he says to one of his favorite bears. "Give it to me, baby." Then to camera: "I can smell death all over my fingers."

As this potent quote suggests, Treadwell (and we must remark also on the irony of such a name, given his rather reckless foray into a landscape where even anglers fear to tread) was at the mercy of a psyche pulled in two different directions: between the life force of the libido and the siren song of the death drive.[2] Indeed, I would add two other agonistic elements at work here: that of the confessional and the Spectacle.

The temptation for the viewer is to psychoanalyze Treadwell, to get to the bottom of the mystery of motivation. Why would anyone give up the creature comforts of Los Angeles for the creaturely discomfort of a tent in Alaska every summer, to commune with a nature that at any moment could tear you to pieces? Herzog tactfully resists this temptation, or at least, he never voices his opinion concerning psychology explicitly; rather he leaves it up to the editing process to make connections between Treadwell's statements, his often bewildering behavior, and his troubled relationship with other humans.

In one revealing scene, Treadwell walks and talks to his camera, clearly needing to unload certain issues regarding his sexuality:

> I don't know why girls don't want to be with me for long. I'm very good in the . . . you're not supposed to say that. But I am. . . . I always wished I was gay—would've been a lot easier. You know. You could just *ping ping ping.* Gay guys have no problems. They go to restrooms and truck stops and [laughs] perform sex, and it's so easy for them. And stuff. But you know what, alas, Timothy Treadwell is *not gay.* Bummer. I love girls. Girls need a lot more, you know, finesse and care and I like that a bit. When it goes bad and you're alone . . . you can't rebound like when you're gay. I'm sure gay guys have trouble too. But not as much as one goofy straight guy like Timothy Treadwell. Anyway, that's my story.

Herzog is quite discreet in allowing Treadwell to speak for himself here; and yet the evidence accumulates that the guardian of the grizzlies "doth protest too much." Indeed, Treadwell's contradictions and mood swings qualify him as a classic unreliable narrator.[3]

Homosexuality is never mentioned in *Grizzly Man,* and yet it is flagged in the rather camp antics of Treadwell (an obsession with his hair, divalike voice, and attitude; references to *Starsky and Hutch,* etc.) and the biographical details that emerge as the film unfolds. One can't help but wonder if an attraction to men, and a revulsion of this attraction, led Treadwell to flee his family in Long Island, change his name, abuse alcohol and other drugs, and ultimately seek spiritual solace in the wilderness. Indeed, the vulgar interpretation would be that Treadwell is simply displacing his repressed homosexual urges onto larger hairy creatures than you find in a leather bar. (After all, *bears* refers to a hirsute subdivision within gay male culture.)

It would be a mistake to discount old-fashioned denial as part of the equation. However, this is not by any means the end of the story; rather the key to understanding Treadwell's fascination with animals, and indeed the general public fascination that greeted *Grizzly Man,* is the slippage or overlap between human sexuality and bestiality, under the gaze of the camera. "I love you, I love you, I love you," says Treadwell, not only to bears but also to bees and foxes. Indeed, this mantra—spoken emphatically, as if his life depended on it—is what struck me most when first viewing Herzog's film. Love is pronounced over and over, dozens of times. "I'm in love with my animal friends," says Treadwell, clearly overcome with emotion. "I'm very, very troubled. It's very emotional. It's probably not cool even looking like this. I'm so in love with them, and they're so f'd over, which so sucks."

In another scene, Treadwell is clearly aroused by a fight between two bears, whom he knows as Mickey and Sergeant Brown, over Saturn, "Queen of the Grizzly Sanctuary" (aka the "Michelle Pfeiffer of the Bears"). On another occasion, our intrepid environmentalist is excited by the fresh feces of Saturn as he grasps it in his hands. "I can feel the poop," he says, in ecstasy. "It's warm. . . . It was just inside of her. It's her life. It's her."

Herzog doesn't always shy away from judging Treadwell and takes opportunities like this to question the grizzly man's "sentimentalized view" of nature:

> What haunts me is that in all the faces of all the bears that Treadwell ever filmed, I discover no kinship, no understanding, no mercy. I see only the overwhelming indifference of nature. To me, there is no such thing as a secret world of the bears. And this blank stare speaks only of a half-bored interest in food. But for Timothy Treadwell, this bear was a friend, a savior.

Echoing this view, a rather blunt Alaskan helicopter pilot who knew Treadwell states, "To me he was acting like he was working with people wearing bear costumes out there, instead of wild animals. . . . He got what he was asking for. He got what he deserved." (One can't help but wonder to what degree Treadwell's childhood obsession with teddy bears carried over to the beasts on which they were based.)[4]

On this same theme, albeit with more tact, Dr. Sven Haakanson of the Alutiiq peoples notes that Treadwell died trying to be a bear. "And for us on the island, you don't do that. You don't invade on their territory. . . . For him to act like a bear the way he did, to me it was the ultimate in disrespecting the bear and what the bear represents. . . . I think he did more damage to the bear, because when you habituate the bears to humans, they think they are safe. Timothy Treadwell crossed the boundary that we have lived with for seven thousand years."[5] The grizzly man is thus cast as a rather careless ontological tourist.

We shall discuss the anthropological significance of bears soon. However, before we do so, it is necessary to register the interplay between sexuality and technology on this invisible borderline between humans and (other) animals. In other words, I want to designate Treadwell's camera as not only the recording instrument that allows us access to his remarkable story and experiences but as a catalytic agent—a participant observer—on equal footing with the grizzly man and the grizzly bears themselves.

Herzog is extremely sensitive to the different Treadwells who inhabit the footage: there is Treadwell the director, Treadwell the actor, and Treadwell the narrator, to name only three. In one scene, our protagonist seems to lose his grip on his own sanity, as he violently curses and denounces the park authorities and other visitors who he believes are actively pursuing and persecuting him. "His rage is almost incandescent, artistic," waxes Herzog in a voice-over. "The actor in his film has taken over from the filmmaker. I have seen this madness before on a film set [referring to Klaus Kinski]. But Treadwell is not an actor in opposition to a director or a producer—he's fighting civilization itself. It is the same civilization that cast Thoreau out of Walden and John Muir into the wild."

In other moments, Herzog is deeply touched by Treadwell's ability to capture unexpected and resonant images of the environment: "I, too, would like to step into his defense," says the accented documentarian, "not as an environmentalist but as a filmmaker." He then goes on to sing the praises of someone who can coax cinematic moments from the natural world "that the studios and their union crews could never dream of." Indeed, as a wild fox and her cubs seem drawn to the camera, Herzog notes, "There is something like an inexplicable magic of cinema."

Though this might sound somewhat hypocritical, in that such a statement could also be construed as sentimental, I believe Herzog is using the word *magic* in a very deliberate and qualified way. He is not talking about the kind of cinematic wonder lauded by Steven Spielberg and friends—which is ultimately an inflated and lazy form of narcissism—but rather a contingent inscription of the wider world, not necessarily by or for humans but conveying a significance or force beyond the banal, reified messages we constantly send ourselves via the media. In other words, one must be an orthodox humanist to be sentimental, and Herzog is no orthodox humanist (by which logic, Treadwell is a humanist who prefers the company of animals—by *humanizing* them). Herzog is, of course, interested in people, but insofar as they skirt, and often plunge over, the edges of their race. Thus he shares the conviction of his compatriot, Peter Sloterdijk, that the real question is not *what* is the human (since this posits an unverifiable essence) but *where* is the human.

Where is the human indeed? Is it something that flares up during moments of compassion, only to disappear when self-interests are compromised? Is it an ontological property found nested within condominiums, or slums, or space stations, or caves? Or is it an unstable element that needs precise criteria and conditions to emerge? Does it in fact cut across current taxonomic species lines, as happens when we seem to communicate with dogs, horses, or elephants? Are we, as the philosophers might ask, merely simulating these conditions of emergence in a controlled experiment? Moreover, is that which we call "the human" really confined to the invisible souls of *Homo sapiens*? Is it projected onto the historical development of these souls, as relentlessly figured in speech, text, and (moving) image? And finally, if humans are the tool users par excellence, then has not our quintessential property been outsourced to objects (as Bruno Latour suggests)?

When approached from the perspective of these wider questions, Herzog's valorization of the cinematic apparatus, qua "nature," suggests that the human constantly reemerges through technologies of representation, reflection, and recognition. In other words, if something isn't captured on film, on what ontological register did it really happen? (One wonders, for instance, if Treadwell talked so much during the first eight expeditions to Alaska without a camera.)

"Sometimes," states the director,

> images develop their own life. Their own mysterious stardom. Beyond his posings, the camera was his omnipresent companion. It was his instrument to explore the wilderness around him, but increasingly it became something more. He started to scrutinize

his innermost being, his demons, his exhilarations. Facing the lens of a camera took on the quality of a confessional.

Treadwell refers several times to a pantheon of deities from world religions, praying for rain so the grizzlies can find fish, and also praying for forgiveness (or at least validation) from above. "If there is a God," states Treadwell confidently, "He would be very pleased with me. If He saw how much I love them. . . . It's good work. . . . I will die for these animals. I had no life. Now I have a life." (Soon after, he adds the caveat, "Lord, I do not want to be hurt by a bear," suggesting that Treadwell would rather have died by the bullet of a poacher or ranger, as a martyr, than by the claws of those he adored.)

At this point, we might return to the structuring absence of the film: the gruesome mauling by "bear 141" on a bleak October day in 2003. In fact, there is another significant aporia here, namely, the presence of Amie Huguenard, Treadwell's girlfriend, whom Herzog calls "the great unknown" because she appears only twice in the hundred hours of raw footage (and even then, her face is deliberately obscured or turned away). The traumatic sound track of the attack tells us that she bravely tries to fight off the bear that has grabbed Treadwell in his hungry maw. (The fact that the camera was on but the lens cap still in place suggests that the device was always poised to record, and yet this attack was too swift and unexpected to capture visually.)

In reviews of the film, Huguenard is often cast as a sacrificial victim of Treadwell's impassioned obsessions and charismatic delusions. (He left several adoring and grieving women in his wake, which does nothing to dilute the homosexual hypothesis.) However, this reading of Huguenard robs this enigmatic figure of any agency or intelligence. She made the decision to accompany and stay with Treadwell, despite the misgivings in her diary. Her death is indeed terrible, especially as it lacks the pathos, coherence, and seeming inevitability of her companion. And yet she was a woman who clearly understood the risks of living in the "Grizzly Maze." Moreover, her documented fear of bears suggests that the attraction to Treadwell was even stronger. In any case, Huguenard both complicates and reinforces the semiotic square that I'm attempting to set up between sex, death, confession, and spectacle, since she clearly shied away from the last two to morally support Treadwell's embrace of all four.

"You should destroy it," says a shaken Herzog to Treadwell's ex-girlfriend, Jewel Pavolak, about the blank videotape that captured the final cries of agony, "because it will be the white elephant in the room all your life."[6] It is worth pausing for a moment to meditate on the term *white elephant* in this context. Why are charismatic megafauna enlisted by idiomatic speech to signify an unspoken-yet-pressing presence? Could it be because our animalistic affiliations and lineage are *the* disavowed foundation for civilization-as-we-wish-we-knew-it? In other words, what are white elephants—or, for that matter, eight-hundred-pound gorillas—trying to tell us, as conspicuous (and possibly concupiscent) cotenants?

To answer this question, it is necessary to zoom in closer to some of our key foci: first, the anthropological archive on human–bear interaction, and then the more structural relationship between sexuality, species, and mediating technologies.

BEARING WITNESS: IF YOU GO DOWN TO THE WOODS TODAY . . .

> If you're going to write about human beings, you might as
> well make them people.
> —Woody Allen, *The Front*

> Man is a fatal disease of the animal.
> —Alexandre Kojève, *Introduction to the Reading of Hegel*

Elsewhere, I proposed the rabbit as the most potent virtual totem, acting as trickster medium for our relationship with seductive, flickering images.[7] On this occasion, I would like to suggest the bear as a close runner-up (relying on Lévi-Strauss's notion that "animals are good to think with"). In his contribution to Reaktion's animal series, Robert E. Bieder emphasizes the "spiritual kinship" between bears and humans in those areas of the globe that they both inhabit.

"Long ago," he writes, "bears lumbered into human imaginings and left legends, stories and myths, which gave rise to ceremonies, rites and observances" (Bieder 2005, 49). For instance, the ancient Greeks believed that bears were born formless and that the mother licked them into shape, hence their scientific name "Ursidae," from *orsus,* meaning "mouth." An unnamed alchemist from the same period believed that "the bear is a shaggy, slothful, wild beast, in all respects like a man, and wishful to walk upright" (21). For their part, the Tlingit of Alaska insist that "people must always speak carefully of bear people since bears have the power to hear human speech. Even though a person murmurs only a few careless words, the bear will take revenge" (38). The Alaskan brown bear, and its close relative the grizzly, are considered by most North American Indians as very powerful "people," on a level with shamans in their ability to control the supply of animals, to heal, to prophesy the future, and to govern the seasons (38–39). The bear was also considered half human to the Finno-Ugrian people (76).

Several cultures in Scandinavia and North America trace their high-ranking lineages back to interspecies procreation and also feature legends of women marrying these beasts and "bearing" their children. "To this day," writes Bieder (2005, 52–56), "there are some [Native American] tribes that refuse to eat bear meat since to do so would be to eat their own ancestors." Listed similarities between bears and humans include "consumption of wide variety of foods, the ability to walk upright, masturbation, similarity of faeces, footprint, physical shape, facial expression and tears" (76).

In his information-rich study, Bieder marks two significant paradigm shifts in humanity's relationship to bears in particular, and to animals in general. The first is at the sunset of the classical period, when the early Church Fathers successfully attempt to wrestle the soul from the metaphysically promiscuous pagans. The second is the switch from nomadic social models to herding and agriculture. From this point on, "the bear became seen as an impediment to progress and was desacralized, made to represent an ogre or a fool, and marked for destruction" (70).

The problem with this neat narrative is that it assumes that "humanity" is a stable category, while at the same time acknowledging the fluid boundaries that exist in certain folkloric traditions. What Bieder (2005, 74) calls "an aura of sexual attraction between humans and bears" vouchsafes the species line that denotes a simultaneous separation and proximity. And so the relationship is depicted as one of mutual resemblance and respect rather than one of ontological overlap or entanglement. A great white bear that prowled the court of Ptolemy II (285–246 B.C.) is offered by Bieder as evidence of the symbolic sexual power of these creatures (and we shall look more closely at why the sexual is a privileged mode later). "On special occasions the beast was paraded through the streets of Alexandria, preceded by young men who carried a 180 foot phallus" (Bieder 2005, 79). With an abrupt shift in gender focus, the book notes that St. Ursula acquired her name when she protected her eleven thousand virgins with the fury of a bear.

It is quite possible, given Timothy Treadwell's charitable mission to educate schoolchildren about the plight of the bears, that he was aware of these complex cross-cultural associations. However, as *Grizzly Man* makes patently clear, he did not *understand* them, in the sense that he "disrespected" the line that separates bear from human. (And yet, isn't this what all the protagonists of the mythological tales did, in marrying and breeding with bears? This suggests another important line influencing the conduct of conscious beings: that between legend and reality.)

So on one hand, we have a narrative about the special bond between bears and humans (or rather the *imagined* kinship that humans believe they have with bears). In this category we could put the Viking berserkers, who earned their name from *ber* (bear) and *serkr* (shirt) and their faith that wearing bearskins into battle would transfer the strength and ferocity of this totem animal to their hearts, limbs, and minds. On the other hand, humans have felt the need to control bears and harness their fearsome power in more crude and cruel ways. Caligula, for instance, stained the Colosseum sand red with the blood of four hundred bears, all killed in one day. Two millennia later, the coronation of Queen Elizabeth II inaugurated a massacre of thousands of black bears in Canada so that their skins could be used for the ceremonial hats of the five elite infantry regiments (Nieder 2005, 115).[8]

Thus, since the dawn of the Christian era, animals have carried a double burden: they have been increasingly marginalized as neighbors in the theological sense and yet obliged to sacrifice themselves in various allegorical passion plays for the pathos-infused benefit of—usually male—humans (with women playing a mediating role between culture and nature).[9] As Bieder (2005, 81) notes, animals were moral entities for the Christian Fathers, each "bearing a message for the human" (pun intended?). The neoreformation of scientific discourse in the nineteenth century did little to displace the structure of this relationship, where animals are still lower on Darwin's revision to the Great

Chain of Being and, soon enough, would be appropriated by the arts and entertainment industries—think Winnie the Pooh, Paddington Bear, and Smokey Bear—to play the role of a distorted reflection for humanity's never-ending mirror-stage.

The circus staple of bears on bicycles, eliciting laughter by mimicking human gestures, has its origins in an earlier and more vicious form of entertainment. Bearbaiting was popular across all classes in medieval Europe, evident in village fairs as much as the cities and courts. London, for instance, had many so-called bear gardens, holding up to a thousand spectators, where these animals were fatally attacked by dogs. Elizabethan playhouses alternated between presenting plays and holding bearbaiting exhibitions. And though this practice was made illegal in 1835 in England, the practice continues today in places such as Pakistan. However, before Anglo readers pat themselves on the back for being more enlightened and progressive than those in central Asia and Eastern Europe, it is worth recalling T. B. Macauley's words from his *History of England*: "The Puritan did not ban bear-baiting because it caused the bear pain, but because it gave the spectators pleasure" (quoted in McConnell 2003, 32).

Bears thus have a special relationship not only to humans but to the highly spectacular and mediated relationship humans have with themselves.[10] These creatures form part of the intricate circuitry that the anthropological machine requires to function properly during any given historical epoch. Bear "academies," bearbaiting, bear pits, bear dancing, bear fights, and menageries were all commercial uses of bears that relied on the dynamic interplay between their similarities and differences to our own behavior. The ontological stakes are higher than with cockfights or dogfights, which is why bears were allowed to tread the boards with other subhumans such as actors.[11] Entertainment involving bears was at once scopophilic, narcissistic, and erotic: the pillars of the twentieth-century Spectacle. And so a totemic continuum links the medieval use of bears in entertaining the public with the more modern antics of P. T. Barnum's early traveling show (which featured James Capen Adams, aka "Grizzly" Adams, and his pet bear Benjamin Franklin) and—in turn—the postmodern angst of Timothy Treadwell.[12]

The ontological line dividing humans from other animals has been evoked many times and suggests a kind of definitive metaphysical horizon or border. However, as has already been suggested, these distinctions depend very much on the cosmologies of different times and peoples. We see residues of earlier, more folkloric traditions in Europe. Take, for instance, the Fête de l'Ours (Festival of the Bear), celebrated every Winter in St. Laurent de Cerdans, France. Here the villagers choose a virile man to become the "bear" for a day, who then, once in full costume, proceeds to simulate ravishing the women of the town, thereby reenacting the tale of a young virgin kidnapped by a bear many centuries before. As with the original tale, the bear's desires and designs are vanquished as a group of men, dressed as bakers (as if to validate the theories of Lévi-Strauss), "cook" or "bake" the ferocious creature back into a human being.

Such symbolic border crossings take us into the disorienting territory mapped by Deleuze and Guattari, whose concept of "becoming-animal" has kept many theorists busy in rethinking the relationship between our alleged überspecies and those on which we rely for food, clothing, knowledge, and/or companionship. As Deleuze and Guattari note, the modern or protomodern attitude toward nature, in which animals are "perpetually imitating one another," fosters a "mimetic or mimological vision" without which a theory of evolution would have been impossible (235).[13] Their concept of becoming-animal breaks molar (especially human) presumptions such as individual sovereignty, conscious autonomy, objective taxonomy, and even "being" as an empirical condition. Becoming-animal, for Deleuze and Guattari, "always involves a pack, a band, a population, a peopling, in short, a multiplicity" (239). Becoming-animal proceeds by degrees and intensities rather than by a clear delineation of properties, depending more on the contingencies of context than on the perceived continuities of the will.[14]

One striking instance of the depiction of becoming-animal is the music video for Björk's song "Hunter," directed by Paul White. This video consists of a single long take of the Icelandic singer in close-up, singing the song and shaking her head in an "animalistic" way. Computer-generated effects enable a kind of digital–genetic transformation to occur in stages so that by the end of the song, Björk has become the object of the hunt: a bear[15] ("I thought I could organize freedom—how Scandinavian of me!").

Deleuze and Guattari (1986, 22) believe that

metamorphosis is the contrary of metaphor. There is no longer any proper sense or figurative sense, but only a distribution of states. . . . There is no longer man or animal, since each deterritorializes the other . . . in a continuum of reversible intensities . . . a circuit of states that form a mutual becoming, in the heart of a necessarily multiple or collective assemblage.

The special effects of the music video seem to both understand and underscore this constant flux, as the cybernetic fur emerging from Björk's face appears like a rash caused by a sneeze, like a *contagion* (which is indeed a key word for the becoming-animal concept). Björk is unclothed and appears sensually affected by the metamorphosis she is experiencing. As Deleuze and Guattari note, "there is a circulation of impersonal affects, an alternate current that disrupts signifying projects as well as subjective feelings, and constitutes a nonhuman sexuality" (233). What's more, "these combinations are neither genetic nor structural; they are interkingdoms, unnatural participants" (242).[16]

Timothy Treadwell may have been accused of wanting to be a bear, but there is no evidence that he actually played the New Age shaman and tried to channel or shape-shift into his totem animal. So credit is where credit's due. And yet the very proximity to these creatures in the Grizzly Maze meant that a kind of feedback loop or resonance machine was at work, both in Treadwell's own mind and in the environment itself. What we could call the "ursine urge," visible with Björk, but also working within Treadwell, qualifies as one of Deleuze and Guattari's "alliances": that being, "a single block of becoming" (as happens with their famous example of the orchid and the wasp). "We believe in the existence of a very special becomings-animal," they state, "traversing human beings and sweeping them away, affecting the animal no less than the human" (237).

Herzog has already mentioned the indifference that he sees in the bears' eyes. Whether Treadwell and his actual and virtual baggage registers on their ontological radar is less a matter for animal psychology than a question of spheres of influence, mediation, and the aforementioned contagion. At one point, the grizzly man moves a mountain of rocks to allow the water to flow and the bears to access the migrating salmon. Outside the sanctuary, his publicity and educational tours bring the bears into a discursive circuit that either threatens or safeguards their survival (depending on your perspective on the potential effects of Treadwell's mission). Thus the Björk music video, as much as *Grizzly Man,* crystallizes the process of, and desire for, becoming-animal. In the case of the latter, this process is inextricably bound to annexed territory (another Deleuzian trope). "The wolf is not fundamentally a characteristic or a certain number of characteristics: it is a wolfing. The louse is a lousing, and so on" (239). This begs the question of a bearing, a bearing down, as well as a filming, a filming of. "There are always apparatuses, tools, engines involved, there are always artifices and constraints used in taking Nature to the fullest" (260).

Of all the ideas posed by Deleuze's overused and abused vocabulary, this last is the most relevant to my project here. What he describes as the "whole anthropocentric entourage" of metaphor and meaning is wagered on the decision to actively engage with the already initiated process of becoming-animal. And yet he delivers a timely warning:

> So much caution is needed to prevent the plane of consistency from becoming a pure plane of abolition or death, to prevent the involution from turning into a regression to the undifferentiated. Is it not necessary to retain a minimum of strata, a minimum of forms and functions, a minimal subject from which to extract materials, affects, and assemblages? (270)

Herzog's film seems to provide a response in the positive, in its subtle suggestions that Treadwell went too far or understood too little of that which captivated him. And yet it also admires the singular energy of a man who refuses to take "the conformist path of a little death and a long fatigue" (285). In the following section, I discuss the terrain and topology that allowed such a larger-than-life death to occur.

ON RESERVES AND RESEMBLANCE

Man is nothing other than technical life.
—Bernard Stiegler, *The Ister*

During the First World War, Sigmund Freud made the following observation in a lecture at the University of Vienna:

> In the activity of phantasy human beings continue to enjoy the freedom from external compulsion which they have long since renounced in reality. They have contrived to alternate between remaining an animal of pleasure and being once more a creature of reason. Indeed, they cannot subsist on the scanty satisfaction which they can extort from reality. . . . The creation of the mental realm of phantasy finds a perfect parallel in the establishment of "reservations" or "nature reserves" in places where the requirements of agriculture, communications and industry threaten to bring about changes in the original face of the earth which will quickly make it unrecognizable. A nature reserve preserves its original state which everywhere else has to our regret been sacrificed to necessity. Everything, including what is useless and even what is noxious, can grow and proliferate there as it pleases. The mental realm of phantasy is just such a reservation withdrawn from the reality principle. (quoted in Damisch 2001, 132)

I take this quote from an essay by Hubert Damisch (2001), who provides the timely reminder that "the creation of a psychic realm of 'fantasy' and the institution of national parks are perfectly analogous" because "both satisfy the same need, topographical if ever one was, to see constituted, as a reaction against the exigencies of the reality principle as manifested in mental life as well as in geography, a domain and a field of activities free of its grip" (143). Nature reserves and national parks are thus spatial liminal zones—cartographic states of exception—that allow citizens to "experience" the Great Outdoors. Significantly, this experience must be without any violent disjunction from the daily movements and rituals of urban or suburban life, which is why Damisch notes the important qualification that "the 'animal of pleasure' to which the parks were meant to appeal is supposed to cohabit peaceably with the 'rational animal'" (143).[17]

In contrast to the "wild," reservations and parks are nature tamed, like bears that have been caught, trained, and forced to dance. Of course, there is a difference between the simulations of Olmsted and Vaux and the annexed territories of somewhere like Yellowstone or Katmai: a difference based on the qualitative effects of scale. Whereas the former is domesticated through design, the latter is processed through the lens. Since national reserves and parks are, on the whole, too large or too costly to sculpt into aesthetic functionality, it is left up to the postcard industry and photographers such as Ansel Adams to document and "capture" the pristine and indifferent beauty of the landscape. Treadwell's instinct to bring his camera to the Katmai National Park can be traced back through the plethora of nature documentaries that have helped narrate the nation since the invention of film. It is in such places, "reserved" for our civilization's fantasies of freedom (like a table "not too close to the band"), that we enframe ourselves in the camera lucida of the outdoors.

Indeed, it is relatively easy for so-called civilized men to reflect on their human qualities in the asphalt jungles of the naked city. That is to say, even in the dehumanized environments of film noir, the dilemmas in which the characters find themselves speak to the pathos of self-consciousness and metacognition. We may sometimes behave like animals, but the story is only worth telling to the degree that we are tormented by a surplus or exceptionalism to the animal state. We may be poor, but we are not poor-in-world, and thus we are responsible for the worlds we make and the situations in which we therefore find ourselves. Remorse and sarcasm are the twentieth-century urban coping mechanisms, providing a metallic sheen to the more bucolic modes of mourning and melancholy.

In contrast to the metropolitan lens, a camera in the wild bears witness to the human extracted from his natural (i.e., artificial–cultural) element. We asked earlier, where is the human? And now we can answer this question: *wherever there is a constitutive technology of self-recognition.* Whether that technology is a camera, a gun, a broken-in horse, a wife, or the U.S. Constitution itself matters less than the capacity to register, record, and transmit this recognition. (Remember Freud's dictum that we never learn something new but remember something we have forgotten—a comment that becomes even more pertinent on the collective level of culture.)

Bernard Stiegler notes that there are three forms of memory for living beings. The first is genetic (DNA), the second is phylogenetic (individual–experiential), and the third is epiphylogenetic (technical–prosthetic–inscriptive). This last type is obviously the kind at which humans excel, being the foundation of pedagogy and other key modes of cultural transmission and reproduction. "Technics," Stiegler insists, "is a process of transmission: from the flint to the video-camera."[18] Agamben's anthro-machine—an optical mechanism of perpetual self-questioning affirmation—would be impossible without the interlocking of these three types of memory. Moreover, he links the current crisis of the machine's operations (i.e., an increasing friction in its functioning) with the immanently sexual transcendence of its operation. For Agamben (2004, 83), sexual fulfillment is "an element which seems to belong totally to nature but instead everywhere surpasses it." Sex, along with food, is a key area in which the human is forced to acknowledge his animalistic aspect, hence the amount of effort lavished on sexuality and erotica (not to mention cuisine) to convince ourselves that we are in the realm of the cooked rather than the raw. Cameras are increasingly penetrating the previously sacrosanct, domestic spaces of the kitchen and the bedroom. Eating disorders and sexual pathologies emerge out of the modern apparatus identified by Foucault, that being the constant managerial pressure for the subject to articulate, delineate, interrogate, and sublimate his or her own subjectivity. Just as bears were said to lick their young into shape, humans do the same, although not with actual tongues but rather with language (which, in French at least, is the same word: *langue*). Sex is no longer something we do but something we *have*, something we *are*: a burden, a stowaway in the modern soul.

Walter Benjamin wrote that "technology is the mastery not of nature but mastery of the relation between nature and humanity" (quoted in Agamben 2004, 83). Confession is a social technology with a long and effective history: a device that became increasingly detailed and codified by the new professions that appropriated its economical approach to information gathering and population control. Confession moved from the confessional to the clinic, the court room, the couch, and—eventually—the movie camera, and now the Web cam. One cannot remove sexuality from the equation because, as I have argued elsewhere, the historically produced libido is "the goat in the machine." Moreover, as Žižek (1997, 178) notes, the camera "not only does not spoil *jouissance,* but enables it." This observation stems from the case of pornography but can be extended to any domain where the sexual is enhanced or encouraged by the Spectacle, since "the very elementary structure of sexuality has to compromise a kind of opening towards the intruding Third" (178), toward an empty place that can be filled in by the gaze of the spectator (or camera) witnessing the act.

Thus we are in a position to posit various Dantesque levels of "the open" in terms of the anthro-machine. On the first level, we have the open of Rilke's (2001) animals (the "pure space" of the outside). On the second level, we have Heidegger's reinterpretation of the open as "the unconcealedness-concealedness of being." On the third level—the one on which we have been dwelling thus far—there is the opening of the human to the nonhuman, as a form of autopoiesis or autointerpellation. On the fourth level, we have the opening of the self to the other, in the most figural, transductive sense. Then, on the fifth level, there is the opening of the camera to the open mouth, confessing itself into being via the moralistically charged *logos.* The sixth and seventh levels are the openings of the vagina and the rectum, signifying the alpha and omega of the body politic, and thus of the world.

Taking his cue from Benjamin, Agamben (2004, 87) looks forward to a dismantling of the anthropological machine through a novel form of erotic ontology: "the hieroglyph of a new in-humanity." This rather messianic configuration would usher in "a new and more blessed life, one that is neither animal nor human," saving us from our cosmic agoraphobia, allowing us to play out in the open without fear. But this is to play the dangerous—or at least rather passive—waiting game of the "to come."

My own theory is that Timothy Treadwell was driven to the open of the Grizzly Maze not only in a futile attempt to escape his repressed sexuality (i.e., his humanness) but because he was rejected by the warm and sticky embrace of the Spectacle. Treadwell's parents (who, incidentally, seem straight out of Seidl's sinister film *Animal Love*) trace their son's most significant trauma to his bitter disappointment at the hands of his own kind: coming in second for the role played by Woody Harrelson in the 1980s sit-com *Cheers* (this, after appearing as a contestant on *Love Connection*). "That is what really destroyed him," says the father somberly. "That he did not get that job on *Cheers*." This may sound glib, and any good psychoanalyst would not trust a word parents say about their children. However, this piece of the puzzle makes perfect sense in the light of my argument, giving equal status to the camera as to the creatures it enframes.

A mere ten years before the first unveiling of the first movie camera, Nietzsche (1967, 57) wrote, "To breed an animal that is entitled to make promises—surely that is the essence of the paradoxical task nature has set itself where human beings are concerned? Isn't that the real problem of human beings?" Mnemotechnics, and the violence they entail for the subject obliged to remember, can stretch in both directions. It can go backward, as a married person who has promised fidelity well knows, but it can also go forward, in the promise of a glorious and triumphant future. Great expectations, like all things human, have a technical basis.

Timothy Treadwell fled the trappings of culture for the trap of nature. But he could not resist bringing his teddy bear and his camera, both of which create a far bigger footprint than any ecotourism operator could measure.

THE INSANE ANIMAL

> I fear that the animals consider man as being like themselves that has lost in a most dangerous way its sound animal common sense; they consider him the insane animal, the laughing animal, the weeping animal, the miserable animal.
> —Friedrich Nietzsche, *The Gay Science*

> In what way can man let the animal, upon whose suspension the world is held open, be?
> —Giorgio Agamben, *The Open*

I began this piece with the specter of snuff movies, referring specifically to films in which humans are killed by animals. However, there are, of course, many more in which animals are killed by humans (*Apocalypse Now* and *Sans Soleil* spring to mind). Indeed, an argument could be made that cinema itself begins with snuff, due to the fact that one of the first uses of celluloid was Thomas Edison's decision, in early 1903, to film the execution by electrocution of Topsy the elephant, who had killed three men in as many years.[19]

Humans are not only producers of media but also created by media. The molar organism is something of a mirage, in our case, because a new, technologized form of symbiosis is created through our symbolic webs, as much as our viral vectors. Mantralike appeals to understand our behavior via so-called human nature do not even begin to address the issue, since we not only have a nature but a *second* nature. Moreover, there is much speculation whether this second nature has reached a new density or point of emergence, whereby our mediated existence fosters a *third* nature—a meta-alienation from the natures we both fear and revere.

These three natures play across the words and actions of Timothy Treadwell—one of our most complex Icarus figures. As Derrida (2008, 29) notes, "the animal looks at us, and we are naked before it. Thinking perhaps begins there." Humans need animals to feel, even to *be,* human.[20] This process of identity-via-(sexual)-negativity would be impossible without the media (aka the anthropological machine), which first shuddered into motion with cave paintings of animals and mythological tales and continued to hum across the centuries, all the way up to *Grizzly Man* and Critter-Cam.[21]

At this point, Agamben is most famous for his redeployment of the ancient Hellenic concept of *Zoë,* bare life, which is held distinct from *Bios,* life recognized—and thus captured and processed—by the law. Bare life is the property of *homo sacer*: he who may be killed but not sacrificed. The question of whether Timothy Treadwell was sacrificed, or merely killed, by bear 141 is a matter that Herzog leaves up to the viewer. And yet the very fact of retelling Treadwell's story weights the scales in the direction of some kind of symbolic exchange or moral lesson (the traditional functions of sacrifice). The eye of god is the camera rather than the narrator; it is a neutral and silent god, thwarted, ultimately, by a stubborn lens cap.

As Nietzsche's epigraph to this section suggests, animals may be (consciously?) resisting being dragged into the symbolic universe, just as tribal peoples eschewed the social coagulations of the state, alongside the complications of capitalism. As Deleuze implies, the very notion of "species" smuggles in a smug form of moralism. Can we trust a classification system created by one of the categories supposedly being classified (a set theory problem, perhaps best left to Alain Badiou)?

The day I write this, *ABC News* is running an upbeat story, "Return of the Grizzly," in which John Kostyak of the National Wildlife Federation states, "We think we can now tell our children and grandchildren that there's going to be grizzly bears in a while for them to enjoy." This last word is an interesting one in the light of our discussion. Žižek never lets the opportunity pass to insist that the injunction of the superego is to enjoy, and as we have seen, Freud links the fantastic topography of the unconscious with the actual landscapes of national parks. Bears are the most symbolically charged figures, functioning as both guardians of, and challenges to, the libidinal checks and balances we make with our own cultures and, by extension, subjectivities. They may not have the genetic or gestural kinship with humans that apes do, but this degree of separation allows us to consider them with more accurate lenses.[22] The complicity between the camera and the human instinct to record can, however, simultaneously work to question the assumptions of those who authorize the capturing of the footage.

"What is Cinema?" asks Akira Kurosawa (1983, 191):

> The answer to this question is no easy matter. Long ago the Japanese novelist Shiga Naoya presented an essay written by his grandchild as one of the most remarkable prose pieces of his time. He had it published in a literary magazine. It was entitled "My Dog," and ran as follows: "My dog resembles a bear; he also resembles a badger, he also resembles a fox . . . " It proceeded to enumerate the dog's special characteristics, comparing each one to yet another animal developing into a full list of the animal kingdom. However, the essay closed with, "But since he's a dog, he most resembles a dog." I remember bursting out laughing when I read this essay, but it makes a serious point. Cinema resembles so many other arts. If cinema has very literary characteristics, it also has theatrical qualities, a philosophical side, attributes of painting and sculpture and musical elements. But cinema is, in the final analysis, cinema.

Humans and (other) animals are different. No one would dispute this, not even Treadwell, who would not have yearned so strongly to be close to the bears if he did not feel the gulf separating him from them. And yet the species are not completely closed off from each other: there are revealing points of both virtual and actual intersection and/ or communication. For while a tick may not care what mood we are in when it drops on our scalp from above, the chemical composition of our blood influences the captivation that the tick experiences (an admittedly loaded term, even within the human horizon). And so there is a push–pull with animals: we want to humanize them, and yet we never quite say *mi casa, su casa*.[23] The animal that mimics the human is a delightful distorted mirror to those who consider themselves to have permanently transcended their animal origins, which is why European royalty liked to listen to parrots, dress monkeys in clothes, and—moving to the New World—put a pygmy in the Bronx Zoo.[24] But an animal that mimics a human to *perfection* is intolerable. It would create the clammy vertigo of the uncanny (as happens when a foreigner speaks one's own language to perfection and with no accent).

Fortunately, for the security of the human nation, no animal has yet appeared on the scene—unless, that is, we count ourselves, which is exactly what both Herzog and Agamben do in their interlocking projects. It is said that the king who thinks he is a king is as mad as a madman who thinks he is a king. And we could well say the same thing about an animal that thinks it is a human.

2

Zooicide: Animal Love and Human Justice

> We do not regard the animals as moral beings. But do you
> suppose the animals regard us as moral beings?—An animal
> which could speak said: "Humanity is a prejudice of which
> we animals at least are free."
> —Friedrich Nietzsche, *Daybreak: Thoughts
> on the Prejudices of Morality*

It is perhaps *the* primal scene of the impending twentieth century. Friedrich Nietzshe, his nerves shredded by spirochetes and spiritual exhaustion, sees a horse being beaten in a Turin plaza on January 3, 1889. He throws his arms around it, weeping and whispering brilliantly incoherent words of solace. The man who wrote *Ecce Homo (Behold Man!),* and who employed animals primarily as figurative beasts of burden for the benefit of the *Übermensch,* reveals an anguished sympathy—or perhaps even empathy—for his fellow creature.[1] As the mythology presents it, witnessing this scene of senseless cruelty broke the emotional dam inside him, and compassion poured out, all but drowning the philosopher's wits and extinguishing the mortal flame within him.

For Gina M. Dorré (2006, 160–61), what remains most significant about the broken body of Nietzsche's horse "is that we can always only see ourselves through it, in which the defenseless animal, beleaguered by the oppressive and exploitive mechanisms of the human world, still functions first and foremost as a metaphor."[2] The question is thus raised from the outset: is the much-celebrated human capacity for compassion a genuine empathy with other (nonhuman) beings, or does it merely *use* these others as a screen on which to project reassuringly narcissistic images of our own finer sensibilities and sensitivities?[3] To begin addressing such a question is to confront the very process of identification itself as the hypothetical premise of all relations ("turtling all the way down," as Donna Haraway calls this universal desire for a solid foundation on which to base, and judge, our beliefs and actions). It is also to take a long look at the technological forms—those "exploitative *mechanisms*"—that at once allow, mandate, and complicate the degrees of mediation between men, women, and animals.

Fourteen years after Nietzsche's collapse, almost to the day (January 2, 1903), and we are confronted with another infamous episode in human–animal relations: the execution of Topsy the elephant for the alleged "murder" of three men (including one abusive trainer, who is said to have forced the poor pachyderm to eat a lit cigarette). This unfortunate event, which occurred in Coney Island, was staged for maximum spectacular effect, as befitted both the time and the location. Thanks to the unflinching—even prurient—lens of Thomas Edison, we all have the dubious opportunity to witness what the crowd of fifteen hundred did on that bleak winter day. Initially, Topsy was to have been hung,[4] but due to an intervention by the American Society for the Prevention of Cruelty to Animals, the decision was made to enlist the assistance of electricity, a supposedly more humane practice that had already been used with human criminals for thirteen years.[5] As Cynthia Chris (2006, 10–11) points out, Edison not only made this early example of the snuff movie but actively lobbied for it, sacrificing Topsy for a commercial stunt designed to prove that Westinghouse's alternating current was more dangerous than his own patented direct current.

Animal sacrifice has a long and complex history and was never simply unthinkingly performed. Wherever there is blood and the vocalization of distress, there are those who will recognize an ethical imperative. Plutarch, for instance, believed that the cries of animals being whipped, slaughtered, or sacrificed were "begging for mercy, entreating, seeking justice" (Steiner 2005, 94): an interpretation vigorously denied by many of his peers and his philosophical forebears

(Descartes being the most conspicuous). For his part, Empedocles attempted to sidestep the problem of pleasing the gods by urging the sacrifice of *pictures* of animals (Steiner 2005, 50). Millennia before the age of celluloid, the venerable thinker could not conceive of an age in which *pictures themselves* would contribute to the suffering and death of a fellow creature—what Derrida (2008, 78) calls "the cinematography of a persecution."

The presence of that baroque tangle of affect, ethics, interpellation, and obligation that we call "compassion" is confirmed—as with a litmus test—in *Electrocuting an Elephant.* Despite the lack of sound or setup, and the anachronistic flickering of archived celluloid, the spectator is confronted with the deliberate snuffing out of individual life.[6] If one is unmoved by the spectacle, then sociopathic, even psychopathic, tendencies are presumed to be lurking within the viewer.[7] That elephants are classed as "charismatic megafauna"—with memories, graveyards, and tear ducts—makes the injustice more palpable than if the creature were, say, a bug or a chicken or a rabbit. Certainly we humans have historically carried around a veritable bestiary in our head of animal totems, classifying each species according to a sliding scale of killability (dogs at one end, sharks on the other, to give only one cultural example).

Yet there is always a certain hypocrisy at work when invoking the word *injustice,* as I did in the previous paragraph. This term is the angel perched on top of the Christmas tree of humanist presumption, as a growing body of scholarship has shown.[8] Even if we claim to be the strictest, synthetically clad vegan, we are inevitably enmeshed in a political economy that not only deems certain fellow species to be expendable but cannot pretend to do otherwise. Though extending human rights to other animals may seem like the most pragmatic step toward addressing the explicit injustices found in sadistic scientific research, zoological neglect, and the ongoing agri-industrial holocaust, such a strategy creates a privileged sphere that radiates from an anthropocentric center. It measures and merits inclusion within this sphere according to criteria such as "personhood" or "consciousness," which are, of course, species-centric categories, to say the least. In other words, the less a creature seems capable of humanesque (i.e., symbolic) activity, the less urgency has its assumed petition for membership in a transspecies United Nations. Of course, there are less conceited grounds for treating animals with respect ("dignity" is a more loaded concept, rooted in Kantian ideas), but they cannot operate under the aegis of "rights" without smuggling in the compromised discourse of political sovereignty, as extended to global "citizens."[9] Who, after all, is the final arbiter of those with rights and those without? (If all earthlings have rights, why bother inscribing and asserting them at all?)

It is remarkable, then, given that our predominant relationship with animals is one of self-authorized exploitation and/or slaughter, that we still have the chutzpah to use the word *humane* in the manner that we do, as if our essential characteristic as a species is one of compassion. Indeed, this is the premise of Philip K. Dick's (1996) Voight–Kampf test in his novella *Do Androids Dream of Electric Sheep?* as well as Ridley Scott's film version, *Blade Runner* (1982). In this dystopic future, humans and androids are biologically indistinguishable. The only way to certify the difference is via psychological testing, which involves a series of questions designed to measure levels of discomfort when confronted with the mental image of a tortoise struggling on its back in the scorching desert sun.[10] If this imaginary tortoise causes distress in the subject, gauged by minute adjustments in the iris, then he or she is human. If not, then he or she is a replicant.[11] Nietzsche, according to this paradigm, was all too human.

No doubt the results would be very different if we were to apply the Voight–Kampf test to a Cambodian Buddhist, and then to a de-sensitized abbatoir worker in Ohio, which puts the lie to any kind of hardwired human response to perceived suffering. Such an interrogation is also something of a trial in miniature, which should remind us that juridical attitudes toward crime and punishment are embedded in historical eras, which themselves reflect evolving attitudes toward the ever-expanding and contracting sphere of rights. Consider how, in our own time, the reflex response to a shark attack is to hunt down and kill the perp. This is a kind of vigilante justice *(lex talionis),* rationalized through the prevention of further human fatality. In previous epochs, however, animals were sometimes obliged to stand trial in both civil and ecclesiastical courts—something that strikes us modern folk as surreal in the extreme.

Most of our knowledge of such proceedings comes to us via Edward Payson Evans's (1998) *The Criminal Prosecution and Capital Punishment of Animals* (1906), which includes scores of examples of nonhuman creatures caught in the spotlight of human justice.[12] These trials span twelve centuries, from "the prosecution of a number of moles in the Valle D'Aosta in the year 824 to the charges lodged against a cow by the Parliament of Paris in 1546 to the [early] 20th-century conviction of a Swiss dog for murder" (in Kastner 2001). In a related piece for *Cabinet* magazine, Jeffrey Kastner observes that "in Evans's narrative, all creatures great and small have their moment before the bench. Grasshoppers and mice; flies and caterpillars; roosters, weevils, sheep, horses, turtle doves—each takes its turn in the dock, in many cases represented by counsel; each meets a fate in accordance with precedent, delivered by a duly appointed official."

Though Evans does indeed summarize an entire menagerie of animals before the bench (including the 1596 case of the City of Marseilles vs. a school of dolphins, for reasons unknown), one instance is worth highlighting, given the intended trajectory of this chapter, namely,

> the 1750 trial in Vanvres of a "she-ass, taken in the act of coition" with one Jacques Ferron. In the latter case, the unfortunate quadruped was sentenced to death along with her seducer and appeared headed for the gallows until a last minute reprieve was issued on behalf of the parish priest and citizenry of the village, who had "signed a certificate stating that they had known the said she-ass for four years, and that she had always shown herself to be virtuous and well-behaved both at home and abroad and had never given occasion of scandal to anyone." (Kastner 2001)

The notion of a character witness for a "she-ass" is ludicrous to today's sensibility, and no doubt this blatant case of anthropomorphism also offended the more enlightened people of the mid-eighteenth century. However, we should not be so hasty as to ascribe mere misguidance, superstition, delusion, or species imperialism to the prosecutors of such cases. Indeed, there is a certain perspective concerning the trial of animals that should give us pause. On one hand, as Kastner notes, "the ritual environments of the trials Evans and others describe no doubt functioned as complex symbolic matrices through which developing modern society worked out its uncertainties about the place of man and beast before God (or was it god and beast before Man?)." Certainly the legal apparatus was being mobilized to reassert humanity's privileged place within the

Great Chain of Being. For Jean Baudrillard, however, the late medieval and late modern practice of hanging the highwayman's horse along with the highwayman actually alerts us to a more intimate and intense respect for animals than we have today. That is to say, the incorporation of nonhumans within the human sphere of Law extends a certain recognition of the Other as capable of responsibility, if not an actual response.

Given the long and almost unbroken history of self-identified humans relegating animals to either soulless clockwork mechanisms, at worst, or retarded cousins, at best, this willingness to bestow our nonhuman companions with a public face could indeed be considered a kind of acknowledgment of spiritual coexistence and kinship, even complicity. Baudrillard (1993, 167) writes:

> There is something else in the punishment of an animal, which this time derives from the *ritual* character of justice. It is the application of a *human* ceremonial to a beast, rather than just the *infliction* of death, that gives the scene its extraordinary atrocity. Every attempt to dress an animal, every disguise and attempt to tame an animal to the human comedy is sinister and unhealthy. By dying, it would become frankly unbearable.... But why this revulsion at seeing an animal treated like a human being? Because then man changes into a beast. In the hanged animal there is, by way of the sign and the ritual, a hanged man, but a man changed into a beast as if by black magic.

For Baudrillard, the root of the scandal is the way in which our ancestors imposed *social* death onto animals, thereby bringing Adam's charges into the kind of symbolic commerce that we are now accustomed to exchanging only with fellow humans. "For man to impose this form on the animal is to erase the limit between the two, and at the same time to eliminate the human. Man is then only the squalid caricature of the myth of animality that he himself has instituted" (167).

The remarkable claim here is that "disgust is inspired in us by the execution of an animal *in exact proportion to the contempt in which we hold it*" (Baudrillard 1993, 168). That is to say, far from being an index of our progressive moral attitude toward animals, the (recent) taboo on zooicide is in fact—against our better instincts—a sign of "deepening human racism."

If we think back to Edison's snuff movie, this is a very difficult claim to swallow. And yet it is equally difficult to dismiss outright Baudrillard's (1993, 168) insistence that "by holding animals culpable, these societies paid them tribute. The innocence to which we consign animals (along with madmen, the sick and children) is significant of the radical distance separating us from them, and of the racial exclusion by which we rigorously maintain the definition of the Human." According to this line of reasoning, our pride in no longer punishing or sacrificing animals rests on the self-serving knowledge that we have, in a sense, domesticated *all* animals, not only cats and dogs. The result is that such creatures are "no longer even worthy of our justice; they are barely even exterminable as butcher meat" (168).

Baudrillard is no stranger to provocative assertions such as this, and yet his logic is worth following, if only to caution us against trusting the clutch of our guts to guide us in ethical matters. No doubt, the case of Topsy is a particularly complicated example, given that she did not have the benefit of a fair trial, or even a kangaroo court.[13] The "indexical" manner of the execution—meaning the way in which an actual, vital presence was spectrally captured by light and celluloid—heightens the haunted aspect of the moment of decreed extinction.[14] Other directors have since rubbed spectators' noses in the traumatic image of animals dying by the hand of humans, as if there were a need to weed replicants out of cinema seats. For instance, the dynamited horse in Michael Cimino's *Heaven's Gate* (1980) or the decapitated monkey in Ruggero Deodato's *Cannibal Holocaust* (1980)[15] were both sacrificed within the frame of the anthropological machine, and *for* the anthropological machine. But as with all sacrifices, it is the duty of the living to make some kind of sense of overcoded death. (Whether we classify such an exercise in meaning making under the rubric of *redemption* is up to our theopolitical discretion.)

We are used to seeing people on our screens, on a daily basis, mimetically cut down in the prime of life. Fatalities that occur courtesy of Hollywood studios are processed by our sensorium differently than those featured in archival footage. However, on the whole (with violent video games being the conspicuous exception), all these last gasps are implicitly deployed to leverage our sense of justice. A death in vain is not an option, for even the most fleeting henchman, gunned down in the top left corner of the screen, has died so that the narrative may continue. Indeed, we would be hard-pressed these days to root for the death of an animal, unless it has been cast in the role of a monstrous villain, as in *Jaws, Cujo, Razorback,* or *Jurassic Park* (and even then, there may be misgivings mixed in with the proxied relief resulting from the triumph of humans).

In 1789, Jeremy Bentham changed the parameters of the debate by finally asking the question, can animals suffer? (as opposed to the far more common question, are they self-aware?).[16] Nearly four decades earlier, William Hogarth published *The Four Stages of Cruelty* (1751), a series of prints designed for the moral instruction of those human brutes who the engraver saw beating animals on a regular basis in the city of London. The first stage depicts a boy, the fictional Tom Nero, torturing a dog. In the second stage, the boy has grown into a man who thinks nothing of beating a horse. Cruelty reaches its zenith in the third stage, in which Mr. Nero indulges in robbery and seduction, culminating in murder. And in the final stage, the vicious tale turns full circle as Nero himself is subject to the severest punishment of the law: the gallows, followed by medical vivisection.[17]

We should not be surprised that a prized piece of visual culture displays more compassion than Edison's contribution, even though it appeared a century and a half earlier. This serves to remind us of the decidedly nonlinear progression of humanity's relationship with its terrestrial cotenants. The death of Topsy is a kind of limit point in the annals of this simultaneously lived and allegorical relationship: a moment of extreme intersubjective and interspecies estrangement that could not be salvaged by Baudrillard's appeal to the extension of symbolic respect to capital punishment. No doubt the Romans turned cruelty into a fine art; however, the same alibi of cultural relativism could be applied here as to bullfighting in Spain or cockfighting in Bali. The point is not to come up with a cruelty graph for different epochs but rather to underscore that Edison's elephant died for the banal dictates of publicity vis-à-vis monopoly, and as such, Topsy's death represents a hinge linking the different biopolitical regimes of the Colosseum, the court room, and capitalism. In approximately ten seconds, the injunctions of entertainment, justice, and profit are zapped into one and the same ideologically saturated body,[18] as if, after the fact, we could cut through one of Topsy's legs like a tree trunk and read the different layers of human hubris in the rings therein.

To even speak, however, of a coherent or consistent relationship between humans and animals, as I have necessarily been doing up to now, is a breathtaking act of reductionism. It sketches a *Punch* magazine cartoon of Man facing Beast. Thus any discussion that attempts to address this relationship in the conceptual singular, must be mindful of the vast array of cultural differences, not just on the human side, but also those of different animals, in different contexts of encounter.

And yet there *is* that allegorical construction that allows the discussion to happen at all: a conceit that creates a conversation between the human race and the other fauna of the planet, conceived as an entire class. This is a metataxonomy of the crudest division between Us and Them, that is to say, between the children of Adam[19] (or Darwin, if you prefer) and those who fall under the category that troubles Derrida so much: "animals" (which is not to say that finer gradations are not possible within these two kingdoms). Consequently, it is revealing to spiral back from the dark heart of modernity to a fascinating text from the Middle East in the Middle Ages that puts not animals in the dock but rather those humans who would presume to treat them as their slaves.

THE CASE OF THE ANIMALS VERSUS MAN

> And Jesus saith unto him, The foxes have holes, and the
> birds of the air have nests; but the Son of man hath not
> where to lay his head.
> —Matthew 8:20

> We deprive a soul of the sun and light, and of that
> proportion of life and time it had been born into the world
> to enjoy. And then we fancy that the voices it utters and
> screams forth to us are nothing else but certain inarticulate
> sounds and noises.
> —Plutarch, "On the Eating of Flesh"

The Case of the Animals versus Man before the King of the Jinn was an "ecological fable" written by the Ikhwān al-Ṣafāʾ (1978), a group of cosmopolitan, mostly anonymous writers—some of whom were Arabs, some of whom were not—centered around Basra in the tenth century. Their name can be translated as "The Pure (or Sincere) Brethren and True (or Loyal) Friends," and their collective writings are known as the *Rasā'il*. These epistles covered topics ranging from mathematics to physics, psychology, philosophy, law, theology, and politics.

This long and detailed fable tells of a tranquil island—"in the midst of the Green Sea . . . near the equator"—that plays host to a group of shipwrecked sailors. The new arrivals think nothing of exploiting the local fauna for their own ends, which provokes the animals to petition the King of the Jinn (spirits) to air their grievances. The king finds their case worthy and summons the men, as well as representatives of each of the animal classes, to his court, while lower jinn comprise his counsel. The important theological nuances that frame the text cannot be addressed here, and for these, I point the reader to the excellent introduction by the translator, Lenn Evan Goodman. Instead, I focus on the transtemporal and transcultural discursive device of clustering and positioning humans over and against animals,[20] a mechanism usually set in place to explore the question of whether the assumed difference between the two groups is one of kind or of degree.

The reader is told that the humans "enslaved such cattle as cows, sheep, and camels, and such beasts as horses, asses, and mules . . . imposing work beyond their powers, and checked them from seeking their own ends, where hitherto they had roamed unhindered. . . . Other animals escaped. . . . But the Adamites set after them with various devices of hunting, trapping, and snaring, for mankind firmly believed that the animals were their runaway or rebellious slaves" (Ikhwān al-Ṣafā' 1978, 51). The newcomers, we are informed, are not mere deckhands but "men of commerce, industry, and learning," who set about constructing a civilized polis within the bosom of Nature, representing the hearts and minds of seventy different lands. As such, they form a solid sample of all the diverse types of men. The humans (or Adamites, as they are known) are the defendants in this trial, as the different animal classes—the beasts and cattle, beasts of prey, birds of prey, birds, swarming creatures, crawling creatures, and water animals—state their own cases against the imperialistic intruders. The latter, however, claim to have both "traditional religious evidence" and "rational proofs" to support their case that all animals are their rightful slaves. (Amusingly, the humans maintain that they were once in possession of title deeds and bills of sale of *all* worldly animals, "but they were lost in the Flood" [79].)

The first witness is a mule that wastes no times in accusing the Adamites of delusional thinking and brutish behavior. One of the bipeds, however, interjects: "Our beautiful form, the erect construction of our bodies, our upright carriage, our keen senses, the subtlety of our discrimination, our keen minds and superior intellects all indicate that we are masters and they slaves to us" (Ikhwān al-Ṣafāʾ 1978, 56). But the mule is unfazed by such logic:

> Beauty of form is different in every species. Our males are not aroused by the beauty of your females, nor our females by the charm of your males, just as blacks are not attracted by the charms of whites nor whites by blacks, and just as boy-lovers have no passion for the charms of girls and wenchers have no desire for boys. So, Mr. Human Being, you have no grounds for boasting of superior beauty. (58–59)

Leaving aside the mule's blatant racism, the beast certainly has a point concerning aesthetic variances according to species.[21] Only the chauvinism of our species can underwrite any assertion concerning the objective and universal beauty of our bodies, and indeed, our art and artifacts.

The Adamites continue to plea their case:

> His are the praise, the thanks and the glory for giving us our uniquely keen spirits, clear minds, and overpowering intellects. We, with God's guidance, have delved into the most recondite sciences; and, through His mercy, we have devised revolutionary new arts. We have developed our lands, dredged the rivers, planted trees, built buildings, instituted government and rule. . . . Thus we are the heart of mankind, mankind is the heart of the animals, animals are the heart of all that grows, growing things are the heart of all minerals, and minerals the heart of the elements. So we are the heart of hearts.[22] (119)

At this point, an objection is raised by an "outspoken jinni," who, on behalf of the animals, forcefully opines, "Had you completed your speech you would have said, 'We are also plagued with burning the bodies of our dead, the worship of idols, images, and apes, the numerous offspring of our fornication and disgrace, and the eating of betel nuts.' That would have tended more toward a balanced account" (121). A fellow jinn, chief of the philosophers no less, agrees that the human "did not mention the sordid natures and foul tongues they have among them, nor their intercourse with their mothers, cohabiting with boys, their worship of fire and bowing down to the sun and the moon rather than the All-compassionate" (128).

The reader of *The Case of the Animals versus Man before the King of the Jinn* already gets the pronounced impression that the Ikhwān offer a singular vision in matters of anthropocentric rationalization and the various objections that could be raised against the self-righteous rhetoric of so-called civilization. And while the overarching premise for guilt or innocence lies in the law of monotheism and the command to worship the One True God, the more secular sensibility can still appreciate the novelty of hearing the animal's side of the story (even if it is an act of ventriloquism, or "virtual subjecthood," as we shall see later).

The bee, acting in his capacity as spokescreature for the swarming things, adds his buzzing voice to the proceedings:

> Your Majesty, this human claims that they have sciences and knowledge, thought and judgment, capabilities for directing and governing which show that they are masters to us and we are slaves of theirs. If they considered, our point of view would be clear to them as well. They would then recognize from the way we manage our own affairs and cooperate to promote our welfare that we too have knowledge and understanding, awareness, discrimination, thought, judgment, and a capacity for ordering and governing which are keener and subtler, more judicious and more exacting than theirs.[23] (145)

The bee then goes on to score points with the jinn jury, noting that humans are strange masters, given that they are "so avid for our leavings" and go to such lengths to procure honey, that is to say, "the spittle of bees." Indeed, "how can a king be so eager to have the refuse of his servants and retainers?" (146).

Such a line of reasoning stings the pride of the humans, so they change tack and sing the praises of their leisure time: certainly a sign of the privilege and *dignitas* of the ruling class. "We have parties," boast the Adamites, "diversions, and entertainments, fun, frivolity, and delight, weddings, banquets, dancing, stories, games, celebrations and receptions, honors and testimonials. We have robes and vestments of honor, turbans, and every other kind of clothing, bracelets, bangles, anklets, elevated furniture, and sunken cups, rich cushions and luxurious carpets, paired couches facing each other, pillows, and countless other such comforts" (Ikhwān al-Ṣafāʾ 1978, 150). Once again, however, the animals point out that this is only half the story, and humans must spend most of their waking hours in toil, "plowing, sowing, working the soil, dredging rivers, digging canals, damming flood channels, making cisterns, digging wells," and so on (151). The list is long and culminates with condemnation of the "search of luxuries and necessities, hoarding and engrossing, niggardly spending—suffering all the rigors of avarice and miserliness." Excess, surplus, fraud, and profiteering are seemingly interchangeable terms for the animals and are denounced as an aberration in relation to the more equitable economy of nature. "You amass what you do not eat and hoard what you do not need" (157).

At this point, the animals feel they have the upper hand. Indeed, they pull no punches in presenting their class-action suit against those who assume dominion, and then exploit that position of dubious sovereignty. "Against the weddings you must exchange bereavements," notes the nightingale, speaking for the birds:

> against the celebrations, wakes, against the singing and rejoicing, wailing and lamenting, against the laughter, tears, against the joy and gladness, grief and sorrow. For your assembly rooms and your lofty and illuminated halls you must exchange dark graves and narrow coffins. In place of your broad courtyards, dungeons, gloomy and constricted keeps. In place of your dancing and animation, whips, beatings, and sufferings. In place of your bracelets and bangles, fetters, tethers, and chains. In place of your praises and honors, humiliation, shame, and disgrace. An evil in place of every good, a torment in place of every pleasure; in place of every joy, a grief, a care, a sorrow or misfortune, all of which are unknown to us. All these are marks of wretched slaves. (Ikhwān al-Ṣafāʾ 1978, 155)

Lust, in particular, is singled out by the animals as a sure sign of human abjection, enslaving mortals day and night by odorous passions. In contrast, and in keeping with the libidinal equilibrium of a master, the animals insist, "We are aroused to mount but once a year and not with an over-mastering passion or at the call of pleasure but for the survival of our line" (157).

At this point in the trial, dogs, bonobo monkeys, and dolphins might conspicuously clear their throats, and avert their eyes, as humans are certainly not the only animals to "indulge" in sexual pursuits for non-procreative ends (i.e., onanistic pleasure, the relief of boredom, social lubrication, etc.). They are, however, the only animal to do so under the auspices of guilt (of which more in the next section). The bear, in fact, harbors a grudge against dogs in particular, whom he considers wretched, lowly, abject, beggarly, and covetous: "despicable qualities" also found in their masters (Ikhwān al-Ṣafāʾ 1978, 87–88). This orsine witness—echoing Deleuze and Guattari's aversion to domesticated dogs—goes on to suggest that curs "were drawn to the neighborhood and habitations of men simply because they are like them in nature and akin to them in character" (87). Cats, too, are singled out for treason and guilt by association. ("May God not bless dogs and cats!" chimes in the lion, obviously feeling no affinity with his domestic cousins [89].)

Eventually, despite the barrage of accusations and character assassinations, the humans gather their wits about them and speak more stridently in their own defense. Their case for global authority comes down to this: "The singleness of our form and the multiplicity of theirs, the heterogeneity of their shapes. For sovereignty and lordship are more in keeping with unity; slavery, more with multiplicity" (Ikhwān al-Ṣafāʾ 1978, 193). No statement could make the chauvinistic assumption more transparent, that the world is arbitrarily divided vertically by Adamites into the human and nonhuman rather than horizontally according to an interconnected web of species. This maneuver does at least three things: first, it ignores that "us" is a pure set, rhetorically, if not biologically, speaking, whereas "they" is simply an empty space stuffed to the gills with everything else; second, it homogenizes heterogeneity under the sign of slavery; and third, it positively boasts about this disingenuous line of reasoning. The shape of the argument bends tautologically: the others are Others because of their otherness (to each other as much as over and against us).

The feathers of the nightingale are unruffled by this devious, yet clumsy, fudging of categories: "Although our forms are many and diverse, our souls are one, while they, these humans, though their forms are one, their souls are many and diverse" (Ikhwān al-Ṣafā' 1978, 193). For those who have been following the epic trial closely, this seems like a knockout punch, and the King of the Jinn must surely release the animals from their bondage and punish the wicked interlopers. Sensing that both sides have stated their case, one of the more noble Adamites stands. He is "a learned, worthy, keen, pious, and insightful man.... Persian by breeding, Arabian by faith, Hanafite in his Islam, Iraqi in culture, Hebrew in lore, Christian in manner, Damascene in piety, Greek in the sciences, Indian in contemplation, Sufi in intimations, regal in character, masterful in thought, and divine in insight" (202). This personification of the Ikhwān themselves asks the king for his final decision, which—after the loquaciousness of both prosecution and defense—is joltingly abrupt. The final lines simply read: "The king then ordered that all the animals were subject to the commands and prohibitions of the humans and were to be subservient to the humans and accept their direction contentedly and return in peace and security under God's protection. Here the fable ends" (202).

Such an unequivocal decision in favor of humans seems to go against the spirit and raison d'être of the fable itself: that being, to oblige humanity to reflect on its unthinking use and abuse of its fellow creatures. Why detail all the foibles, follies, and failings of our species simply to vindicate them in a single, dismissively bureaucratic sentence? One editorial endnote in the text, aware of the anticlimax that awaits the curious reader, tries to salvage the situation by insisting that "man then is placed in the end in the role of stewardship over nature—given freedom to use the benefits nature affords, but always under the overseership of God, who remains the animals' protector as well as their provider, to whom man himself will be accountable when his epoch of stewardship is at an end" (258). However, there is nothing in the king's words that suggests such a conditional subtext. It is an extrapolation from the trial in toto, one through which the king himself seems to have slept.

If I have quoted this fable at length, it is to examine in some detail what amounts to a prototype of today's anthropological machine. The writings of the Ikhwān compose an operating system that is no less efficient for being textual, in terms of obliging the human reader to recognize her humanity within the distorted optics of the allegory that forms its contours. Half a millennium before Shakespeare's "invention" of the human, the antagonism between humans and everyone else is framed as a form of "divide and conquer," despite the animal's ability to rally together for a common cause. As a result, we see, in a particularly legible form, the ambivalence of our own kind, that is to say, a critical appreciation of the Machiavellian rhetoric that supports our assumed hegemony, combined with the philosophical equivalent of a New Jersey shrug: *whatchagonnadoaboutit?* It is this blithe fusion of comprehension and indifference that creates the fundamental human error that is our primary focus throughout this book—along with the technical apparatus that sustains it—an error that can be traced from the Garden of Eden to *The Planet of the Apes.*[24]

The Case of the Animals versus Man before the King of the Jinn covers a different trial than that of Hiasl the chimpanzee, who was recently the subject of a celebrated court case in Austria, but the stakes are essentially the same: which of the beings of this earth are to be granted access to the privileged subset of the human sort? Lawyers representing Hiasl were attempting to grant the chimp human rights on account of his "personhood," that is, the capability "of owning something himself, as opposed to being owned" (Connolly 2007). In a modern-day echo of the Brown Dog Affair,[25] Hiasl was smuggled into Vienna from Sierra Leone under the auspices of a shady vivisection lab.[26] Customs officers thwarted the crime, but now that the animal sanctuary to which Hiasl was sent faces bankruptcy, there is a good chance he will be doomed to medical experimentation after all. Those who petitioned on the chimp's behalf thus wanted a judge to grant Hiasl a legal (human) guardian, which would grant him the same theoretical protections as a human child.

Written before the trial began, *The Observer* reported:

> One of their central arguments will be that a chimpanzee's DNA is 96–98.4 per cent similar to that of humans—closer than the relationship between donkeys and horses. They will cite recent findings that wild apes hunt with home-made spears and can fight battles and make peace. In New Zealand, apes—gorillas, orangutans, chimpanzees and bonobos—were granted special rights as

"non-human hominids" in 1999 to grant protection from maltreatment, slavery, torture, death and extinction. (Connolly 2007)

According to Professor Volker Sommer, an evolutionary biologist
from the University College London (who gave evidence at the case),
"it's untenable to talk of dividing humans and humanoid apes because
there are no clear-cut criteria—neither biological, nor mental, nor
social." The judge, however, in a gesture evoking the King of the Jinn,
denied Hiasl the right to a legal guardian because she was concerned
such a ruling may "create the public perception that humans with court-
appointed legal guardians are at the same level as animals."[27]

The fear here is clear and reeks of the kind of insecure and paranoid
mental frog-leaps that sustain the Ku Klux Klan and its nefarious activities. It is nailed deep into the Westernized totem pole. Rather than
raise others to the level that "we" assume we have achieved, granting
access is seen as a fall to the debased status of the Other.[28] (Never do
those who belong to the exclusive class consider the Groucho Marxist
phenomenon whereby animals may not even want to belong to a club
that would have them as a member.) For the Ikhwān, too, there is indeed an ontological difference of kind between humans and animals,
despite the fact that their respective relationships to artifice, expression,
and the Godhead are a matter of degree. The king's verdict proves that
though animals may deserve respect, there is a glass ceiling in terms
of upward mobility for nonhumans, denying them the right to enjoy
the freedom of their masters.

This glass ceiling was first installed by those industrious fellows at
Socrates, Plato & Aristotle, a contracting firm that conducted business
in marked contrast to the pre-Socratics, who—on the whole—preferred
not to presume any special status regarding sentience, moral value,
and cosmic significance of humans. Aristotle's *Nicomachean Ethics,* in
particular, was to influence thinkers for two millennia on the notion
that intellectual pleasures are inherently superior to the sensual (and
thus brutish) kind,[29] leading John Stuart Mill to write that "human
beings have faculties more elevated than the animal appetites" (quoted
in Steiner 2005, 9). This, in turn, would lead contemporary deontologi-
cal philosophers, such as Tom Regan, to pronounce, "A million dogs
ought to be cast overboard if that is necessary to save . . . four normal

human beings" (Steiner 2005, 11)—and this from a famous animal rights activist![30]

Countless generations of humans have concurred with the king's verdict by subscribing to the supposition that humans enjoy freedom and self-determination, and thus *eudaimonia,* whereas animals wallow in their own fixed natures: a flagrant case of pride and prejudice. If we are not 100 percent mindful, goes this logic, we are nevertheless striving to become so, or aware of the imperative to do so, however dimly. Homer and Hesiod, by contrast, considered human–animal relations as operating on a continuum. For Homer, the essential difference is between divine and mortal beings, and as instances of the latter, humans and animals are essentially in the same boat. Hesiod takes a step closer to the situation with which we are familiar by drawing a distinction between humans and animals according to the possession of justice, a gift to the former by the gods. "Hesiod's is a view according to which human beings enjoy a status that elevates them above animals, but they are entirely dependent upon the gods for that status and for the fruits which come with it" (Steiner 2005, 43). Humans, ironically, are pets of the gods, in a sense.

In his introduction to the text by the Ikhwān, Lenn Evan Goodman (1978, 221) notes that "the matter of speech and language has been pled traditionally both in *[sic]* behalf of animals and against them—on grounds that inarticulate creatures, lacking reason, must have no rights comparable to those of humans, or on the contrary, by the canon of condescension, that poor, 'dumb' animals, lacking speech to communicate their needs and hurts, must be treated all the more seriously for that."[31] It must therefore be remembered that mute people were often deprived of basic human rights in the Middle Ages because of their inability to plead their own case and were thus relegated to the status of "dumb" animals, which is all the more reason, according to Goodman, to accede to the obligation to "assume a *virtual subjecthood* in all things" (16; emphasis added). That is to say, "all other beings deserve to be treated . . . as ends in themselves, not by virtue of any subjectivity they possess but by virtue of their existential claim to subjecthood, that is, because their very existence makes a claim upon existence, a striving, as Spinoza called it, to preserve and promote their own being" (16). For though "it is natural for human beings to speak of needs, interests, resources, challenges, even tendencies in a language which reflects our own interests and concerns . . . it is quite plain that nothing in the logic of such terms requires their restriction to the human case" (16–17). Virtual subjecthood is thus the portal to a qualified connection with the other: a heuristic device for speaking on their behalf, in a language to which they have no access, or, perhaps, simply in which they have no interest.

According to Goodman (1978, 22), "the ethical purpose of ethical projection is not the rhetorical (emotive) arousal or heightening of sympathy but the attainment of moral recognition of another's subjecthood." Nietzsche would no doubt balk at this deployment of morality, and yet it was a type of moral recognition that prompted him to fling his arms around the horse's neck. The possibility of ethical projection will continue to concern us subsequently, especially the question of whether this is a genuine attempt to transcend anthropocentrism or merely a more refined, ultimately delusional attempt to access alterity in the name of opportunistic, narcissistic knowledge.[32]

SCHRÖDINGER'S HUMAN

> If a man lies with a beast, he shall be put to death; and you shall kill the beast. If a woman approaches any beast and lies with it, you shall kill the woman and the beast; they shall be put to death, their blood is upon them.
> —Leviticus 20:16–17

In 1994, it was almost impossible to escape the huge alternative hit "Closer," by Nine Inch Nails. Despite the explicit lyrics, or probably because of them, this song was all over the airwaves, allowing disaffected young people everywhere to channel the inner zoophile they never knew they had. Even when cleverly censored through judicious fade outs, for the sake of public consumption, the lyrics were quite striking: "I wanna fuck you like an animal, / I wanna feel you from the inside, / . . . My whole existence is flawed, / You get me closer to God."

To my ears, the key line "I wanna fuck you like an animal" did not convey an urgent, bestial fervor; rather it evoked mental images of the bored dogs that I occasionally saw humping desultorily in the park, tongues hanging out, perhaps watching a distant Frisbee. To fuck someone like an animal, I reasoned at the time, is precisely to withhold the human aspect: that very facet that fuels what we call "passion"—jealousy, insecurity, anger, resentment, neurosis, latent cannibalism, and so on. To have sex inside this psychic tornado is precisely what makes us human. Freud, no doubt, would not wish me to make the human–animal distinction so hastily since, according to his view, *all* living creatures are subject, as some level, to the death drive. And thus, in theory at least, animals may also grasp at their sexual partners with some kind of affective surplus, beyond the anatomical motion required to inseminate, or be inseminated by, the other. After all, as we have already noted, procreational sex by no means represents the full extent of animal sexual behavior. (I hesitate to say "sexuality," at least until animals are trained to express their sexual behavior in a self-reflexive way, preferably lying down on a hay-strewn couch.)

What Trent Reznor, the singer–songwriter of "Closer," raises, then, is this very issue of the role and location of the human at the moment of intense physical intercourse. On one hand, we have the notion that sex is a rather shameful evolutionary residue—the beast with two backs, as Shakespeare calls it—and the sooner we can upgrade to pills and pressed palms, as Jane Fonda does in *Barbarella,* the better. Alternatively, sex can be seen as the privileged space of human expression and love, as countless adult-oriented health manuals would lead us to believe[33]: transgression on one hand, transcendence on the other. The human is thereby flanked on the left by the grunting, salivating, pungent creature and on the right by the luminescent, scentless, serene angel. At least when it comes to official public discourse, the human is thus more of an empty bridge between two ideological constructs than an embedded, situated, materially identified participant. As soon as we try to measure the subject, she either becomes subhuman or achieves Godhead: Schrödinger's human.[34]

Of course, Reznor is speaking via analogy. He wishes to penetrate his partner *like* an animal. He does not say he wants to have his way *with* an actual nonhuman creature. Yet his angst-pop anthem taps into a long history of bestial or quasi-bestial scenarios that seek the sacred not in our own human souls but in the alterity of animality. One such person is Kenneth Pinyan, aka Mr. Hands, who died in a Washington State hospital in 2005 from acute internal bleeding due to perforation of the colon. The instrument of perforation was a stallion's penis.[35]

By day, Pinyan was an engineer for some of Boeing's more top-secret projects, and by night, he was an active "zoophile," part of a distributed subculture whose hub was a ranch located in the rather sinisterly named town of Enumclaw. In keeping with our overarching narrative, detailing the cultural history of the anthropological machine, it was not enough for Mr. Hands to be the passive partner of interspecies anal sex but—before the fatal occasion—he was also consentingly documented on videotape. This footage was popular currency among his fellow "zoos." (After all, what use is transcendence or transgression these days if it cannot be captured for posterity, to provide some visual trace of the event?)[36]

The scientific term *zoophilia* was given its official baptism by Krafft-Ebing in his landmark study *Psychopathia Sexualis* (1886). Several decades later, *The Kinsey Reports* (1948/1953) would make the rather far-fetched claim that approximately half of rural teenagers had some kind of sexual experience with a (nonhuman) animal. Whether this is really the case, the prevalence of human–animal "husbandry" in Greek myths, Indian sculptures, Japanese woodcuts, surrealist literature, or the fantasies of American housewives has not made bestiality any less of a universal taboo.[37] Fascinating exceptions certainly exist, such as the (alleged) Lebanese law, in which men are permitted to have sex with an animal, as long as it is female. (Sex with a male animal is said to be punishable by death.)[38] But these are premodern holdovers that serve to underscore Baudrillard's point explored earlier: that the status of animals fluctuates according to epoch, and ours is perhaps the most militant in classifying them according to a tacit act of ontological apartheid.

The documentary film simply titled *Zoo* (2007) attempts to render and reenact the events surrounding the death of Mr. Hands. It is built around a compelling fugue of interviews with the people intimately involved: three zoos (Coyote, H., and the Happy Horseman) and one "horse rescuer," Jenny Edwards.[39] Coyote, a paramedic from rural Virginia, is the first to confess that he and his fellow zoos have "a whole lot more affinity with nonhuman animals than their own kind." For his part, H., a horse trainer, is perplexed by the condemnation that followed the revelation of his role in the scandal, insisting that he is not a bad person. He wonders why "all of a sudden I'm no good, just because I love the horses?" Preemptively heading off the charge of animal cruelty, H. asks, "Do they look neglected? No. . . . It's the love of animals. That's what zoophilia is. It's just like you love your wife or your kids. It's the same thing. I took better care of my animals than I ever did myself."

As the layers of the story unfold, gender distinctions begin to emerge. The rescuer is female, the persecuted zoophiles all male. Ms. Edwards tells of her long, intimate nights with horses and how this helped her immeasurably during a frightening bout with cancer. The implication is that there are healthy and unhealthy ways to fraternize with our equine friends, and men are much more likely to tip toward the latter, given their tendency to sexualize whenever possible. (It is thus worth recalling the words of Ingrid Newkirk, former president of People for the Ethical Treatment of Animals, who asked rhetorically, "If a girl gets sexual pleasure from riding a horse, does the horse suffer? If not, who cares?" [quoted in Cassidy 2009, 105].)[40]

Ms. Edwards is the voice of the wider society in the film, condemning the men for abusing an animal, but also trying her hardest to research and understand the perversion and what might lie behind it. When asked to describe the man she met on the ranch during her rescue mission, she says, "He struck us as a child molester type. Just a really creepy kind of guy." Her instinct to parse this stranger through the grid of a popular media archetype[41] perhaps says more about her own moral sorting engine than anything insightful about zoophilia and those who put it into practice. Indeed, the film finishes with a painful irony, when Ms. Edwards is so concerned about the horse's status as "victim" that she makes the snap decision to geld him. The footage of Strut the horse in an operating theater, suffering surgery in a sterile white room, while breathing through a plastic tube—for no other reason that he may be adopted later by another happy horseman—certainly makes the viewer wonder which is the more compassionate context for the creature.[42] Is this merely replacing the frying pan with fire?

As the Happy Horseman notes in his voice-over, "us humans are just so conditioned from the time we are born to start categorizing. . . . Animals are just not going to do that. You're either a good person or a bad person." (Of course, this is still an example of categorization: probably the most prevalent in watchers of the Fox Network.)[43] This utopia of nonjudgmental sociality extends to the zoo subculture itself, as the men gather at the ranch for potluck dinners and blender parties, comfortable in each other's company, with all caste distinctions between executives and truck drivers checked at the property gate. It is described as "a classless society of our own small world," with no "alphas, omegas or betas." This small world, to my mind, was reminiscent of the people in that other remarkable documentary, *Southern Comfort*, that follows a group of transsexuals who live in the bosom of intolerant rural Georgia. Despite our own prejudices or aversions, both groups qualify as a true community, that is, a subculture that crystallizes around the Lacanian refusal to relinquish one's desire.

According to the film, these ranch parties were homosocial, banal, and innocuous, at least until one of the men said, "Hey, let's go to the barn and pester the animals." Of course, the zoophiles involved are different people, who explain their behavior in different terms. H. warns, "Just be careful, cause if you stand too long in one place it's gonna happen. If you just stand there, they'll walk up behind you and put their head on your shoulder . . . they're gonna pick up that pheromone your body's putting off—they're going to mount you."[44] Were this really the case, of course, we would probably be witness to a swift revival of those medieval trials of horses for sexual assault. Ms. Edwards, in contrast, had no problem with this kind of behavior from her animal companions, which leads the viewer to believe this particular zoo is either suffering from a profound delusion or merely adept at self-rationalization.

In the wake of the arrests in Enumclaw, Pam Roach, a local politician, pushed for new legislation outlawing bestiality, noting, "I can never believe that an animal would do that on their own."[45] Again making the parallel between zoophiles and pedophiles, she goes on to say, "Children cannot consent; they are innocent. And so are animals."[46] But as we have seen, this highly charged construct of animal innocence is a relatively recent invention that can be dated to 1906, when the last nonhuman in the West was charged for a crime. This is a *historical* innocence, and not a metaphysical one, because we fickle humans are the ones who deputize each other to patrol the borders of this ever-shifting terrain. (Interestingly, conservative radio host Rush Limbaugh—in a clip included in the film—implies anatomical evidence in defense of the zoos, asking, "How the hell do we know that the horse didn't consent? Can this happen without consent? . . . If the horse didn't consent, then none of this would have happened.")

A more palatable example of self-rationalization is provided by Coyote, who explains his attraction in terms of a vital sympathy:

> You're connecting with another intelligent being who is very happy to participate, be involved. You're not going to be able to ask it about the latest Madonna album. It has no idea what Tolstoy is, or Keats.[47] You can't discuss the difference between Monet or Picasso. That just doesn't exist for their world. It's a simpler, very plain world. And for those few moments you can get disconnected. It's a very intense, wonderful kind of feeling. I don't think anything can really compare to it. There's no pain.

The key word here is *disconnected*. Even in the backwoods, twenty-first-century life is defined by and through technological connection. After all, these horse lovers all gravitated toward each other online. "I didn't even know what zoophilia was," says Coyote, "till I got on the Internet." In contrast to the alienation of modern life (circa 1848–1989), whereby atomic individuals felt emotionally disconnected from each other within the claustrophobic confines of the concrete jungle, post-modern people today are *all too connected* to each other. Communication is felt to be constant and instantaneous, allowing little room to perform the daily ablutions of self-reinforcement. This creates a kind of meta-alienation, whereby the contours of the very individual who feels amiss and adrift overlap and dissolve into a transcendent, incoherent, networked alterity. In a world of ubiquitous media, the urge to unplug is strong (as both MTV and *The Matrix* showed in the 1990s—a final blip before surrendering completely to the TheyTime of MySpace).

Disconnecting from the grid thus becomes a powerful gesture, albeit a temporary one. And in this extreme, particular case, it speaks of the desire to turn away from the human–machine interface and reorient the self toward the neglected third term of the cybernetic triangle: the animal. "Sex was just a small component of it," insists the Happy Horseman. "I'm talking to you [i.e., the horse] at the same level that you're staring at me: mammal-to-mammal." The other warm-blooded ones thus represent a powerful combination of the organic and the unmediated.

Before his untimely death, Mr. Hands worked as an engineer, over-seeing a secret military project involving antennas—the traditional symbol of modern global communication. Indeed, the ongoing situation in the Middle East pulses subtextually beneath the skin of the movie, sometimes rising to the surface through radio reports and in direct reference to Mr. Hands's job at Boeing. The subliminal implication is that Pinyan may have been an indirect victim of the Iraq and Afghan wars. Were he employed in a more wholesome environment, one that didn't treat humans as targets or military drones, then perhaps he wouldn't have felt such a hardcore desire to unplug from the machinic phylum and be plugged by the zoological one. However, the military–industrial complex is not so easily escaped. Mr. Hands's crime was discovered, and the scene of the crime identified, by tracing through surveillance footage from the hospital back to the ranch. (Who knew the back roads of the rural Northwest were part of Homeland Security's "ring of steel"?) For her part, as a representative of the state, Ms. Edwards diligently remembers to turn on her "internal camera," her "headcam," when visiting the ranch to remove the horse from the premises. She is well aware that in our technoscopic era, every glance is potential evidence.

The director of *Zoo*, Robinson Devor, is also acutely aware, as we might expect, of the influential role of the camera in reconstructing a story. Many of the reviews of the film, which followed in the wake of its successful run on the festival circuit, described it as "beautiful," and indeed, the cinematography is classical and austere, shunning the grainy, guerilla-video textures of the Zeitgeist. Its ominous score, muted lighting, and ponderous pace reach for a Lynchian ambience but—despite the subject matter—fall somewhere short, closer to Tim Burton territory, circling the enigma but restraining itself from plunging toward the pumping heart.

But why the urge to beautify? Were we to curate a documentary double-feature on uncomfortable interspecies congress, Ulrich Seidl's film *Animal Love* would be the perfect companion piece to *Zoo*. Equally aestheticized, but in a very different style, Seidl sets up a series of striking static tableaux of animal lovers from the margins of Viennese society. In contrast to the American horsemen, these people are themselves often more grotesque than their pets, seemingly too caricatured to be real—that is, if one had not already had the opportunity to see such people while sitting in the cafés and train stations of central Europe. (The human grotesque is in fact Seidl's bread and butter, as he illustrated in a similar film on aspiring supermodels that leaves no doubt in the viewer's mind that the director holds no special esteem for his own species and indeed has only a contemptuous fascination for the hyperreal nature of its creaturely life.)

Though there are no overt or explicit references to bestiality in *Animal Love,* it hovers above every frame, like an unfamiliar musk.[48] There are three occasions in which humans gambol with their pet dogs on a bed, in quasi-sexual ways. However, if a couple of screenings in my own classes are anything to go by, one scene in particular repulses beyond the others. This features an overweight, middle-aged man— wearing only a G-string and mottled with tattoos—playing with his tiny, fluffy white dog on a modest bed, overlooked by a sculpture of a pair of breasts. The shot lingers, and the sound is diegetic, allowing as little mediation as possible between the viewer and these two creatures, cavorting with each other to the point of breathlessness. But as the scene goes on, and on, the human is clearly the dominant partner, and things become increasingly awkward as the play threatens to turn fully sexual. Is this frottage? Is it not? The sadistic frisson of the scene lies in its asymptotic undecidability. Several silent questions are thus posed by the filmmaker: at what point does loving one's companion animal devolve into deviance? Where is the tipping point between healthy and unhealthy play? Moreover, can it really be called "bestiality" when humans are just as beastly as their pets?

WHEN ANIMALS ATTRACT

> We have never been the philosopher's human, we are bodies
> in braided, ontic, and antic relatings.
> —Donna Haraway, *When Species Meet*

> Animal is a word that men have given themselves the right
> to give.
> —Jacques Derrida, *The Animal That Therefore I Am*

In his opinion piece "Heavy Petting," first published by *Nerve,* celebrated animal rights philosopher Peter Singer (2001) details his belief:

> The taboo on sex with animals may . . . have originated as part of a broader rejection of non-reproductive sex. But the vehemence with which this prohibition continues to be held, its persistence while other non-reproductive sexual acts have become acceptable, suggests that there is another powerful force at work: our desire to differentiate ourselves, erotically and in every other way, from animals.

In other words, if we are to be judged by those with whom we consort, and if we do not wish to be judged harshly, then we should not go slumming (or stabling or kenneling). The taboo on interspecies sex is thus an unspoken flashpoint for collective identity policing, functioning according to the same principles as social pressure discouraging love between the classes and laws prohibiting marriage between races, which existed in certain states until only a couple decades ago. (Of course, legal same-sex marriage is still a long way from being universally recognized.)

But where there is taboo, there is also the powerful dialectic of repulsion and fascination. That *King Kong* qualifies as a love story between a giant male ape and a blonde female human alerts us to the cultural ambivalence surrounding this kind of unconventional relationship, while the same can be said for the various iterations of *Beauty and the Beast.*[49] The latent power of bestiality—or at least the discourse surrounding bestiality—is the projected possible future, in which we live and love within a harmonious "parliament of things" (Latour 1993). Nobody wants to be the historical chauvinist who is exposed as such due to the increasingly inclusive values of society. Nobody wants to be put in the same position as the closed-minded one who scoffed at the very suggestion of interracial marriage during the age of slavery. And yet very few of us are comfortable with endorsing attempts to literalize Greek myths or tastefully anthropomorphized erotic daydreams.[50] In the previous chapter, I gestured toward the many legends and fantasies uniting maiden with bear, while Timothy Treadwell flirted with the same notion, to his ultimate end (making him a spiritual sibling to Kenneth Pinyan, in that sense). The seductive aura of the animal embodies an otherness that is nevertheless capable of returning one's gaze—the very definition of Benjamin's aura. The risk involved, of course, depends on the animal in question.

In a remarkable statement, Singer (2001) declares that were we truly to acknowledge our own animality, after several millennia of denial and disavowal, then humanity would be more at ease with itself and less fearful of losing its white-knuckle grip on mastery. He writes, "This does not make sex across the species barrier normal, or natural, whatever those much-misused words may mean, but *it does imply that it ceases to be an offence to our status and dignity as human beings*" (emphasis added).

Singer's argument, consistent with his utilitarian stance, is that zoophilia is not unethical if there is no harm to the animal. Moreover, he is quite willing to concede that "sex with animals does not always involve cruelty."[51] In a moment of surprising candor, he goes on to ask, "Who has not been at a social occasion disrupted by the household dog gripping the legs of a visitor and vigorously rubbing its penis against them? The host usually discourages such activities, but in private not everyone objects to being used by her or his dog in this way, and occasionally mutually satisfying activities may develop." But who, we may ask, other than "child molester types" and creepy zoophiles, inhabits this stigmatized subset of the "not everyone"? Must we pay them mind? Can't we stick to the liberal, yet evasive, policy of "whatever they do in the privacy of their own home is no business of mine"?

Well, not if we want to engage with celebrated cultural scholar and critic Donna Haraway, whose recent writings about her relationship with her dog, Ms. Cayenne Pepper, raise some very pointed questions about intimate ontological overlaps between species. Her most recent book, *When Species Meet,* could be considered a direct critique of Aristotle's ancient claim that we cannot have friendships with animals simply because "there is nothing common to the two parties" (quoted in Steiner 2005, 62). Her work is a spirited refutation of the assumptions embedded in such an observation: on one hand, that there is an insurmountable gulf between human and nonhuman psyches, and on the other, that commonality need be the privileged foundation of friendship. Initially famous for her "Cyborg Manifesto" in the mid-1980s, Haraway (2008) has extended her (primarily feminist) interest in the cybernetic triangle, shifting focus from machines to animals, albeit remaining sensitive to the technologies that create, frame, and mediate them. She begins with a deceptively simple question: "Whom and what do I touch when I touch my dog?" (3). Were we mere slaves of our own incurious natures, we could answer this question in 399 fewer pages than she does by replying with the name "Cayenne." But of course, this answer is woefully insufficient for someone who enjoys getting her hands dirty grappling with the complex "lively knottings" (vii) that compose the "becoming-with" of companion species. She seeks to return and read the gaze of her pooch not in the manner of "elevated thinker" confronting "enigmatic object"—within the genealogy of Western metaphysics—but within the actual, material, capricious, contingent, situated, and mundane moments of encounter. The difference is one of attitude and openness, shedding the residues of hubris that she even finds in Derrida, who himself sought to avoid the traps of human exceptionalism. What's more, this difference relies heavily on the poetics of the exchange, suggesting an impatience with any discourse that tries vainly to distinguish form from content. Thus Haraway seeks to chalk the choreography that occurs in those "mortal world-making entanglements" that she calls "contact zones" or "attachment sites."

Hence the claim that "we have never been human," in any verifiable sense. Moreover, that humans have been convinced that they *are* human, for so long, is an indictment of their parochialism, their inability to be worldly. For one thing, Haraway notes that "human genomes can be found in only 10 percent of all the cells that occupy the mundane space I call my body," a humbling scientific fact that makes her smile. Her target is thus "the culturally normal fantasy"—what she calls elsewhere "the outrage"—of human exceptionalism. "This is the premise that humanity alone is not a spatial and temporal web of interspecies dependencies" (Haraway 2008, 11).

But what triggered this specific ethical experience since all such passions have an origin story? Haraway is not afraid to begin with the graphically personal: "Almost eight years ago, I found myself in unexpected and out-of-bounds love with a hot red dog I named Cayenne.... It has been an awakening to track how many sorts of kin and kind this love has materialized, how many sorts of consequences flow from her kiss. The sticky threads proliferate from this woman–dog tangle" (Haraway 2008, 300). Haraway's own designation of "out-of-bounds" certainly begs the question of just how intimate she has been with Cayenne: a question I do not raise out of any prurient curiosity but rather to show how the anthropological machine is being reconfigured by our present moment to consider "bestiality" as not merely an unsavory taboo but also a term that can no longer contain the myriad forms of "animal love" that could hitherto be conveniently shelved under its name (with all its associated pathological overtones).

Haraway (2008) seems to relish being explicit about this and not leaving any doubt in the reader's mind as to the extent of her affection, as when she discusses Cayenne in intimate terms: "Her red merle Australian shepherd's quick and lithe tongue has swabbed the tissues of my tonsils, with all their eager immune system receptors.... We have had forbidden conversation; we have had oral intercourse" (16).[52] Close readers of "A Cyborg Manifesto" should not be surprised at such provocative depictions of experiences that Rush Limbaugh would probably call "lesbian bestiality." For even back then, she wrote, "Cyborgs signal disturbingly and pleasurably tight coupling. Bestiality has a new status in this cycle of marriage exchange" (Haraway 1991, 152).[53] To Haraway's mind, there is no doubt that this complex and profound feeling is, to the degree that it can be, mutual: "Significantly other to each other, in specific difference, we signify in the flesh a nasty developmental infection called love . . . a historical aberration and a naturalcultural legacy" (Haraway 2008, 16). This particular instance of love, however, is not to be confused with the common domestic ritual of emotional blackmail that all too frequently goes under the same moniker. The kind of owner–pet connection that can be witnessed at any dog show, or between coiffed women on the Upper East Side and the trembling, hairless gremlins peeping out of their handbags, does not give Haraway any confidence about the possibility of authentic communication across the taxonomic divide. "If not fashion accessories," she writes, "pets are taken to be living engines for churning out unconditional love—affectional slaves" (206)—which is why she prefers the term *companion*.

For Haraway (2008, 97), "to be in love means to be worldly," that is to say, "to be in connection with significant otherness and signifying others, on many scales, in layers of locals and globals, in ramifying webs." Along with Lacan, I have grave reservations, however, about that initial equation.[54] No question, we all operate under different assumptions of what "love" might be when we are under its influence and what it is capable of. But those differences are tethered together by the common word and the complex, yet coherent, discourse and history that compose its cargo. Haraway is essentially claiming that her love for Cayenne is more enlightened and ethical than, say, Paris Hilton's love for Tinkerbell. On the face of it, this is not a very controversial assertion. But to conflate love with worldliness (or what she calls elsewhere "cosmopolitics"[55]) is to quarantine 90 percent of the behaviors that are triggered in its wake: monomania, projective narcissism, and so on. Indeed, for those lovers who reject the world to spend more quality time with their lovers (i.e., almost all of them . . . and yes, I'm still looking at you, Irigaray), then to be in love is to be as parochial as can be. Granted, the metonymy at work when we are enthralled by our beloved can mean that they function as a prism for more worldly concerns. The cherished one can "stand for" all that we admire about the set to which they belong (usually "humanity"). But as a rule, the centripetal forces far overwhelm the centrifugal ones.[56]

In any case, Haraway's spiritual, intellectual, and physical love for her companion is an extremely powerful lens for exploring the "taxonomic conveniences" we use to navigate the world.[57] Again and again, for Haraway (2008, 64), the crucial, generative force comes down to the *actuality* of encounter: "In their personal bodies themselves, the dogs and people are freedom-making technologies for each other. They are each other's machine tools for making other selves. Face-to-face encounters is how those machines grind souls with new tolerance limits."[58] Kudos to Haraway for not leaving technology out of the mix because much too frequently, the issue is reduced to a molar Mexican standoff. Deleuze and Guattari, however, might ask about the kinds of animals that are not endowed with a face, as we conceive it. What would a face-to-face encounter with a jellyfish look like, for example? But Haraway has little patience for such Parisian pedantry. Instead, she is at pains to note that we must learn "to be 'polite' in responsible relation to always asymmetrical living and dying and nurturing and killing" (42).

So what would it mean to be *polite* to our animal friends and, presumably, foes? Well, the first step is to recognize that "animals are everywhere *full partners* in worlding, in becoming with" (Haraway 2008, 301; emphasis added). They are decidedly not ornaments, pets, therapeutic devices,[59] or mute reflections of our psychic or social status. While Haraway does not put it in these terms, animals embody a post-Kantian imperative to recognize our fellow critters[60] as ends in themselves, while simultaneously appreciating the multifaceted symbiosis that enables all of us to *be,* however temporarily, in the first place. But this is not a pretext to promote animals into our human ranks for the important reason that "resistance to human exceptionalism *requires* resistance to humanization of our partners" (52). The supreme challenge is therefore to respect difference in its full alienness, while simultaneously appreciating the miracle of "nonmimetic sharing" (75) between species.

Hence the aversion to the kind of "animals are people, too" logic of Peter Singer and company: "We do not get very far with the categories generally used by animal rights discourses, in which animals end up as permanent dependents ('lesser humans'), utterly natural ('nonhuman'), or exactly the same ('humans in fur suits')" (Haraway 2008, 67).[61] Indeed, "possessive individuals (imagined as human or animal) are the wrong units for considering what is going on" (70). To put it another way, we should not begin with the beings in question and then map their relationships but rather *begin with the relationships* to better understand the kinds of beings that emerge. It is a matter of the parallax view.

And so, were we to boil down Haraway's sophisticated love letter to her dog into one sentence, it would read, "Multispecies flourishing requires a robust nonanthropomorphic sensibility that is accountable to irreducible differences" (Haraway 2008, 90). Indeed, tracing such a nonanthropomorphic sensibility is not only the principal concern of the current book but a common theme uniting such different projects as those designed by Derrida, Agamben, Foucault, and Deleuze and Guattari. Haraway, as I have already suggested, has precious little time for such attempts, which—in the last instance, at least—she believes to be rooted in misogyny, fear of aging, a disguised incuriosity about animals, and a (typically male) horror of the flesh (30). (Given her fierce love for Cayenne, it's no surprise that she would be aggrieved by Deleuze and Guattari's statement that "anyone who likes cats or dogs is a fool"—a provocation that loses its teeth a little, now that we know about Deleuze's lifetime affection for his pet cats.)[62]

Indeed, the trajectory of the long twentieth century looks quite different if we decide to bookend Nietzsche's horse with Derrida's cat, as opposed to Haraway's dog (or vice versa). As we have established, Haraway is not one to blush when discovered naked by her fellow creature. So what is it in Derrida's account that makes him ashamed in front of his feline friend? Well, let us hear it from the horse's mouth, as it were:

> I have . . . trouble keeping silent within me a protest against the indecency. Against the impropriety *[malséance]* that can come of finding oneself naked, one's sex exposed, stark naked before a cat that looks at you without moving, just to see. The impropriety of a certain animal nude before the other animal, from that point on one might call it a kind of *animalséance*: the single, incomparable and original experience of the impropriety that would come from appearing in truth naked, in front of the insistent gaze of the animal, a benevolent or pitiless gaze, surprised or cognizant. The gaze of a seer, a visionary or extra-lucid blind one. It is as if I were ashamed, therefore, naked in front of this cat, but also ashamed of being ashamed. A reflected shame, the mirror of a shame ashamed of itself, a shame that is at the same time specular, unjustifiable, and unavowable. (Derrida 2008, 4)[63]

In a bathroom sequel to Genesis, Adam is now all too aware that clothes maketh the Man. Only this time around, the mastery bestowed on him by God is castrated by a personal and historical distance from such an authorizing God as well as by the micropressures of domestic space, politics, and cohabitation. To figuratively blush in front of an other is to experience the ontological feedback loop created by the subjective acknowledgment of his or her presence. This presence can be actual or virtual, hence the possibility of feeling ashamed in front of one's parent or guardian or spouse, even when he or she is absent. Of course, as Haraway has shown, one need not feel ashamed to register the presence of an other; one merely has to show politeness. However, if someone blushes under the gaze of some *thing,* then that something is at once an honorary human and an entity that troubles the very category to which it has been given an entry pass.

The cat, in contrast, does not seem ashamed. It does not meow a mortified "sorry" before backing out of the bathroom. And so Derrida is obliged to marinate in metashame, taking on enough nakedness, obscenity, and exposure for the both of them. After all, only humans can be "naked" in the sense of self-consciously feeling so because of the absence of covering (proving once again that children are only quasi-humans, after all).[64] No doubt, even long before Freud, cats have been associated with a singularly feminine form of narcissism, and it is perhaps no surprise that Derrida's cat is female. However, it would be an injustice to the subtlety of his thought merely to conclude that the great thinker is simply ashamed of his literal exposure and that Haraway—by way of contrast—avoids related issues because she has no phallic panic to which to measure up.

For Derrida (2008, 11), "nudity is nothing other than that passivity, the involuntary exhibition of the self." What is more, since "clothing derives from technics," we would "therefore have to think shame and technicity together" (5). The human, as we have seen, is the species without qualities. Discursively speaking, there is a fault, default, or lack at our origin that subsequently constitutes our being-in-the-world from *episteme* to *episteme.* (Humanity, for Derrida [2008, 14], is "above all anxious about, and jealous of, what is proper to it.") We have compensated for this lack of perfection practically with technics and philosophically by emphasizing what we presume we have over and above animals or machines (soul, language, consciousness, rationality, etc.). In any case, the human is always framed and figured as an animal plus or minus *n,* and on this occasion, the *n* corresponds to clothing. Thus the humble, organic fig leaf becomes drafted into the technological world as soon as it is used deliberately to obscure, shield, or mask the most patently animalistic part of the human. (Yet another example of technology comprising a relationship between elements rather than anything essentially "artificial.")

Derrida (2008, 11) uses his shame as a springboard to think about "this absolute alterity of the neighbor," itself "an existence that refuses to be conceptualized" (9). For him, the ever-present "question of the animal" has been both settled and unsettled by several key hearings in the history of thought, which he designates in shorthand as Descartes, Kant, Levinas, and Lacan. One of the most persistent distinctions self-identified humans have made against their animal others is that between a reaction and a response, the assumption being that only the former are capable of the latter. The most scandalous issue for Derrida, however (leaving aside, for the moment, the issue of its effect, namely, "the unprecedented proportions of this subjection of the animal" over the past two hundred years, and the disavowal accompanying it),[65] is the matter of the definite article and the singular: *the* animal. "The animal is a word . . . a name they have given themselves the right and authority to give to the living other" (23). What Derrida finds so remarkable is that *all* philosophers have drawn a clear and unbreakable line in the sand and that "*all* philosophers have judged that limit to be single and indivisible, considering that on the other side of that limit there is an immense group, a single and fundamentally homogenous set that one has the right . . . to distinguish and mark as opposite, namely, the set of the Animal . . . in the general singular" (40–41).

The very project of anthropogenesis, for Derrida, is based on this conceptual violence, this ontological apartheid, which he goes so far as to call not only a crime but "a kind of species war." His linguistic intervention to begin reducing the unthinkable scale of this crime, following the reasoning that our words reformat our thoughts when used enough, is to replace the word *animal* with *animot*. The virtue of this is encapsulated in the French pun, homophonically blending the plural *animaux* with the chimera, *ani-mot* (*mot* meaning "word"). This has the duel benefit of reminding us that there is no such figural homogenous phantasm as *the* animal, as if spiders and bears and luminous deep-sea fish belong to the same category, while also serving to deconstructively point to the linguistic nature of the convenience: that *animal* is a very simple word, obliged to represent an extremely complex explosion of referents. "*Ecce animot,*" writes Derrida. "Neither a species nor a gender nor an individual, it is an irreducible living multiplicity of mortals" (41).

And yet, despite Derrida's rather unprecedented gesture in the history of mainstream philosophy, Haraway is not convinced it is enough. "Derrida failed a simple obligation of companion species," she writes. "He did not become curious about what the cat might actually be doing, feeling, thinking, or perhaps making available to him in looking back at him that morning.... Instead, he concentrated on his shame in being naked before this cat. Shame trumped curiosity, and that does not bode well for an autremondialisation" (Haraway 2008, 22).[66] One would think that exposing the profound anthropocentric remainder inside the supposedly antihumanistic turn of postwar Continental philosophy would be enough to allow Derrida entry into Haraway's pantheon of animal allies. But she interprets such gestures differently, valuing an emphasis on an attempt to know the unknowable: to reach out and intersect in actuality rather than between the pages (and occasionally between bathings).

Haraway's alternative utopia is, fittingly, a very mundane one—the team sport of "agility"—in which a human and a dog compete together as a team against the clock, while navigating an obstacle course. She is, of course, aware of the kind of discipline such an activity requires as well as of the Foucauldian concerns one might raise in this context. (Indeed, I find it odd that in a book that name-checks so many animal-centered television shows, there is no mention of *The Dog Whisperer,* a show with a slightly misleading name, since the whisperer himself, Cesar Millan, is candid about the much more urgent need to train the human owners than the troublesome canines.)[67] But this utopia is firmly embedded in time and space. "There is no happy ending to offer," she states unflinchingly, "no conclusion to this ongoing entanglement" (39). To share the same world with an animal, without imposing our own telos, is the key to a less ethically bankrupt relationship (the kind that leads to heedless exploitation, experimentation, and slaughter).

In this provisional, pragmatic paradise—a technically advanced, atheological, perhaps even matriarchal Garden of Eden—"no one gets to be Man" (Haraway 2008, 82). This is another way of saying that we can be quite certain that Haraway does not serenade her dog Cayenne with any Nine Inch Nail songs.

THE HUMAN TAINT

> No wonder of it: shéer plód makes plough down sillion
> Shine, and blue-bleak embers, ah my dear,
> Fall, gall themselves, and gash gold-vermilion.
> —Gerard Manley Hopkins, "The Windhover"

Despite its open, curious, worldly intentions, Haraway's love for her dog still shows subtle signs of circulating within a familiar libidinal economy, involving the kind of struggles around difference and recognition that can lead to passive-aggressive sulking because of perceived miscommunication. A very different model of human–animal passion can be found in J. A. Baker's (2005) singular book *The Peregrine*, which comprises diary entries of the author's monomaniacal pursuit of hawks during a hunting migration in East Anglia during the 1960s. Like the birds that he describes in such exquisite and poetic detail, Baker himself is a mysterious figure, leaving barely a trace of his actual existence besides this book (and one other), leaving only speculation concerning his life, work, and (probable) death. The enigma of Baker's biography dovetails provocatively with Lacan's assertion that animals are distinct from humans in their inability to erase their own traces,[68] for it places this author, who so stridently sought to shed his humanity and become-bird, in an awkward position. On one hand (or should that be *talon*?), Baker wants to disappear into the pure, mindless motion of the swoop; on the other, he is engaged in one of the more profound aesthetic experiments of the postwar period. What could be more human than wanting to control one's own trace? ("Footprints in snow are strangely moving," he wrote. "They seem an almost shameful betrayal of the creatures that make them, as though something of themselves had been left defenceless" [138].) And yet Baker's words are obsessed with, indeed haunted by, the possibility of effacement, of defacing himself as a member of his own species.

Early on he tells us:

> I have always longed to be a part of the outward life, to be out there at the edge of things, to let the human taint wash away in emptiness and silence as the fox sloughs his smell into the cold

unworldliness of water; to return to the town as a stranger. Wandering flushes a glory that fades with arrival. I came late to the love of birds. For years I saw them only as a tremor at the edge of vision. They know suffering and joy in simple states not possible for us. Their lives quicken and warm to a pulse our hearts can never reach. They race to oblivion. They are old before we have finished growing. (Baker 2005, 10)

Like Haraway, Baker is allergic to any sentimentalizing of the animal kingdom, preferring to see the environment and those who populate it through the lens of his own evocative precision rather than through Disney's rose-colored kind:

I shall try to make plain the bloodiness of killing. Too often this has been slurred over by those who defend hawks. Flesh-eating man is in no way superior. It is so easy to love the dead. The word "predator" is baggy with misuse. All birds eat living flesh at some time in their lives. Consider the cold-eyed thrush, that springy carnivore of lawns, worm stabber, basher to death of snails. We should not sentimentalise his song, and forget the killing that sustains it. (14)

And yet the tone is very different to Haraway's. Rather than warm, drooling tongue licks and a rather enmeshed, reaching, potentially claustrophobic mode of contact, we get an altogether more distanced and sparse ontology. Though the latter could be seen as a more masculine mode, as observation at arm's length, I suggest that gender is a red herring in this encounter, since something more fundamental is at issue—something concerning the returnability of the gaze of *all* ocular beings.

Jakob von Uexküll told us in 1934 that each creature exists in its own perceptual bubble, thus creating its own mode of time and space. He also acknowledged that the trickiest part of his radical bio-phenomenology is to account for the interactions that occur *between* these bubbles (say, between a dog and a woman, a hawk and a man). One can certainly appreciate the notion that a tick, which exists only to register and react to the scent of butyric acid (a sign of the presence of mammalian blood), lives in a drastically different universe to the one we do. Moreover, we may even grant Uexküll his relativistic cosmology in that there is no single universal objective time–space continuum functioning as a backdrop that different bodies experience differently but rather only the chain of onto-bubbles separating species from species (a scenario that has the benefit of avoiding the desire to carve up the world into two homogenous, cartoonish groups). But what happens when two different animals experience an exchange via the eyes or, at least, seem to? Is this a case of two bubbles bouncing off each other, offering a glimpse of a limit that threatens to disappear but constantly reasserts itself? Or is there truly a moment in which the bubbles pop, allowing an authentic, nonlinguistic, mutual communication?

Baker would no doubt endorse Haraway's (2008, 236) belief that "among beings who recognize one another, who respond to the presence of a significant other, something delicious is at stake."[69] He may also agree that "it is no longer possible scientifically to compare something like 'consciousness' or 'language' among human and nonhuman animals as if there were a singular axis of calibration" (235). And yet, in choosing a bird of prey over a domesticated dog, the tone of his own obsession speaks of intimacy on a different scale (speaking both spatially and musically). For all the respect paid to uncanniness and alterity in Haraway's ode to the other, we are left with dog food, pet pills, and recreational obstacle courses. Her project is thus to balance the mundane with the taboo. Baker, following a different route, could perhaps be accused of romanticizing Nature, were his diary entries not so brutal, abstract, and formalist.[70] The remarkable thing about reading *The Peregrine* is the way in which the narrator renders the potential tedium of repetition (after all, there is no plot to be found here) into an accumulative, atheological epiphany. The reader—or at least *this* reader—is constantly astonished that endless descriptions of birds and landscapes are not soporific but exhilarating. In its fuguelike structure, we are offered a sense of what it might be like to become-animal, that is to say, to be *entertained* by something other than human intrigue.[71] Thus Baker's balancing act is between his own potential self-transcendence and the wavering indifference of the auratic other.

From the outset, we are told, "Like all hunters, the peregrine is inhibited by a code of behavior. It seldom chases prey on the ground.... If the code is persistently broken, the hawk is probably sick or insane" (Baker 2005, 26). The narrator is careful to caution himself against

Orwellian anthropomorphisms, suggesting that this particular use of the term *code* really does refer to a nonhuman etiquette rather than a phantasmatic fusion of prince with falcon.[72] Indeed, today's ethologists would no doubt scold us for presuming that we are the only creatures with the capacity for social graces (i.e., legible behavioral protocols between the same genus).

Though the published fragments that make up *The Peregrine* only represent one season, Baker notes that he has found 619 kills in ten years, all diligently documented by species. Clearly we are dealing with a compulsive personality here, albeit one with an infinitely more subtle grasp of "the Open" than Timothy Treadwell.

Baker (2005, 35–36) continues:

> Like the seafarer, the peregrine lives in a pouring-away world of no attachment, a world of wakes and tilting, of sinking planes of land and water. . . . The peregrine sees and remembers patterns we do not know exist: the neat squares of orchard and woodland, the endlessly varying quadrilateral shapes of fields. He finds his way across the land by a succession of remembered symmetries. . . . He may live in a world of endless pulsations, of objects forever contracting or dilating in size.

The introduction to the book provides us with a rare nugget of biographical information, namely, that Baker had purportedly been diagnosed with a serious illness around the time of writing, perhaps inspiring him to record the thoughts that had occupied him only internally for nearly a decade. And once in possession of this piece of unverifiable intelligence, there is the temptation to read the influence and proximity of mortality between the lines. Yet this should not be considered an overdetermined reading but merely a reminder of the *Dasein* (i.e., being-toward-death) that conditions *all* self-identified, or self-proclaimed, artistic projects.[73]

Essentially we are dealing with at least three Bakers: the enigmatic author, the virtuosic narrator, and the whatever-twitcher[74] character. At the center of the text, around which these three avatars circulate, lies the event of the kill, and Baker intends to remain faithful to each and every one: "A hawk's kill is like the warm embers of a dying fire" (Baker 2005, 67). There is no recognition here of the old philosophical chestnut that animals do not die but merely expire because dozens of avian species are—according to the narrator—ruled by a palpable fear, one that overflows anthropomorphic projection: "One bird fell back, gashed dead, looking astonished, like a man falling out of a tree. The ground came up and crushed it."[75]

For whereas Baker sees reflections of men in some birds, as happens when an owl appears to him as a comical shrunken knight, the trajectory of the book is more concerned with the reverse, as he engages in his own idiosyncratic version of Keats's "negatively charged lyrical consciousness" (Khalip 2006, 899)[76] (i.e., effacing oneself into another being via poetic projection—itself a mode of virtual subjecthood, discussed earlier):

> I found myself crouching over the kill, like a mantling hawk. My eyes turned quickly about, alert for the walking heads of men. Unconsciously I was imitating the movements of a hawk, as in some primitive ritual; the hunter becoming the thing he hunts. I looked into the wood. In a lair of shadow the peregrine was crouching, watching me, gripping the neck of a dead branch. We live, in these days in the open, the same ecstatic fearful life. We shun men. We hate their suddenly uplifted arms, the insanity of their flailing gestures, their erratic scissoring gait, their aimless stumbling ways, the tombstone whiteness of their faces. (Baker 2005, 95)

Being the proverbial descendent of Epimetheus and Prometheus, however, Baker is obliged to rely on the artifice of technology to compensate for his species's insufficiencies. "Binoculars, and a hawk-like vigilance, reduce the disadvantage of myopic human vision" (96) (to which we may add the mnemotechnology of alphabetic depiction). As we have seen throughout, technics is often considered the element that allows us to extend beyond our humanness, branching out in two different directions along the sides of the cybernetic triangle: toward the animal and toward the machine. To render it somewhat differently, however, our species's systematic deployment of and within technology *creates* the human as an emergent property inside the overlap of the Venn diagram between animal and machine (hence the now increasingly common claim that we are all cyborgs). But in this particular case, Baker uses his binoculars and his pen to launch himself on the asymptotic trajectory of becoming-peregrine. Sometimes it is difficult to tell whether he is approaching one particular hawk or a synthesis of different ones—a significant point as we move closer toward a discussion of types qua individuality. It is also worth noting that Baker does not display an Adamic urge to give them names. In any case, he begins not only to experience a metamorphosis but to *bestow the bird of prey with a possible acknowledgment of such*: "The predictability of my movements may have made him more curious, and more trusting. He may associate me now with the incessant disturbance of prey, as though I too were a species of hawk" (125). And yet the narrator is not laboring under any delusion of symmetry: "I think he regards me now as part hawk, part man; worth flying over to look at from time to time, but never wholly to be trusted; a crippled hawk, perhaps, unable to fly or to kill cleanly, uncertain and sour of temper" (162). And further still: "He has found a meaning for me, but I do not know what it is. I am his slow and moribund companion, Caliban to his Ariel" (176).

The role of subject, that is to say, the one who enjoys an honorary Cartesian subjectivity, flickers between the narrator and the peregrine, each feeling the other out, as it were, the human clearly involved in both deference and transference, aware of the horizontal hubris of the latter. "Standing in the fields near the north orchard, I shut my eyes and tried to crystallize my will into the light-drenched prism of the hawk's mind" (Baker 2005, 144), an attempt redeemed by the sincerity of its own intensity but that—like the ascendancy of Icarus—is doomed to fall short.[77] (This is not necessarily the same thing as failing, it should be noted—after all, Icarus *did* fly.) "I watched him with longing, as though he were reflecting down to me his brilliant unregarded vision of the land beyond the hill" (140). Any telepathic connection, however, is constantly shadowed by the profound uncertainty of the "as though."

As a human, Baker is entering this milieu at a terrible disadvantage: "As so often on spring evenings, no birds sing near me, while all the distant trees and bushes ring with song. Like all human beings, I seem to walk within a hoop of red-hot iron,[78] a hundred yards across, that sears away all life. When I stand still, it cools, and slowly disappears" (Baker 2005, 185).[79] And yet our narrator is not always imprisoned inside this lethal radius, for he can shrink the circle by renouncing his own condition.[80] "Like the hawk," he writes, "I heard and hated the sound of man, that faceless horror of the stony places" (144) (a description reversing Levinas's anthropocentric ethics, which denies the face to the animal, even Bobby the Kantian dog).[81]

The stakes are revealed in the gaze, a temporal supplement to the mirror stage, played out in this case on the level of the species rather than person to person. "Hawks are reluctant to fly while they are being watched," he tells us. "They wait till the strange bondage of the eyes is broken" (Baker 2005, 97).[82] Several weeks later, Baker and the peregrine meet again: "For more than a minute we both stayed still, each puzzled and intrigued by the other, sharing the curious bond that comes with identity of position" (141). And here, in the phrase *identity of position,* we encounter a compelling description for a relationship that avoids all those narcissistic snares that tend to haunt the human world. It is a geometric relationship: fragile, contingent, yet undeniable. It is (th)us—albeit fleetingly. Indeed, the peregrine becomes so familiar with Baker's presence that he or she (gender is not consistently given) eventually feels comfortable enough to stay and sleep (191).[83]

And so, eight centuries after Anaximander of Miletus asked, "What does a falcon see?" Baker answers by way of a would-be ahuman poetics.[84] As such, his book is deliberately designed to sabotage the Enlightenment's anthropological machine. What's more, as readers, we are not in the presence of a wrenching compassion, as we are with Nietzsche; neither are we witness to a self-reflexive shame spiral, as we are with Derrida; nor to a curious ethics of occasional lust, as we are with Haraway. Rather we are confronted with a kind of desolate melancholy, as perfected by W. G. Sebald, one of the three poet laureates of "creaturely life"—according to Eric Santner—along with Rilke and Kafka.[85] Baker has composed an energizing requiem for both the noble lineage of the hawk and for himself.[86] In doing so, he has exposed the possibility of fixating on one specific creature, in the singular, as an ambassador for the *animot,* in the plural.

IMPERSONAL INTIMACY

> Have we ever had a single experience which convinces us
> that man alone has been enlightened by a ray denied all
> other animals?
> —de la Mettrie, *Machine Man*

Is Baker's book narcissistic? Absolutely, but not in the banal, personalized, self-absorbed sense. Instead, it represents a rare portrait of what Leo Bersani and Adam Phillips (2008) call "impersonal intimacy," that is, a "new relational mode" that does not hate or fear otherness and that does not take difference *personally*. ("Difference," writes Bersani, speaking psychoanalytically, "is the one thing we cannot bear" [viii].)[87] Impersonal intimacy is a way of being, becoming, and/or belonging, free of the rather dismal subject-centric narratives of love (to use the clearest example as our test case). For where depth psychology posits a sovereign self who must successfully bond her established ipseity with other such entities,[88] psychoanalysis—at least the kind that interests Bersani and Phillips—begins with the premise that "the It in the I transforms subjecthood from psychic density into pure potentiality" (25).[89] In other words, we should switch our focus from the defensive armature of the self's psychological apparatus to inaugurate an orientation that does not mistake the "accidents of personality" (82) for something worth cherishing and preserving, no matter the mental cost.

Bersani's illustration of impersonal intimacy is extreme and, to some, repulsive, that being the death-baiting male homosexual subculture of "barebacking" (i.e., anal sex, sometimes collective, without condoms). While acknowledging the extremely problematic nature of his own example, Bersani is attracted by what he sees as "the ascesis of an ego-divesting discipline": a discipline "necessary in order to be replaced, inhabited by the other" (Bersani and Phillips 2008, 51). One hopes, however, that one need not fly quite so close to Thanatos to purge Eros of its contaminated aspect. Baker's relationship to the peregrine certainly involves the frisson of death—this much has been established. And yet no animals, human or otherwise, need necessarily be harmed in his rendition of "sublime self-abnegation," outside the established feeding cycle.

As modes of Keatsean poetic projection, the difference between barebacking and bird-watching seems patently obvious. In the former, the "bottom" (passive partner) is filled physically and—according to Bersani at least—spiritually by the other. He becomes the host of "some monstrously appetitive god" (Bersani and Phillips 2008, 50), thereby transforming himself into the locus of "pure love" (or at least a modern twist on the medieval notion of the same). The self is erased or transcended by the solicited invasion of radical difference.[90] By contrast, Baker's vision of escaping the confines of subjectivity is through an ontological leap *into* the other. The self is erased or transcended by the willed absorption into alterity. But in fact, these are two perspectives of the same architectonic process. Though the agents involved are engaged in very different activities, they are initiates of impersonal intimacy, otherwise described as "indefinitely suspended being" (Bersani and Phillips 2008, 29). And yet there is a difference we need to register, for while one wallows within "awesome abjection," the other hovers above the gravity-bound world of the psyche. That is to say, barebacking uses *shame* as a tool of liberating self-shattering. Hawk-chasing, by contrast, attempts to leave shame (i.e., the shame of being human) far behind. Mr. Hands, of course, sacrificed himself to the impossibility of doing both at once: of allowing the embodied integrity of his human narcissism to be violated by a different species.

While recognizing that shame can fortify the fearful self, if processed defensively, Phillips writes that such an experience "is like a threshold from the personal to the impersonal, from consent to abandonment, from cherished and horrifying self-images to those images of oneself that one could never have before the experience" (Bersani and Phillips 2008, 111). Haraway's critique of Derrida, for instance, is that his other-induced shame of nakedness did not jolt him out of his philosophical training but rather sent him into a narcissistic critique of the terrain with which he is most familiar and comfortable. In any case, Phillips goes on to note that "the first intimacy" (i.e., that of motherhood) is one "with a process of becoming, not with a person" (114). That is to say, the baby's experience is of nourishment, cradling, and the entire "aesthetics of handling," which only later coalesce into an individual by the name of "Mama." The question then becomes, "why is this relation so difficult to sustain, so easily sabotaged by the drive to take things personally?" (114).

Phillips's implied answer to his own question is the bildungsroman implanted in our own heads via cultural narratives: "our idealization of growth and development," which is, in his view, "an attempt to conceal from ourselves that we are going nowhere." After all, "the joke of evolution is that it is a teleology without a point" (Bersani and Phillips 2008, 114). The reason we can therefore combine psychoanalysis with poetry, under the sign of zoology, is because "the self" is constituted not only through human intersubjectivity but within networks of nonhuman others. Pulling the point-of-view camera back to include such others is perhaps *the* task of our age.

Bersani and Phillips (2008, 37) condense their approach into one provocative comment by French novelist Guillaume Dunstan: "When no one really exists, there is room for everyone." Their own unpacking of this striking idea is more rigorous but less pithy, seeking "a universal relatedness grounded in the absence of relations, in the felicitous erasure of people as persons" (37).[91] The implications here are vast and vertiginous. To begin with—and to adapt their human scene into a more expansive one—we get a sense of why the drive to include chimps or orangutans as legal "persons" is the wrong way to go. Simply adding more "people" to the mix will not extend justice but rather dilute a pond already polluted by rampant wrongdoing; rather we should be involved in self-divestiture, en masse. This could conceivably lead to a "universal singular" of creatures, to be negotiated one by one rather than through transcendental categories. (To paraphrase Haraway, *No one gets to be Man, man.*) In this radical utopia, "the very opposition between sameness and difference becomes irrelevant as a structuring category of being" (86), at once stemming from, and resulting in, a "generous narcissism."

The pleasure to be found in Baker's book is the way it soars above the fog of personal narcissism and human psychology. Though it is indeed an example of human imagination, it is more rigorously the scene of an impersonal intimacy: one not interested in leaving an individual trace, in the manner of a Joyce or Nabokov. "Writers, painters, filmmakers," writes Bersani, "frequently move in their late work not toward a greater density of meaning and texture, but rather toward a kind of concentrated monotony that designates a certain negativizing effect inherent in the aesthetic" (Bersani and Phillips 2008, 25). In other words, mature artists attempt to flee their own rather arbitrary idiosyncrasies, for they understand that the "self is a practical convenience; promoted to the status of an ethical ideal" (96). As a further consequence, they strive for the far more forceful and enduring resonance of the universal, the formal, the abstract, the archetypal.

"What is different about others (their psychological individuality) could be thought of as merely the envelope of the more profound (if less fully realized, or completed) part of themselves which is our sameness" (Bersani and Phillips 2008, 86). Here Bersani literally brackets off the psyche. But if only it were that simple! Of course, this is much more easily said than done, given that the entire process of triumphant hominization is based on inflating the self to the size of the State, leading to an era in which corporations now have the rights of individuals (if not vice versa). Nevertheless, I—along with Bersani and Phillips—believe we must nurture these conceptual seedlings in the hope that they take root somewhere, somehow. For the Trojan horse of fetishizing the individual "for who they are" is merely another name for the anthropological machine in its most seductive, irresponsible mode. This is not to advocate an army of people-bots: a gray Orwellian future of individuals afraid to mark themselves as different. Rather it is to lobby against a common baseline or criteria for parsing that very difference, to urge against *universal* measuring sticks to distinguish the line of demarcation between the merely eccentric and the insane, between genders, between species. (The invention of provisional, local, contextual, unofficial systems of judgment would be half the fun of living in such a novel situation. "The world will always successfully resist projects that aim to erase its otherness" [Bersani and Phillips 2008, 121], states Bersani, which is all the more reason to nuance that very resistance.)

True, Bersani and Phillips don't follow me this far, since they are not interested in the question of the animal (at least, not in this book, although Bersani does appear with a small bird on his shoulder in the author photo, which makes me believe he would be sympathetic to my project). To the question, "how can we allow ourselves—or, how can we remind ourselves—of our passion for sameness"? (108), they answer, "impersonal intimacy."[92] But how might this question apply to animals, that is, all those *other* beings who are *not*, ostensibly, trisected and self-alienated by the antagonisms of language, identity, and social imperatives. Is it easier for us to empathize with animals, according to a law of narcissism of major differences? Or is the absolute alterity of a different species something with which we must struggle only after transcending the narcissism of minor (i.e., human) differences?

Toward the end of his epic lecture on the *animot,* Derrida (2008) answers his own question, "is there animal narcissism?" (51), with a qualified yes, supporting such a conclusion with another rhetorical question: "Who can deny that phenomena of narcissistic exhibition in seduction or sexual combat, the 'follow me who is (following) you' deployed in colors, music, adornments, parades, or erections of all sorts derive from such an auto-deixis?" (95)[93] (*auto-deixis* being the assumed exclusive human capacity to turn the index finger toward the self and thus create the power of the "I"—cogito, *ego* sum). Derrida is careful, however, not to get carried away with the kind of argument that claims that animals are just like people, or at least can be, in profound, wide-angle ways. He states, "It would not be a matter of 'giving speech back' to animals but perhaps of acceding to a thinking, however fabulous and chimerical it might be, that thinks the absence of the name and of the word otherwise, and as something other than a privation" (48). Or further:

> The critical or deconstructive reading I am calling for would seek less to restitute to the animal . . . the powers that it is not certain to possess (even if that sometimes seems possible) than to wonder whether one could not claim as much relevance for this type of analysis in the case of the human—with respect, for example, to the "wiring" of its sexual and reproductive behavior. Etc. (173)

In cruder terms, why pull animals—or for that matter, robots—up the evolutionary or theological ladder, when we can just take humans down a few pegs? ("The real problem," wrote B. F. Skinner in 1968, "is not whether machines think but whether men do" [quoted in Milton 1996, 95].)

Sex is the most semiotically potent site because it is where the human is stretched to the breaking point between the angelic and the bestial and must therefore engage itself in a flurry of activity to stop the structure from collapsing in on itself (a disaster in which the human could disappear completely—but would it really be such a disaster?). For Agamben (2004, 83), the sexual is "an element which seems to belong totally to nature but instead everywhere surpasses it." As such, it is "the hieroglyph of a new in-humanity." Agamben's explicitly messianic vision relies on our ability to sabotage the anthropological machine, which is today on autopilot, idling without direction or directive, having helped established the historical emergence of Man but, through its sheer presence, now preventing us from experiencing "a new and more blessed life, one that is neither animal nor human" (87):

> To render inoperative the machine that governs our conception of man will therefore mean no longer to seek new—more effective or more authentic—articulations, but rather to show the central emptiness, the hiatus that—within man—separates man and animal, and to risk ourselves in this emptiness: the suspension of the suspension, Shabbat of both animal and man. (92)

And yet there is a faint whiff of anthropocentrism here, as in all melancholic projects, probably. (This is something I will explore in more detail in the next chapter, on creaturely life.) The inhuman, ahuman, or posthuman dream is based on a collectively narcissistic metarecognition of "mutual disenchantment," something within which Derrida's cat and Haraway's dog can only be included by dint of patronage.

In any case, all those elements at play and at stake in "sexual behavior" cannot be definitively attributed to any one particular species, especially because humans can be as Pavlovian as their pets, and animals can be as neurotic as their putative masters.[94] For Derrida (2008, 59), there is a mirror effect "wherever there is sexuality properly speaking, wherever reproduction relies on sexual coupling." Contra Lacan, as well as scientific studies that rely on *actual* mirrors, Derrida sees some erotic "hetero-narcissistic 'self as other'" (60) circuit at work in the dances of bower birds, the courtship of seals, and indeed, the premating rituals of Parisians. This is not to promote the kind of pop sociobiology of Desmond Morris (1967) ("We are all just naked apes") but to appreciate the power and potential of the trace across species lines, as they are currently drawn. In other words, being captivated by the image in front of us, whether virtual or actual, need not be a paralyzing captivation but an enabling condition for an unprecedented form of worlding to occur. And this worlding (essentially a process of dynamic interaction: an improvised "language" that is then dismantled and reassembled differently on each encounter) can thus be shared on a plane that does not merely reinforce the worldview of the participants but punctures the illusion of a stable "world" that can be viewed, and thus *mastered*. (Think of the classic mid-twentieth-century plastic toy, the ViewMaster.) An impersonal passion for sameness-within-difference (rather than beyond it) fosters a mutual attunement, always threatening to go off station, rather than a predetermined harmony. And it can trace the circumference of a revised zoosphere, "the dream of an absolute hospitality and an infinite appropriation" (Derrida 2008, 37).

Bersani's impersonal intimacy seeks to "emerge on the other side of the sexual," but as he himself swiftly asks, "where is that?" (Bersani and Phillips 2008, 27). Even if we were capable of shedding our egocentric skins, for the sake of transcending the terrorized and terrorizing regime of the personal, what would be the positive incentive to do so? The answer is hard to imagine in our current hyperalienated trance, but it certainly addresses that which Bersani believes "may be the most profound 'mistake' inherent in being human: that of preferring our opposition to the world we live in over our correspondence, our 'friendly accord,' with it" (124). Bersani has flagged perhaps the most entrenched of human errors. But is this encoded within our essential species-being? Or is this rather a mistake attributable to us moderns? One would hope that this is a mistake from which we can learn and which we can avoid repeating, ad infinitum.

As I write (2008), one of the most popular viral videos circulating on the Web is a scene taken from a 1970s nature program that documents the return to the wild of Christian the Lion.[95] The clip begins with some text, explaining that the two gentlemen on screen helped raise Christian as a cub in London and have now returned to the Kora National Park in Kenya to see how he is faring as an adolescent. The viewer is told at the beginning of the clip that the men expect no recognition as their former charge has now presumably reverted to his "wild nature" and "feline instincts." At first the big cat seems wary, and then he races toward them. We fear that they are vulnerable and foolish, about to become lion lunch. But in a moment of undeniable recognition—with a resonance extending all the way back to Homer[96]—Christian jumps up and playfully nips at his ex-guardians.[97] Edited according to the same principle as two separated lovers, rushing toward each other on a beach—but avoiding cliché thanks to of the interspecies twist—this video rarely fails to bring a heartfelt smile to the viewer, if not a flood of tears. (As Nietzsche once wrote, "I want to have my lion and eagle near me so that I always have hints and omens that help me to know how great or small my strength is" [quoted in Chamberlain 1996, 209].)

YouTube thus supplants, or at least supplements, the kaleidoscopic mirror stage (which has been carefully stage-managed for many centuries) between humans and animals. Though it may be experienced simply as the joy communicated to others when one creature loves another, the sincerity of viewer response (or should that be *reaction*?) speaks of a complex knot of guilt, shame, disavowal, estrangement, curiosity, compassion, and desire concerning this relationship. The intensity of such a vicarious encounter can either lead us toward a straightforward, kitsch, self-indulgent glow or prompt us to try to begin dismantling a network in which "one can be somebody only if someone else is something" (Haraway 2008, 206).[98]

But the desired alternative to zoophobia is not zoophilia because it is all too easy to indulge in a love of animals at a distance, while participating fully in the intensifying anthropocentric program of disavowal and destruction. Without even broaching the enormous question of what is to be done about the abuse, exploitation, and extinction of animals of all kinds, there is the phenomenon of fetishizing Nature as the exoticized other. This maneuver is, as Timothy Morton has so eloquently shown, akin to patriarchy's celebration of idealized Woman, while using such a figure to facilitate the oppression of actual women (a phenomenon we discuss at length in chapter 4). What Nietzsche, the Ikhwān, Haraway, Derrida, Mr. Hands, Bersani, Phillips, and Baker have all shown us are diverse ways of communicating with natures rather than communing with Nature. Though some are more extreme than others, and though we may not want to adopt any one orientation or strategy wholesale for ourselves, they all point to the potential of inhabiting the highly charged and affectively rewarding space of the becoming-with.

Speaking of Nietzsche's madness as a type of "grace," Lesley Chamberlain (1996, 207) writes that the philosopher referred to himself as a "beast" to indicate his interest in "cultivating the animal in himself." For "he had spoken of himself . . . as an animal who was constantly being hurt and who received no human word. He had pity for himself as an animal, for by the mark of illness he was one cast out of civilization and its comforts, though a creature of sensitivity and feeling" (207). To employ Nietzsche as a figure embodying all humanity, and its vexed relationship with its cocreatures, would be disingenuous, given all the work we have done in this chapter to avoid a staged face-off between dusty chess pieces. Yet the persistence and potency of the mythology remains, obliging us to return to the original question: are humans capable of looking at animals as animals, and not as screens or mirrors?

Haraway and Derrida, among others, would answer in the affirmative, and yet they would disagree as to the right way of looking. No matter the ethic or stratagem, to behold alterity is to make a wager with oneself concerning the very fine line between recognition and misrecognition. It is to be suspended in the undecidability between these two possibilities, even if one is obliged to respond or react immediately ("Is that a real snake in my lunchbox, or a rubber one?"). Pan-species intelligence emerges from the assorted ways an individual or society makes this wager and negotiates both the pragmatic and ontological forms of exposure that it creates.

To err is human; to forgive, equine.

3

After the Beep: Answering Machines and Creaturely Life

And we ought not to confound speech with the natural
movements which indicate the passions, and can be imitated
by machines as well as manifested by animals.
    —René Descartes, *Discourse on Method*

Man can sink lower than any animal.
    —Martin Heidegger, *The Fundamental*
    Concepts of Metaphysics

The song "A Simple Process of Elimination," by the Glaswegian band
Aerogramme, ends with a telephone message that reportedly appeared
out of nowhere one day on the drummer's answering machine, during the recording of their second album. The voice is female, possibly
drunk, and incredibly distressing. "Hello. Please get in touch with me.
Oh, please... *please*. I need you to help." The woman's voice breaks in
the second sentence in a way that few actors could mimic or simulate,
and it sounds, quite simply, like the penultimate whimper of a dying
animal. Though the inclusion of amusing, threatening, or boastful
phone messages on an album, often between tracks, is a staple of contemporary music of diverse styles, this example stands out in its harrowing effect on many, if not most, listeners. It is immediately apparent
that we are hearing a desperate SOS signal, broadcast from the core
of the real, no matter how many degrees of digital separation. While

the quality of the message conveys the mediation of the machine, the plea tugs at the heart of the listener due to the pathos-heavy presence of "humanity." (Where is the human, one may ask? In this message, might be the reply.) To add salt to the wound, this cry for existential assistance is punctuated by a robotic voice providing the time stamp: "Tuesday, 12:26 A.M." The contrast between messy emotion and precise automation could not be more clearly juxtaposed.

The ethical implications of including such a sound bite on an album for public consumption are quite significant, but I will not be following that route; rather I will be unpacking the contradiction already implicitly flagged earlier, in which a person's distress call is at once "like a dying animal" and a quintessential example of *human* suffering. The human capacity and potential to suffer has been taken for granted throughout history, although this aptitude (some would say poisonous gift) has obviously been ignored on a daily basis, and on a horrific scale. Animals, on the whole, have not had their cries of pain heard by humans, except for isolated cases such as by the pre-Socratics, Nietzsche, Jeremy Bentham (who, as we have seen, was the first person of authority to go on record to ask if animals suffer), and compassionate individuals who fight against maltreatment, either formally or in their own personal lives. The philosophers in particular have believed that the squeals of the pig or the whimperings of the dog are little more than a cosmological ruse, designed to fool our sometimes overgenerous sympathies.

The writings of René Descartes, which deny animals the capacity to suffer, represent the polar position of those who today fight against animal experimentation and slaughter on the grounds that this is akin to harming fellow humans.[1] For Descartes, animals cannot suffer because they lack both soul and language and therefore cannot *respond*.[2] To support this claim, the philosopher invents his own version of the Turing test in *Discourse on the Method* (Descartes 2006). Such a test allows him to proceed with confidence when he is obliged to distinguish between humans and ingenious mechanical simulations of the same, that is to say, to delineate the difference "between men and brutes." Speaking of the latter, Descartes insists:

> They would never be able to use words or other signs by composing them as we do to declare our thoughts to others. For we

can well conceive of a machine made in such a way that it emits words, and even utters them about bodily actions which bring about some corresponding change in its organs (if, for example, we touch it on a given spot, it will ask what we want of it; or if we touch it somewhere else, it will cry out that we are hurting it, and so on); but it is not conceivable that it should put these words in different orders to correspond to the meaning of things said in its presence, as even the most dull-witted of men can do. (46)

According to Descartes, if you cannot transmute your suffering into intelligible discourse, then you are not really suffering. Thus, despite any objections we may receive from the mute or from humans schooled in different languages (or indeed from Elaine Scarry [1985][3]), the cards still lie face up on the table: consciousness—including a consciousness of pain—is the ability to code and communicate information according to the context and within the protocol of the master receiver.

Derrida seizes on this thought experiment conducted by Descartes, which not only seems scandalous in retrospect but had its opponents at the time of writing.[4] In his lecture on the *animot,* Derrida (2008, 85) notes that for Descartes, the animal is an "automatic responder *[répondeur automatique]* and therefore without response."[5] Interestingly, the French phrase *répondeur automatique* translates as "answering machine" into English, drawing a solid connection between the voice, the recording of that voice, and its ethical call to, or for, the other. (Thus we find ourselves in terrain mapped, as it were, from one side by Friedrich Kittler and from the other by Emmanuel Levinas, in which new technologies complicate the ethical obligation to—even definition of—the neighbor.) Today we have all sorts of "answering machines," broadly conceived, from voice mail to automated phone agents to spouses who read the newspaper while pretending to listen to our stories for the umpteenth time.[6] Though it may be true that an actress could not perfectly capture the agony in the message left by the anonymous woman on the Aerogramme track, our sampling technologies are now so exquisite that we can simulate a dog howling, a baby crying, or a woman pleading for help. This once again leads us to Turing test territory (i.e., a certain uncertainty concerning concern itself).

Ignoring the cognitive question of the extent to which our own empathic response to distress signals is hardwired into our nervous systems, there is—in any case—a surplus of compassion (or a measurable lack of it, in cases deemed exceptional or sociopathic). In Descartes's time, the beating of an animal was, in most cases, the beating of a machine, akin to thrashing an unreliable car that would complain merely by beeping its horn. Compassion for animals was seen as a misguided and extravagant anthropomorphism. Today, we have widened the circle of empathy, depending on our cultural and individual sensibilities, although not yet to the extent that we would throw our arms around a photocopier were we to witness it being assaulted by an overworked librarian. Hollywood, however, is preparing us to complete the empathic circuit via all three sides of the cybernetic triangle.

Take, for instance, Steven Spielberg's film *A.I.* (2001), in which human rednecks of the not-too-distant future gather in the woods to pass the time by torturing Mechas (i.e., mechanical people) in an open-air stadium—a bush-league echo of the Roman Colosseum.[7] When the protagonist of the film, a young Pinocchioesque Mecha, who wants to become human, squeals in authentic pain during one of these spectacles, the audience is unsettled.[8] (That a woman is the first to intervene at the sign of distress—"Mechas don't plead for their lives! Who is that? He looks like a boy"—suggests that the motivation is maternal: a trope consistent with the cloying trajectory of Spielberg's oedipal melodrama.)[9] The inference here concerns a certain threshold of intelligence—or, in this case, emotional sophistication—whereby the *simulation* of humanness becomes indistinguishable from the hitherto unprogrammable and seemingly infinite subroutines of its mortal blueprint. The android has become "a real boy"—at least to the satisfaction of a Benthamite twist on the Turing test (in which the question is not, can this entity communicate in a convincingly human way? but rather, can this entity feel pain like we do?).

The stakes, as Descartes insisted, are between experience and expression. A tree, for example, may suffer when chopped by an axe, but it lacks the faculties for transmitting such suffering to the specific sensorium of the species swinging the axe. (The same lack of conductivity would apply in the case of a woodpecker, I imagine.) In other words, the dice are loaded when the onus is *always on the other* to prove to *us* that they are suffering. As things stand, the anthropocentric assumption is "insentient unless proven otherwise." But equally, if not more, important is *our* ability, indeed *our* willingness, to respond to distress, wherever it may be located and on whatever frequency it is being broadcast.

HIS MASTER'S VOICE

> Remember, that I am thy creature; I ought to be thy Adam; but I am rather a fallen angel, whom thou drives from joy for no misdeed.
> —Frankenstein's monster

> Yes. He is a nice creature.
> —Laura Jesson, *Brief Encounter*

In the case of the anonymous woman pleading for help on the Aerogramme song, our own distress is heightened by the fact that there is no tangible source of the anguish. Though the voice feels acutely contemporaneous, its status as recording-of-a-recording means we cannot come to its aid. What's more, even if we were to later find out the identity of the woman, *this particular* emergency has passed, for better or for worse. And so we have little recourse but to wring our hands, captured by a nuanced case of quasi-Pavlovian conditioning. Just as the dogs who were trained to salivate at the sound of a bell, even without the satisfaction of dinner, we may shed a tear with no concrete signified to justify our response. Human and dog alike converge in the classic logo for His Master's Voice, searching the gramophone's orchid-shaped amplifier for sign of the absent master himself (a cross-species instance of the fort/da game, which Freud understood as enabling the child's developing independence, that is to say, surrender to subjectivity).

For a perceptive critic like Eric Santner, the force field created by abjection, suffering, alterity, the body, and phantom presence–absence—as expressed in the voice on the answering machine—is indeed intimately bound up with a Lacanian understanding of the Master, or Big Other. His book *On Creaturely Life* (Santner 2006) argues that the psycho-fetal moment of curling up into the self because of the intolerable charge of exposure to "the world" is best described and understood via the phrase that makes up his book's title. How to tag the human, then, in these extreme cases, which nevertheless structure even our most banal daily encounters (since, after all, the most splendid outing can turn into trauma within a heartbeat)?[10] How to confidently locate the watermark guaranteeing the authentic currency of humanity when dealing with misery, confusion, humiliation, shame, desire? For these are states usually reserved for human psychology, by virtue of our self-conscious exceptionalism, and yet they carry within themselves the power and the violence to jolt us into a nonhuman zone ("I felt like a piece of meat" or "I was trapped like an animal" or "I was sick as a dog").

Creatureliness, in Santner's (2006, 13) definition, is "a uniquely human form of animality" generated by the increasingly refined natural-historical emergence of the political. Its exemplary portraitist is Kafka (2008–9), whose writings show how "creatureliness is a by-product of exposure to what we might call the *excitations of power,* those enigmatic bits of address and interpellation that disturb the social space—and bodies—of his protagonists" (24). We become creaturely, in other words, when we are trapped in a self-conscious feedback loop with an authority figure who represents not merely the repressive mechanisms of power but the ecstatic potential of (perverse) pleasure. We are immobilized and dehumanized by a cryptic, unspoken demand, but one that weighs on us nevertheless by the sheer existence of a system that preceded and eludes us. Thus "'Creature' is not so much the name of a determinate state of being as the signifier of an ongoing *exposure,* of being caught up in the process of *becoming creature* through the dictates of divine alterity" (28)—a "radical subjection" to the ultimately unreadable Law.

The question may be asked if Derrida became creaturely, in this sense, when caught naked in front of his cat, and furthermore whether this experience provoked a revised ethical relationship to alterity.[11] But though this is a somewhat tempting analogy to make, it reverses the asymmetry of Santner's account since—blushing and nudity aside—Derrida is in the place of the Master, at least according to the domestic contract. In terms of human–animal relations, it is the former that hoard sovereign *jouissance* for themselves, by virtue of assumed authority and ownership. But when it comes to human–human relations (Santner's primary concern), the question of who wears the pants—in its most nuanced and metaphysical sense—becomes harder to identify with any certainty. Creaturely life is less a primal scene of encounter, allowing an allegorical tableau for our edification, than an ongoing and agonistic process of inquiry, negotiation, and plea-bargaining by those who have not received the Golden Memo from above or beyond (i.e., pretty much all of us, with the possible exception of Oprah).

In any case, we have all, at some time or another, been pinned humiliatingly in place by an intolerable exposure to a set of abstract demands or expectations that we either simply do not recognize or with which we identify to an excessive (and thus unforgivable) degree. This experience does not "belong" to us but rather takes us to the threshold of our own psychic borderline between ourselves and the outside world. In my own case, I remember laughing at something or other so much during a dinner party that it made everyone else in the room uncomfortable, and the more awkward the situation became, the more I laughed, and the more palpably shameful the outburst became, so out of ratio with whatever witticism inspired it (of which I can't even remember), until it was patently clear to everyone present that I had almost evaporated in the cascade effect of figuratively, if not literally, wetting myself. During that moment, I was not human and was acutely aware of the creaturely life that can possess us: a life that does not lurk within, as a Darwinian residue of animality, but is invoked or summoned from without, as a Kafkaesque metamorphosis or metalepsis of the cultural. (I half suspect that computers can feel creatural, as when an explosive mise en abyme of pop-up windows fractally ejaculate themselves all over the desktop, and whereby closing one window merely opens a host of others. As a college professor, I have also seen more than one student morph into something "infrahuman" [Santner 2006, 26] when called on to answer a question in class.) Paradoxically, the human is thus glimpsed most clearly the moment it collapses into the animal, or creaturely, in the double exposure of the shame spiral. And so the creaturely, as manifested in the human, is "a form of exposure that both intensifies and constrains life" (Santner 2006, 128).

"Human beings are not just creatures among other creatures," writes Santner (2006, 26), "but are in some sense *more creaturely* than other creatures by virtue of an excess that is produced by the space of the political and that, paradoxically, accounts for their 'humanity.'" The inhuman or nonhuman or infrahuman aspect unfolds within "the peculiar proximity of the human to the animal at the very point of their radical difference" (12). This phrase is thus not the place to base an ethics according to a vital continuum between all of God's or Darwin's creatures, nor is it the hinge on which to hang both human and animal rights, because it cannot be enlisted as a witness to testify to a shared capacity for suffering. Rather it pertains "to a biopolitical *animation* that distinguishes the human from the animal" (39).

The most important function of Santner's deployment of the term *creaturely life* is thus to use it as yet another conceptual stick to draw the line in the sand between the human and all other animals. It would be too reductive and polemical to accuse his book of being a more subtle, sophisticated updating of Descartes's dismissal of the suffering of animals, and yet it does once again place the human at the top of the totem pole, by the very gesture of placing it at the bottom. What Derrida might therefore consider an "irony"—humans being more creaturely than creatures—is justified as a paradox, whereby the exceptional species recognizes itself as such in the very moment that it seems to least resemble the dignified *zoon logon echon*. Oh, the humanity, indeed! For Santner (2006, 39), "where we diverge from the animal is in our peculiar capacity for that pleasure-in-pain that Lacan refers to as 'jouissance.'" But the stakes in perpetuating this divergence are exceedingly high, for it amounts to a rather perverse anthropocentrism, in which we are unique in our capacity to appropriate the abjection of the animal to the nth degree.[12] Santner is essentially echoing Heidegger's claim that man—and only man—can sink lower than the animal. Though Heidegger himself was a rigorous antihumanist, and would not say anything as gauchely neo-Kantian as "animals have no dignity to lose," he would support such a sentiment if we were to replace the word *dignity* with *Dasein*. The substance of the human is changed, but its structural relation to nonhumans—figured symptomatically in the negative—remains the same.

Santner (2006, 105) writes, "What ultimately subjects man, in an emphatic sense, to the destructive forces of natural history is precisely his aberrant place in the 'great chain of being.' Man's subordination to the course of natural history is a consequence of a spiritual supplement that separates man from animal while in some sense making him more animal than animal, this 'more' being the very seal of his 'creatureliness.'" Once again, the human is animal plus or minus n, in either case, an exception that proves the rule. We might also take note of the "spiritual supplement," which extends the religious and philosophical heritage of the West, while simultaneously "abjectifying" it. (For this supplement is not a sacred gift from the heavens, nor an enigmatic social by-product of the evolutionary process, according to Santner, but an indication of an excess animation that he calls "undeadness" [106]. In other words, we are not merely alive, but our existence is what is at issue: a self-conscious, excitable, and constrained vitality that renders us closer to the zombie, taxonomically speaking, than Rilke's or Blake's tiger.)[13] Ultimately, however, this is to romanticize the human in a decadent sense as the creature with the capacity for genuine disgrace.

And where does Santner locate this spiritual supplement? Well, not surprisingly, in our sexuality, or more specifically, in "the mechanical stupidity of our jouissance" (Santner 2006, 147). Consider, for example, the uncanny experience of addiction, that is, of acting against one's own best interests, as compelled by the obscure dictates of the libido. "There is nothing that throws more into question our status as living beings," writes Santner, "than the sheer, quasi-mechanical automaticity of the compulsion to repeat" (191). And yet, in a case of taking with one hand but then returning with the other, he writes of the excessive "inhuman" vitality that sets us apart from the animal and in some sense first makes us distinctively human. In other words, the more our behavior resembles a machine stuck on repeat, or an ape captivated by its own routine or reflection, the more some kind of elusive metaphysical residue rescues us from collapsing or congealing into either of those categorical states.

Think, for instance, of the horrendous climax to von Sternberg's film *The Blue Angel* (1930), in which the disgraced and erotically enslaved professor shrieks like a wounded cuckoo bird for the dismal amusement of the cabaret crowd. The animal is once more enlisted to prop up and highlight the pathos of the human. A shrieking bird would not tug at our heartstrings the same way, for there would be an essential patronage—an ontological asymmetry—in our sympathetic response. Because of the specifically human presence of libido, however, we cannot create a comfortable buffer zone between us and this professor, destroyed by the quixotic and foredoomed attempt to realize desire. We can condescend, as the other characters do in the film, but it is a disavowal that will inevitably come back to haunt us.

"We become sexual in the human sense," Santner (2006, 194) continues, "when we have, so to speak, been made over as creature, when our bodies have been intensified, amplified, by exposure not simply to the space of signification, the symbolic order, but to the point of exception that sustains this space." We can thus never know what the Master expects of us, especially now that the Big Other has deputized so many little others and ventriloquized Himself by means of telepresence. He can reach out, and we can be touched, whether we want to be or not. (Indeed, one key symptom of creaturely life is a profound ambivalence, or confusion, about our desires regarding this very question.) And though we may attempt to annex some of the Master's power for ourselves, we are forever trapped in the master–slave dialectic, which ensures that even the most enfranchised are haunted by the uncanny authority of parental ghosts, theological chaperones, or shadowy political adversaries.[14] The silver lining to such paranoia, as Schreber understood, is fleeting access to sexual ecstasy, or *jouissance.*

Ventriloquism, however, is a human trait (provided we remember to ceaselessly put the term under erasure).[15] Our species may not be definitively distinguished by language—for who can say for certain what the sonic signals of birds or whales do or do not say.[16] By the same token, we may not even be the only creature that can speak on another's behalf, by proxy, as it were, due to another's absence, given the complex functions of bee dances and various chemical codings in the insect world. Even Chomsky has revised his original, uncompromisingly anthropocentric conclusions about language capabilities recently.[17] And yet, according to our own matrices, the human is the only creature who has been wrenched from the natural order by the artifice of culturally forged languages, that being, the appropriation of the vocal apparatus by the technology of speech, to enable the kind of response so valued by Descartes and his ideological offspring.

Santner himself, in his book, ventriloquizes the Lacanian theorist Mladen Dolar (2006), who observes that "by speech [the] mouth is denaturalized, diverted from its natural function, seized by the signifier (. . . by the voice which is but the alterity of the signifier). The Freudian name for this deterritorialization is the drive" (Santner 2006, 139). The tongue is thus figured as the most uncanny guest in the human body, rendering the "natural" organism into something historical, symbolic, alienated, self-conscious. (Though, as a species, we are getting used to seeing images of ourselves, it is still something of an ordeal to hear recordings of our own voices.) Animals may have voice, as the ancients recognized, but—so the story goes—they do not have speech. And speech is that which, owing to its capacity to dissimulate as well as communicate, mutates our animal instincts into human drives.

For Friedrich Kittler (2001), the fusion of voice and (written) language achieved a certain apotheosis in 1800, under the sign of a literacy ordained by Nature, itself figured as maternal: "Where speaking takes place, there the Other of the soul begins" (8). Since the internalization of language began with the external source of the mother's mouth, *She* (transmuted into capitals) embodied the Spirit or Soul of (specifically German) Poetry, and thus of humanity on a self-conscious quest for expression through an increasingly democratic, international technique. Words change their texture on the tongue once they can be rendered and reproduced in note form. Indeed, the analogy of language and music is a crucial one since texts and scores were the only impersonal mode of cultural transmission until the later nineteenth century, with the advent of electrical storage technologies. Earlier that same century, however, students would learn to speak in a manner as one might learn an instrument. As contemporary pedagogue Heinrich Stephani noted, the mother's mouth must become "an instrument upon which we are able to play certain meaningful tones that together we call language" (quoted in Kittler 2001, 33).

According to Kittler, the voice is a harbinger of the Real. By extension, the gramophone—the ability to record the voice—has a profoundly uncanny, haunted element to it, because our quotidian existence can cope with only the most microscopic traces of the Real, before it begins displaying severe psychosocial symptoms.[18] For Kittler, the "bottleneck of the signifier" means that only a fraction of the Real becomes symbolically encoded. There is simply more of the traumatic material of existence out there than can be captured, recorded, processed, and rendered by our machines.[19] However, "once the technological differentiation of optics, acoustics, and writing exploded Gutenberg's writing monopoly around 1880, the fabrication of so-called Man became possible. His essence escapes into apparatuses" (Kittler 1999, 16). With these magical, diabolical new machines of capture, the organic age of humanity seemed to be drawing to a close, and the reproduction of our most essential qualities seemed imminent:

> And that the symbolic is called the world of the machine under-
> mines Man's delusion of possessing a "quality" called "conscious-
> ness," which identifies him as something other and better than a
> "calculating machine." For both people and computers are "sub-
> ject to the appeal of the signifier"; that is, they are both run by
> programs. "Are these humans," Nietzsche already asked himself
> in 1874, eight years before buying a typewriter, "or perhaps only
> thinking, writing, and speaking machines?" (Kittler 1999, 17)

The year during which I write, 2008, witnessed a remarkable discovery: a sound recording that predated Thomas Edison's "Mary Had
a Little Lamb" (captured on tinfoil and previously considered the first
technological reproduction of the human voice) by nearly two decades. Scientists at the Lawrence Berkeley National Laboratory used
"a dash of digital fairy dust"[20] to convert analog visual sound waves,
first created in 1860 by the French inventor Édouard-Léon Scott de
Martinville on a device called the "phonautograph," into a signal capable of audio playback.[21] These same scientists were dumbstruck
on hearing—through the cobwebs of a century and a half—a brief
snippet of an anonymous woman singing the folk song "Au Clair de
la Lune." This sound file was then released to the world with much
fanfare, sending many chills up spines at the resurrection of a ghost
from the presumed vanished past, within little more than graphite on
paper.[22] The most remarkable thing about this story, however, might
not be the melancholy afforded by a trace of an unknown individual
human life (one that lingers as an aural version of Barthes's *punctum*)
but rather that we take the recording and broadcast of intangible, immaterial aspects of ourselves for granted. What originally struck people
as an infernal ventriloquism of humans by machines[23] soon appeared
as nothing more than a merry jape. "What hath God wrought" soon
became "put something else on, this is boring" (to rather flippantly
fuse the telegraph with the phonograph).

The point is that technology allows a form of afterlife that we, as
a species, have swiftly rendered prosaic in exact ratio to its capacity
to shock and disturb. When both a pleasant folk song and a heart-
wrenching cry for help can be captured and replayed at will, we are
in the presence of an ontological echo that refuses to diminish or die
out. On the plane of the intuitive, it defies the laws of physics. It is

negentropic. Moreover, as the Greek myth makes plain, an Echo is intimately—problematically—bound up with the desire of Narcissus. The melancholy pleasure we receive from hearing these ghosts is an index of our narcissistic investment in recognizing ourselves in them. We weep at the human capacity for music in the midst of perplexing mortality, and we also weep at the suffering that drives us to write such music in the first place. As with *Execution of an Elephant,* in this nineteenth-century song, we are confronted by an event that requires a response. The heavily mediated, yet indexical, echo of presence (which in itself—in the human case at least—implies suffering, as the screaming newborn attests) demands recognition, redress, succor, justice, assistance. One wonders why it takes such extreme examples to remind us of that which we are so busy collectively attempting to repress: that the Spectacle, which now functions as the idling engine of history, is fueled by the ectoplasm of the dead and the ever-thinning blood of the living dead (hence the recent interest in media *hauntology*—a term coined by Jacques Derrida [1994] in his book *Specters of Marx*).

Humans are thus not only answering machines (of varying sophistication) but also *questioning* machines. And though our responses are often automatic (think of a sports star answering a reporter's questions, or a politician, for that matter), our questions also tend to stick to the script provided by the discourses that shaped us.[24]

E.T. PHONES COLLECT

> Back when I was a child and happy, the voice of a colorful
> green parrot lived in a house off the courtyard next door. On
> rainy days his talking never became mournful, and he would
> cry out—sure of his shelter—a constant sentiment that
> hovered in the sadness like a phonograph before its time.
> —Fernando Pessoa, *The Book of Disquiet*

But what of an encounter for which no stable script has yet been written (at least, not outside Hollywood fantasies of so-called first contact)? The case of alien visitation would certainly be a fascinating test of how humans respond to a radically unfamiliar form of alterity. We do indeed have plenty of films to preempt our behavior, from the horror of *Alien* (1979) to the reassuring kitsch of *E.T.: The Extra-Terrestrial* (1982) (which themselves derive from science-fictional novels and short stories, representing an alternative history of the Big Cosmic Other that swiftly followed in the wake of the Victorian assassination attempt on God). But though certain scripts for human–alien encounter have been cobbled together from the rough materials of speculation, they have not been lived in the sense that we apply to our association with each other, or with animals, or with machines. Nevertheless, over the last few decades, official representatives of our species have taken it on themselves to send out greeting cards into deepest space in the hope of playing host to alien visitors at some point in the future. That is to say, despite the fact that our relationship with intraterrestrials is so shamefully predatory, and our rapport with human "aliens" so suspicious and exclusionary, we continue to comb the universe for yet more creatures to offend and appall.

To this end, the well-meaning folks at NASA put together a unique time capsule in 1977 known as the Golden Voyager Record: a phonograph LP that essentially represents a best-of of earth-based images and audio up to that year, as selected by a committee chaired by the eminent astronomer Carl Sagan. This record was placed in both Voyager I and II space probes, which have recently traveled past the farthest reach of our sun's influence (the so-called termination shock[25]) and thus beyond the solar system itself. In the words of then-president of the United States Jimmy Carter, "this is a present from a small, distant world, a token of our sounds, our science, our images, our music, our thoughts, and our feelings. We are attempting to survive our time so we may live into yours" (quoted in Genta 2007, 246). Or, as Dr. Sagan himself noted, "The spacecraft will be encountered and the record played only if there are advanced space-faring civilizations in interstellar space. But the launching of this bottle into the cosmic ocean says something very hopeful about life on this planet" (quoted in Stewart 2002, 182).[26]

But what exactly does it say about life here on earth, other than our hope that aliens are vinyl junkies and have not moved on to compact discs or MP3s?[27] Well, one message it encodes—even if the chances of decoding are astronomically slim—is that there are all sorts of citizens of this planet, who live in a holistic, though fragile, ecological and economic network. However, the narrative of the disc is, inevitably, profoundly anthropocentric, including only seventeen images of non-human animals in their own habitats (as opposed to sixty-nine featuring humans) and only two audio tracks of nonhuman sounds, out of thirty-one in total.

In terms of the auditory, the record includes a twelve-and-a-half-minute-long track called "Sound of Earth" that moves sonically through Teilhard de Chardin's different registers, beginning with the geosphere itself: volcanoes, earthquakes, thunder, mud pots, wind, rain, and surf. The samples then move to the biosphere, represented by crickets, frogs, birds, hyenas, elephants, chimpanzees, whales, and two dogs, one wild and one domesticated. The privileged human component of the biosphere is encapsulated in the sounds of footsteps, heartbeats, laughter, and the kiss between a mother and her child. Of course, nature is not the only thing that abhors a vacuum, and here ideology rushes in where there is the attempt to have human traces and artifacts, free of the bias of culture. Just as most people succumb to vanity by brushing their hair or putting on makeup before taking an official photograph, here NASA has captured humanity from its best angle. (There are no sounds of argument, temper tantrums, crying, sneezing, fornication, or flatulence here.) The soundscape finally takes a technological turn to the noosphere as it traces an arc from the first tools through herding sheep, sawing, blacksmithing, and riveting, and as it also connects the historical dots between a horse and cart, Morse code, a ship's horn, a tractor, a bus, a train, a car, a jet fighter, and—in a self-reflexive twist—a rocket ship launch. (Again, this is terrestrial propaganda, conveniently leaving out the sounds of war.) In addition to these environmental noises, the record includes a spoken greeting in fifty-five languages as well as a sample of so-called world music, from a pygmy girl's initiation song from Zaire to Bach and Beethoven to the "Melancholy Blues" by Louis Armstrong and his Hot Seven[28] (a choice that would please Santner, no doubt).

The Voyager Golden Record was a more considered and curated version of the plaques that were placed on the Pioneer probes of the early 1970s, as visual messages designed to explain their origin to any intergalactic interceptors. Though the plaques featured a scientific rendition of pre-Lapsarian Man and Woman, any curious aliens who encountered this relic may have found news reports of the time more revealing as to our species's culture, given that debate raged around the inclusion of naked illustrations to the extent that the images were censored and the simple vertical line denoting the vagina removed. (For some reason, possibly related to Michelangelo's *David*, the penis was not deemed so offensive.) The authorities at NASA, pressured by the argument that they were using taxpayer's money to send pornography into space, settled on this compromise and crossed their fingers that E.T. would not consider this an obscene message.[29]

In any case, we would be hard-pressed to find a purer expression of the anthropological machine than the Voyager Golden Record and the Pioneer Plaque: a multimedia *dispositif* designed both to comprehend and to compensate for the endless identity crisis known as humanity, that is, "an ironic apparatus that verifies the absence of a nature proper to *Homo*, holding him suspended between a celestial and a terrestrial nature, between animal and human—and thus his being always less and more than himself" (Agamben 2004, 29). What is more, these examples remind us that the anthro-machine need not be primarily optical but can be auditory—and indeed, no doubt, haptic, gustatory, and olfactory. Sent beyond the heliosphere, farther away from earth than any other human artifact, the cargoes of Voyager and Pioneer represent more of a mirror or self-portrait than an invitation to open a dialogue with our interstellar cousins. Some may even see a cry for help in our PBS-style wonder, didacticism, earnestness, and tempered hubris. But as with the anonymous woman who has haunted this chapter, there is very little chance of an adequate response to our distress signal.[30]

Were NASA in the financial position or reflective state of mind to repeat the experiment today, I suspect they would approach the process as less of a cultural time capsule or symbolic statement and as more of a genetic Noah's Ark, including samples of DNA from the remaining species of plant and animal that have survived the recent spike in planetwide biocide. Such a project bears repeating, albeit in a more Copernican spirit regarding the archived content, since it should remind us that we are closer to chimpanzees, chromosonically speaking, than different species of gibbon are from each other (Diamond 2006, 25). And perhaps we should not see ourselves as spokespersons for the earth, of which we are presumed steward by virtue of our humanity, but rather we should see that we have been calibrated by technics to the point of being able to relinquish the chrysalis of this now obsolete term. It would be fascinating to know what kind of taxonomic system extraterrestrial visitors to earth might come up with, were they to have the opportunity. To whom would the phrase "greetings, Earthlings," be directed, for instance? To us, or to other animals, or to our machines, or to all at once? And given the symbiosis and dependence and over-laps between these categories, would they even recognize an entity that could be called "human," or would they rather see a mobile nest for parasites, or a host for DNA, as Richard Dawkins once did. Our holism may very well be different from theirs.

But beyond such whimsical thought experiments, there is something to be said for employing the term *Earthling* to replace the compromised term *human* or *humanity* (realizing, of course, that we are too attached to the name now to let it go; autointerpellation is complete and ongoing). Though the word *Earthling* has B-grade sci-fi connotations at present, it is at least inclusive and uncoded by self-righteous morality or the conceited legacy of organized religion. Yet it retains the engagement with the fragile, the finite, the ethically implicated. Thus—whether we use the word *Earthling, creature,* or something even less loaded—we should strive to avoid conflating sentience and sensitivity with the human. Intelligence, compassion, comprehension, humor, suffering, melancholy, love, and all those many traits with which we self-identify are not always exclusive to our species. Today more than ever—but, in fact, since the beginning of hominization—these traits have depended on technology to manifest and perpetuate themselves. Considering ourselves as the source of that-which-we-call-human, and viewing animals or technics as mere conduits—as means to that end—is a fallacy. It is to see mastery where a vital, complex, ahuman dynamic reigns. It is to mistake the anthropological machine for an objective verification of status and thus to succumb to the parochialism of all conspicuous consumption.

It is, in short, a human error.

4

The War on Terra: From Political Economy to Libidinal Ecology

Landscapes and trees have nothing to teach me; only people in the city can do that.
    —Socrates, in Plato's *Phaedrus*

I'd rather be a zombie than a tree hugger.
    —Timothy Morton, *Ecology without Nature*

It is an article of faith that human beings are exceptional creatures in terms of our relationship to the environment. For while we are not the only animals to "terraform" the ready-made objects of nature into dwelling places or social levers, we are seemingly alone in comprehensively adapting the planet's resources to our own agenda rather than the other way around, to a degree at which the natural balance is lost. To put it glibly, we have turned a functioning ecosystem into a toxic and precarious ego-system.[1] Hospitality—for ourselves as much as others—is not something we moderns are very practiced at, since we tend to vandalize our domicile with the concern and consideration of a teenage rock band on crystal meth in a hotel room. And yet home extends beyond the heart and hearth to our dealings with all other agents—familiar and foreign—as grasped within the word *economy*, derived from the Greek word *oïkos*, itself meaning "home." (The traditional high school classes pitched to future housewives known as home economics are thus a tautology.) To have one's intimately domestic affairs in order is to be involved in a healthy economy, a concept that lost its sense of intimacy as economics evolved and inflated into both a global business and a dismal science. As such, a concept of economy has been reified into its own linguistic sign since the earliest times of writing, especially because writing itself is considered to have originated in the marketplace as a necessary outgrowth of the merchant's request, "Can I get this in writing?"[2]

In contrast, *ecology*—which shares the same root and denotes the study of home-as-environment—does not emerge in Romance languages until the last quarter of the nineteenth century with Ernst Haeckel, suggesting that though the checks and balances of daily life have been acknowledged since time immemorial, the world-as-object does not occur to the human mind until it is radically divorced from it.[3] As Heidegger (1977) argues in his famous essay "The Age of the World Picture," the environment is taken for granted in premodern times: neither the background to action, nor the fetishized source of fascination, but an organic extension of the self and an unconscious reflection of being itself. It is the scientific quest for objectivity, perspective, and mastery that results in today's heedless manipulation of the planet (*manipulation* meaning literally "to control with the hand").

It is remarkable, then, that the cybernetic understanding and practice of home (i.e., regulating feedback mechanisms to maintain a productive equilibrium) predates its scientific acknowledgment and management by so many centuries. Clearly we are only at the incipient stage of accounting for our more generalized transactions with nature (a stock-taking process encouraged by Arendt's [1998] repeated references to "nature's household" in *The Human Condition*). Since the age of global colonialism, those with the means and will to do so have exploited everything they have found, to the extent that the accumulating tab must now be recognized, lest humanity itself become only the most recent victim of its own rapaciousness and inability to balance the biological books.[4] But what happens to this familiar tale of Adam losing his mind after the Fall—getting an engineering degree, and building a thousand skyscrapers of Babel—when we let go of the now obsolete (yet exceedingly persistent) distinction between *phusis* and *nomos*, nature and culture?[5]

Some provocative answers to this question can be found in Timothy

Morton's (2007) book *Ecology without Nature*. For Morton, "the environment was born at exactly the moment when it became a problem" (141). As a result, the ongoing romanticization of nature is one of the most significant stumbling blocks to ensuring the actual health of the planet. In a sobering parallel, he states, "Putting something called Nature on a pedestal and admiring it from afar does for the environment what patriarchy does for the figure of Woman" (5). Such a hypostatizing fetish sets the tone for our relationship to the environment and the other life-forms found therein.[6] Indeed, the very term *environment* is part of the predicament, symptomatic of the crisis provoked by the conceptual distance we have from our surroundings. "Our notions of place," Morton writes, "are retroactive fantasy constructs determined precisely by the corrosive effects of modernity" (10). Hence the intriguing title to his book, which suggests that "the very idea of 'nature' which so many hold dear will have to wither away in an 'ecological' state of human society" (1). Nature is dead—long live ecology!

In Morton's (2007) philosophy, Nature is *always already* a discourse—at least for humans—before it is actual badgers, rocks, pine needles, and sunsets: "an arbitrary rhetorical construct, empty of independent, genuine existence behind or beyond the texts we create about it" (21–22). It is thus "a transcendental term in a material mask" (13), useful to ideologies of all kinds in its refusal to maintain any consistency. "Practically a synonym for evil in the Middle Ages," uppercase Nature became (in a startling reversal) "the basis of social good by the Romantic period" (15). And since then, it "has been used to support the capitalist theory of value and to undermine it; to point out what is intrinsically human, and to exclude the human; to inspire kindness and compassion, and to justify competition and cruelty" (19). Quite simply, "Nature loses its nature when we look at it head on" (63).[7]

The crucial aspect of this slippery (non)-category is its undeniable alterity, its uncompromising Otherness. And for Morton (2007), its essence comes down to all those "things that are not identical to us or our preformed concepts" (7). Here there is almost a Levinasian dialectic at work, but without the need for a face (since a waterfall has no such thing yet still places a kind of demand on us—"please do not kill me . . . please do not let me run dry"). Nature, for Morton, is nothing more than "the flickering shapes on the edges of our perception, the strangers who disturb us with their proximity, the machines whose monstrosity inspires revulsion" (81). So to reduce his sophisticated argument to a simple paradox, nature does not exist because *every-thing* is (now) "the environment."[8] And yet it persists in the enigmatic solicitations of existence.

As a result, *Ecology without Nature* is as much about technology as it is about trees; it is as much about cultural aesthetics as it is about biological ethics. (To put it as Heidegger might, "the essence of nature is nothing natural.") Coming from a background in romantic literature—and with a keen interest in contemporary music—Morton (2007) finds examples in both domains of what he calls "ambient poetics": the *formal* attempt to grapple with the environment as an uncanny, dynamic principle rather than as a static foundation (the latter of which he calls the "nonexistent measuring stick" [27]). Morton explains that art need not explicitly reference animals or mud slides or what-have-you to evoke the environment (which, again, does not exist outside the "crisis" of humanity's relationship with it). As such, foregrounding ambience complicates the notion of nature as an ontological backdrop, on which *real* Being (e.g., *Dasein*) can be pinned. It also complicates the paradigmatic metaphysical orientation device—used by humans immemorial—of Inside versus Outside.[9]

For purposes of contrast, Morton (2007, 180) cites indigenous cultures that have no use for nature figured as modernity's alter ego. He provides the example of the Apache people, who posit no difference between a place and the social stories that they associate with it. Thus there is no "nature" in the primitivist terms Westerners tend to think of it, inherited from Rousseau & Co. Nor indeed is there nature in the radical terms presented by Deleuze and Guattari because in Morton's estimation, the rhizome functions as an all-too-convenient poststructuralist fantasy, effectively "do[ing] away with the strange, bumpy divisions between things" (52). Morton's alternative for avoiding both the nostalgic and naive mode is "ecocritique," whose guiding slogan is "not afraid of nonidentity" (13) (or to put it more positively, an ability to cope with—even rejoice in—unbridgeable difference). One way to navigate such novel philosophical terrain is to render the challenge of nonidentity into a contingent, inclusive project, one that could forge new types of connections across fundamental differences. "Ecocritique," Morton insists, "could establish collective forms of identity that include other species and their worlds, real and possible" (141). That is to say, "if we knew what to do with animals and their kin, we could take a break from the painful exertions of consciousness. We could shout 'We are the world!' and it would be true" (100).

This is, of course, impossible if life-forms are trapped within their own hermetically sealed environments, as Uexküll maintained. But for Morton (2007, 100), "strangers undermine the very *Umwelt* that uses them to establish its boundaries." The problem with celebrating "nature"—whether as an activist, poet, or Alpine hiker—is that this very notion "gets in the way of looking out for actually existing species, including the human species" (164). (After all, the Nazis were avid nature enthusiasts and passed several laws protecting animals and forests.) So we have not fallen from a secular Eden into the artificial paradises of modernity; rather "the ecological 'paradise' *has not occurred yet*" (162). Morton thus subscribes to what he calls a "nostalgia for the future."

Indeed, there is no going back. Truth be told, there was never anything to go back to: *il n'y a pas de rapport environmentale*. But this melancholy certainty should not make us retreat further into our own besieged sense of species-being but rather prompt us to be actively mindful of all the other ontological orphans out there. It is necessary to "muck in," as Morton (2007) puts it. And just because there is no avoiding the fact that "a national park is as reified as an advertisement for an SUV" (164), it does not necessarily follow that ecological questions are moot; quite the contrary.[10] Indeed, "if we could not merely figure out but actually *experience* the fact that we were embedded in our world, then we would be less likely to destroy it" (64). So though we may have lost the comforting mythology of Nature, we have gained the more immersive perspective (if that isn't too much of a pleonasm) of ecology. A continuing humanist approach, by contrast, "would leave the environment just as it is, as an Other 'over there,' a victim" (188).[11]

One spectacular instance of this latter attitude is the global biodiversity census first proposed by celebrated sociobiologist E. O. Wilson and executed by a network of scientists and research teams. This hugely ambitious project—which seeks nothing less than the cataloging of every living thing "over there"—amounts to a modern-day Domesday Book for all nonhuman biota on the planet.[12] So though it is humans themselves who are busily sending species into oblivion (at an estimated rate of seventy-two a day)—through their precious habits, addictions, and sheer numbers[13]—they are also carefully registering those that have thus far been spared the anthropogenic apocalypse: the "completion of the 'Linnaean enterprise' into a 'Catalogue of Life'" (quoted in Youatt 2008, 397):[14]

> One critical role that information technology plays in organising the global biodiversity census is in its ability to suggest a panoptic biological future. "Imagine an electronic page for each species of organism on Earth," Wilson asks us, "available everywhere by single access on command." Genealogically related to projects like Diderot's *Encylopedie*, the modern "Encyclopedia of Life" is the endpoint and ultimate goal of the censusing project, organised in a technology that claims to outrun space and time. (398)

As Rafi Youatt notes in his article on the implications of such a massive (and problematic) task, "the global biodiversity census is as much about power and political life and the boundaries between nature and society as it is about scientific information gathering for conservationist ends" (394). Indeed, "the biodiversity census provokes us to think about the ways that biological nonhumans are embroiled in, and challenge, the technologies of power that see life itself as a political object" (394).

Youatt (2008) approaches this initiative from the angle of biopower and biopolitics to highlight the ways in which political ecologists administer living beings in both repressive and enabling ways. What happens to both the discourse and the process, he asks specifically, when we extend Foucault's influential concepts to nonhumans (given that these concepts are usually deployed in anthropocentric contexts)? What happens when "nonhumans are regulated and rationalised in matrices of knowledge and science, through which they are readied as productive resources for capitalism and mined as repositories of genetic information" (394). Interestingly, Youatt does not condescendingly wring his hands, decrying nature-as-victim. Instead, he takes careful note that "biotic nonhumans are constantly challenging the normalising will of biopower" (395). For on one hand, "the discursive power of the census is connected to economic life, in the way that it renders nonhuman agents ready for postmodern capitalism as semiotic constructions (as in genetic codes for bioprospectors or images in nature videos)" (398); but on the other, "nonhuman entities are both *active and complicit* in these practices of power" (409; emphasis added).

Certainly few anthropological machines are as explicit or obvious in their autoreinforcing mission as the global biodiversity census. These return Adam to his sovereign role—the namer of animals—albeit under a secular vocabulary.[15] Nevertheless, Youatt (2008) sees potential in the project for a less chauvinistic future, since "a biodiversity census will help construct new ideas of a multi-layered and multi-species global community" (405). Unfortunately, he chooses contemporary political lobbying as a model: "For present-day aspirants to statehood, a census remains an important marker of a consolidated national citizenry, as in the push for a Palestinian census as a way towards achieving a de facto Palestinian state. Similarly, then, a global biodiversity census might be understood as part of constructing a global biocitizenry and in forming a global ecopolitical community" (405). This, for me, is where animals splat against the glass ceiling. Other life-forms are only being granted access to such a community on human terms (and very narrow ones at that, i.e., the established protocols of liberal democracy). There is an inability or unwillingness to conceive of the kind of challenging, clammy, and uncanny *mitsein* to which Morton alludes, opting instead for metaphors that no longer function in the present (if they ever did at all), let alone in the future. This is also the flaw in something like Peter Singer's attempt to integrate the great apes into human personhood, or even Latour's conception of a Parliament of Things. Ultimately, these well-meaning exercises of inclusion fail to acknowledge the profound alterity of *nonhuman life* (itself a far too negative and anthropocentric term). As with the United Nations and global statehood, ethnicity is recognized only if it speaks the same political language as the status quo. Harmony can only be achieved if the same musical score is decided on in advance, inevitably by a powerful minority.

Youatt (2008) certainly anticipates this kind of criticism, as when he insists that "the force of human/nonhuman hybridity is not in introducing the nonhuman into the human; it is [in] pointing out that it is already there and always has been. The matter is one of undoing discursive denials" (411), and likewise when he states that "the global biodiversity census offers a way of re-territorializing the category of 'human,' grounding it relative to other species and to the wide variety of local ecosystems that make up the global ecosystem" (408). As with Aristotle's zoological writings (so the logic goes), focusing on the biological will oblige humans to be less presumptuous about our own ontological status and condition and therefore less unblinking in our sense of global entitlement. But the agency ascribed the nonhuman here stems from the human initiative itself. And for all of Heidegger's latent centrisms, his critique of the deeply compromised enframing of science—at least science unchecked by aesthetics or philosophy— summarizes the hazards of placing faith in its outcomes. Youatt writes, "Whereas biopower tends to take nonhumans as a kind of cinematic 'bluescreen' against which human dramas unfold, an ecological view of biopower gives nonhuman actors active roles" (407). Notice, however, who is doing the giving, in true Adamite tradition. The nonhumans only have roles in a play directed by Man.

As we shall see in more detail throughout the following pages, the modulations between economy and ecology occur on the register of the political and the libidinal,[16] which is to say that technocratic capitalism, as the mode of organization that has most egregiously reified and plundered the natural world, complicates the well-meaning attempt to atone for our profit-driven sins. It is not only a matter of the exploitation of planetary resources but the rampant consumerism it allows, which—in a predictable twist—is presented as a crisis solvable through the same combination of ingenuity, technology, and so-called smart spending habits. (Hence we have *greenwashing*—the attempt by corporations to reassure consumers that they are helping the environment while continuing to accelerate the machine that led to the crisis in the first place.)[17] As Morton (2007, 110) notes, "green consumerism made it possible to be both pro-capitalist and green."[18]

The symptomatic schizophrenia alluded to previously—in which humans carefully catalog nonhumans for posterity, while heedlessly harming them—reaches its outrageous apotheosis when luxury handbag manufacturer Hermes admits that it is breeding its own crocodiles to meet the demand for its exotic accessories (over three thousand orders a year for fifty-thousand-dollar items) (Jones 2009). No doubt, the people buying Hermes products are not the ones recycling, so it could be argued that the schizophrenic split is between types of people and not the individuals themselves. And yet Morton (2007, 139) insists that compassionate people today are intrinsically and inescapably consumerist—no matter how green—and "any attempt to tear off this skin will reproduce existing conditions." He says this not to be defeatist but to burst the insidious illusion that it is possible to exist outside neocapitalist imperatives, which are now, like PCBs, inside the very fiber of our being.

For someone like Žižek, the new green movement thus represents merely the latest in many strategically deployed opiates of the masses. "How to prevent the privatization of ecology?" he asks, during a lecture in New York[19] (for him, a pressing question, in a time in which Bill Gates and Rupert Murdoch are the bastions of socially responsible thought). As a fan of Morton's work, Žižek echoes the notion that "the only way to confront ecological catastrophe is to get even more denaturalized"— even more technologically alienated. Yet to denaturalize ourselves is still to assume a state of nature from which we are progressively, even if deliberately, estranged.

As it happens, Mère Terre may not be so easy to shake off.

OLD MOTHER HUBBERT

> To grasp oil as a lube is to grasp earth as a body of different narrations being moved forward by oil. In a nutshell, oil is a lube for the divergent lines of terrestrial narration.
> —Reza Negarestani, *Cyclonopedia*

> There is virtually no point any more in trying to work out a critique of modernity: depletion does it for us, relentlessly, derisively, definitively.
> —Allan Stoekl, *Bataille's Peak*

In the wake of George Bataille's (1993) monumental study of symbolic exchanges in *The Accursed Share*, it has been impossible to make any precise distinction between economy and ecology. For Bataille, desire (figured as biological exuberance) is, and has always been, intertwined with the regulation of expenditure (figured as wealth and/or waste). According to this cosmic perspective, indigenous societies have forever concerned themselves with their obligations to the gods, to the sun, to their ancestors, and to the gifts of nature. Yet these debts are not to be metaphorically confused with the invoices of a "restricted" or capitalist society that attempts to narrow and control the field of transactions to capture and force the unnatural surplus of profit. Against the modern, urban drive to accumulate dead objects in the form of commodities, Bataille deploys the potlatch—a ceremony performed by the northwestern Native Americans, designed to sacrifice excess wealth in exchange for prestige.[20] Yet while there is a nostalgia pulsing through Bataille's heterodox Marxism, it is not a typical primitivism because he sees the dialectic between the general (gift) economy and the restricted (market) economy as ongoing and not necessarily a matter of historical chronology. The Marshall Plan, for instance, authorized by Harry Truman to rebuild Western Europe after the Second World War, is read by Bataille as a contemporary manifestation of the potlatch: a symbolically charged gift from one culture to a cluster of others. More traditional economists and historians have presented this moment as a rational exchange: large sums of capital for the suppression of communism and the stability of the region (which in turn allows for a future profit). Bataille, however, sees a more primal motivation at work, beyond whatever individual psychologies contributed to the architecture of the plan.

In other words, *the* economy—invoked as a mantra by so many politicians, experts, and victims of the same—is in fact only one type of possible economies: an arrangement that has been increasingly naturalized through discourse and habit, even as the means to sustain it become more and more unnatural (i.e., divorced from the scenarios of past logics and experience).[21] Writing in 2009, one year after the global financial collapse, the disillusion with capitalism is palpable, even to those who formerly championed the free market. Having been aggressively groped one too many times by the invisible hand, people are exploring local barter economies, alternative currencies, peer-to-peer exchanges, and other nonprofit ways of not only making ends meet but changing the ends themselves (i.e., from a zero-sum game to a more symmetrical imperative).

Yet what Naomi Klein has called the "biggest heist in monetary history"—the bailout of private banks with astronomical amounts of public money—is still not enough for the system itself to lose faith in "crony capitalism."[22] For as long as the cronies themselves still see profits to be made, the core mythologies will continue to perpetuate themselves: that markets heal themselves for the benefit of the majority, that a healthy economy translates into healthy lives, and so on. But there is one shadow looming on the horizon that threatens to make the subprime meltdown look like a mere bout of seasickness on the *Titanic*—this shadow is known as peak oil.

First identified by M. King Hubbert, a Texan geoscientist working for Shell, peak oil is the highest point on the graphic curve representing barrels of crude available for extraction in any given oil field. Now known also as Hubbert's peak, this apex augurs the downward slide of reserves, signifying that from such a moment on, the cupboard is only going to become increasingly bare. Many prophets have ascended this peak and returned with apocalyptic, *Mad Max*–style visions of the future.[23] Others see inside such gloomy forecasts the opportunity that often lurks within disaster,[24] while others still—those chirpy, delusional cheerleaders of capitalism-with-a-human-face-(mask)—place their faith in human ingenuity to come up with new technologies to get us out of the mess created by the old ones.[25]

"The problem is enormous," notes Wade Adams, the director of nanotechnology research at Rice University, in the documentary film *A Crude Awakening* (2006). "Fourteen terrawatts of energy by 2050. We need a new source of that much energy. That's equivalent to 220 million barrels of oil per day." The quantification of energy is a key factor in the efficiency that followed in the wake of the Industrial Revolution.[26] One barrel of oil embodies the working equivalent of twelve humans for an entire year, which, give or take some cents, translates to one dollar for twenty-five thousand hours' worth of labor. The explosive growth of the twentieth century would be unthinkable without the discovery and exploitation of fossil fuels, which themselves are organic material deposits (i.e., dead creatures) resulting from two fortuitous spikes in global warming 90 and 150 million years ago, cooked by the so-called kitchen effect. Known colloquially as the excrement of the devil, the blood of the dinosaurs, and the blood of the world economy, oil has literally fueled the modern world we now take for granted, creating a universe of machines and products as well as the mobilities and conveniences they afford. The benefits, however, were not distributed evenly. Until the early 1970s, over half the world relied on the energy provided by beasts of burden, including humans. With the Chinese experiment in communist consumerism lurching forcefully toward the latter, and other so-called developing nations, such as India and Brazil, expecting the kinds of lives advertised on their television sets, Hubbert's peak—laughed at in his own time as an absurdity—is now creasing the brows of even the most upbeat of business commentators.[27]

In the documentary film *A Crude Awakening*, oil geologist and energy consultant Colin Campbell speaks of "another great depression, comparable to the one of the 1930s, if not worse, because this one is imposed by nature, rather than being a speculative bubble." As Old Mother Hubbert himself said back in the 1950s, "it's the most disturbing thing that's ever happened to the human species. It's responsible for our technological society, and in terms of human history it's a very brief epoch." As he does so, Hubbert points to his chart, which is far more phallic than any subsequent representations of his bell curve. No doubt, any arch-Freudian of the same epoch would seize on such a graphic to elucidate the fear of the paternal phallus and its perceived power to spoil the party. And yet this is Nature at issue here, figured as a phallic mother, or monstrous feminine, wreaking revenge on the children who ravished her so, without so much as a phone call the next morning.[28]

One tale in particular, published as an army of oil wells was first penetrating the upper crust of Texas, renders this rather confronting sexual scenario explicit: Arthur Conan Doyle's (1928) "When the World Screamed." The protagonist, Professor Challenger, is one of the author's reoccurring characters, lacking the nuance and sympathy of Sherlock Holmes and yet embodying the relentless drive of hard science's will to power. Galled by what he perceives as the indifference of his material environment—and operating on the educated hunch that the planet is a morphologically macroscopic instance of a sea urchin—Challenger decides, in effect, to rape Mother Earth. He does this by sending an enormous iron shaft into the exposed "nerve ganglion," causing her to scream in pain.[29] (The gender of the planet is never in doubt.) "The world upon which we live," states Challenger, "is itself a living organism, endowed, as I believe, with a circulation, a respiration, and a nervous system of its own." To prove his point, the renegade scientist enlists an expert in Artesian borings to rig a specially designed drill eight miles below the earth's surface: "But it is essential . . . that you should let me know what soil the drill is to penetrate," insists the expert. "Sand, or clay, or chalk would each need different treatment." "Let us say jelly," replies Challenger. "Yes, we will for the present suppose that you have to sink your drill into jelly."

The flagrant gynophobia of Doyle's story revels in the classic attraction–repulsion complex associated with the sexual sublime. After traveling down into the shaft, the narrator parts the labial tarpaulin protecting the deepest excavation site and states:

> It was a wondrous place, on a very much larger scale than I had imagined. . . . Beyond it lay the open mouth of the shaft, a huge yawning pit, some thirty or forty feet in diameter, lined and topped with brick and cement. As I craned my neck over the side and gazed down into the dreadful abyss, which I had been assured was eight miles deep, my brain reeled at the thought of what it represented.

Insofar as it is true that a six-inch Artesian borer is sometimes just a six-inch Artesian borer, the rhetoric of the nascent oil industry—as framed in Doyle's story—relies in significant measure on personifying, domesticating, and oedipalizing the environment through the newfound vulnerability of Mother Earth–Nature. In the final sentence quoted, the author seems to be deliberately, even rather salaciously, winking at the reader, just in case she was chaste enough to miss the abundant references to "protective secretions" and "curious slimy scum." The chief engineer, holding aloft his lamp, confirms, "There have been shiverings and tremblings down here. I don't know what we are dealing with. . . . It's all new to me." As if attempting to outdo the chthonic gothics of H. P. Lovecraft, the story mimics the fascination of its protagonists:

> It was a most extraordinary and terrifying sight. The floor consisted of some greyish material, glazed and shiny, which rose and fell in slow palpitation. The throbs were not direct, but gave the impression of a gentle ripple or rhythm, which ran across the surface. This surface itself was not entirely homogeneous, but beneath it, seen as through ground glass, there were dim whitish patches or vacuoles, which varied constantly in shape and size. We stood all three gazing spell-bound at this extraordinary sight.
>
> "Does look rather like a skinned animal," said Malone, in an awed whisper.

And further:

> It was an amazing sight which lay before us. By some strange cosmic telepathy the old planet seemed to know that an unheard-of liberty was about to be attempted. . . . A dark purple fluid appeared to pulse in the tortuous anastomoses of channels which lay under the surface. The throb of life was in it all.

After this narrative buildup, the climax comes under the gaze of the assembled press and dignitaries (all male) in the form of the "terrible cry" emanating from the shaft, which becomes both cervix and throat. "It was a howl in which pain, anger, menace, and the outraged majesty of Nature all blended into one hideous shriek. For a full minute it lasted, a thousand sirens in one, paralysing all the great multitude with its fierce insistence."

Much to Challenger's satisfaction, an "enormous spout of a vile treacly substance of the consistency of tar" erupts from the ground. One wonders if Doyle wrote himself into some kind of perverse peak, as he depicted the ejaculation of fourteen lift cages from the shaft into the blue heavens, like pellets out of a blowpipe, followed swiftly by a "gush of putridity" to cover the crowd in filth. Such scenes are part of the popular imaginary: oil workers covered in heavy sump, the whites of their eyes the only sign that they are human and not creatures of the black swamp. The crudity of oil is at once scatological, menstrual, and ejaculative and thus triply obscene. To coax it out of the earth in such a manner is analogous to the early Victorian doctors who invented vibrating machines to bring their female patients to a climax to cure them of hysteria.[30] And yet the response of Challenger's peers is not disgust but the jubilant comradeship of a successful gang bang, conducted in the name of science. "From every part of the field there came the cries of admiration, and from his hillock he could look down upon the lake of upturned faces broken only by the rise and fall of the waving handkerchiefs. . . . He rose from his chair, his eyes half closed, a smile of conscious merit upon his face, his left hand upon his hip, his right buried in the breast of his frock-coat."

Here the story betrays its own restrained respect for the man, who says, "I propose to let the Earth know that there is at least one person, George Edward Challenger, who calls for attention—who, indeed, insists upon attention." Challenger is thus the first man whom Mother Earth had been compelled to *recognize*—a key aspect, we should recall, of the anthropological machine. The hideous shriek that emanates from the core of the planet seems to bare aggrieved witness to the orthodox feminist insistence that rape is more about power than sex (as if the two could be neatly separated—their very inextricability in popular culture being the very issue and stake). Challenger is thus the personification of Heidegger's critique of modern technology, that the technocratic condition makes an "unreasonable demand of nature," only in this science-fictional case, humanity has gone beyond unreasonable to outrageous—even vindictive.

With his allegorical name and phallocentric agenda, the symbolism is so clear-cut that it does not so much invite interpretation as contextualization. The story itself was published in 1928, five years before Freud wrote the following: "The id of course knows no judgements of value: no good and evil, no morality. The economic or, if you prefer, the quantitative factor, which is intimately linked to the pleasure principle, dominates all its processes. Instinctual cathexes seeking discharge—that, in our view, is all there is in the id" (from *New Introductory Lectures on Psychoanalysis*, in Guattari 2000, 92). There is thus an "attention economy," which plays out today, not only in the marketing man's attempt to grab eyeballs but also more existentially— that is to say, libidinally—between agents who require recognition as much as they need food and water.

Here Man is the supreme narcissist, and Nature is cast as the ambient presence who refuses to participate in the attention economy (and we will have more to say about narcissism shortly). There are at least three ways to refuse to acknowledge another: (1) consciously, as a matter of strategy; (2) semiconsciously, as a matter of indifference; or (3) unconsciously, as a matter of incapacity. While most would believe the earth to ignore our claims on it as a case of the third possibility, Challenger proves it to be rather a case of either the first or second. As a result, the disrespectful one has been forced to *respond*.

To view the earth as a living organism, capable of at least reacting in pain to the same degree as an animal, is anathema to positivist science. So there is an atavistic impulse in Challenger's challenge to *terra firma*. Holistic developments in environmentalist sciences since the 1960s, however, have encouraged the view that the planet can be considered a vast, interrelated, self-regulating entity, designed to stabilize temperatures and control chemical compositions. Known as the Gaia hypothesis, and first proposed by James Lovelock, this vision of the global environment is suspended somewhere between mythic metaphor and verifiable biocybernetics.[31] Yet, after being initially laughed out of the building, this theory has—in this time of accelerating environmental crisis—only garnered increasing interest by the scientific community. Lovelock (1990, 100) himself insists that nowhere in his own writings does he express the idea "that planetary self-regulation is purposeful, or involves foresight or planning by the biota," thereby reassuring certain minds put off by the New Age evocations of the Gaia name and its appropriation by activist environmentalists. Nevertheless, he warns of dire consequences of climate change, in addition to the threat of oil depletion, leading to the "big die-off" (also known as power down or the ongoing anthropogenic species extinction event [Youatt 2008, 404]), in which two-thirds of the human race may simply expire within fifty years due to a collapse in food production.[32] This Malthusian nightmare is thus considered as a biological market correction for an overproduced stock: the end of hydrocarbon man. Perhaps Mother Earth seeks her revenge for the Challengers of this world after all.[33]

For Allan Stoekl (2007, x), the discourse and debate around the environment are a sure sign that energy, after a long period of dormancy, "has been rediscovered." As a consequence, it is especially revealing to reread Bataille with fresh eyes, alert to the situation of both peak oil and global warming, since this eccentric thinker was unique among twentieth-century philosophers in placing energy in the center of his system. That is to say, Bataille appreciated and understood energy "in its vastness, its violence, its defiance, its elusiveness, its expenditure" (xiii). At first glance, this redeployment of Bataille's oeuvre seems at once brilliant and necessary but also counterintuitive. For on one hand, Bataille's writings sought to understand "an economy on the scale of the universe" (xiv), while on the other, he is the last candidate on earth to rationally discuss sustainability or conservation or any other cornerstone of the green movement. Bataille, after all, was a big fan of profligate spending, in all its senses. So how exactly is this champion of squander a useful guide to living in the age of scarcity?

Stoekl imagines what Bataille would have made of today's ecowarriors and environmental activists, anticipating that the Dionysian Frenchman would have found their talk of austerity, simplicity, and authenticity a collection of puritanical values parading around in tie-dyed disguise. "Such a cult," argues Stoekl (2007, xv), "refuses certain basic human urges to consume or destroy, and in the process involves the affirmation of yet another humanism." (*Humanism* here, as elsewhere, functions as a synonym for *pious delusion*.) From the perspective of sustainability, Nature is still viewed as a "standing reserve" for its edifying value for humans so that the logic of the state park or nature reserve is merely extended to cover the globe.[34] For the ghost of Bataille, "the problem becomes how best to *expend* rather than how best to envision the consequences of shortage" (Stoekl 2007, 33; emphasis added).

Bataille—like Doyle before him (albeit in more sophisticated terms)—foregrounds the libidinal economy that in large part powers the market economy and is yet suspended outside of it, as an open secret. But though both the libidinal and the political economies boil down to supply and demand, we shall see that they cannot be reduced to each other or conflated in any definitive way. For the general economist, energy stems from the transgression of structural limits and is thus beyond human use (Stoekl 2007, xvi). The cosmic imperative is thus "the recognition of an energy that does not do 'work' for the maintenance of the human" (Stoekl 2007, xvii). As Stoekl (2007, 32–33) explains, "man is not so much the author of his own narrative, or the subject that experiences and acts, as 'he' is the focal point of the intensification or slackening of energy flows." Thus humans "are no different from any other animals, though their wastage of energy might be more intense through its very self-consciousness."[35]

Our species is not exempt from the general laws of concentration and release—for Bataille, physical processes with sacred implications or incarnations. And yet, in our pathetic hubris, we try to master these forces and regulate them according to our own schedule: itself an artificial suspension of desire. "The future," writes Stoekl (2007, xix),

> is fundamentally resistant to planning; blind expenditure entails not an obsessive and centralized prognostication, authored by a head that is always the supreme metonym and referent of social intelligence, but rather the playing out of aftereffects in which social practices may very well "save the earth" in spite of themselves (save it not for conservation but for lavish consumption).

In other words, "an economy on the scale of the universe implies an earth on the scale of the universe" (xix).

Such logic is so foreign to our habitual way of doing and viewing things that its provocative wager takes a great effort to fully absorb. Here survival is not an end in itself, as is taken for granted by both the Left and the Right and most people in between. Rather it is a means of perpetuating yet more glorious expenditure. Bataille is no tree hugger, berating Man to attune himself to the harmony of the universe. Instead, he rejoices in the human capacity to push Nature's exuberance and excess to the nth degree, beyond itself, as it were. As a consequence, the perpetuation of the species does not rely on rationally pulling back from the brink but rather on a more bodily understanding, in which energy is conducted more profoundly through the quasi-divine circuits of this errant animal, with its strange intelligence, mirroring, and magnifying of the undeniable economies of life and death. Hence Baudrillard's (1990, 186) argument, influenced by Bataille, that our unconscious desire to witness the terrible spectacle of nuclear war will most likely ensure that such a thing never actually happens, or in Stoekl's (2007, 46) words, "survival . . . can be read as the fundamentally unintentional consequence of expenditure rather than its purpose."

For Stoekl (2007, 37–38), then, Bataille's ethical challenge is to "somehow distinguish between versions of excess that are 'on the scale of the universe,' whose recognition–implementation guarantee the survival of society (and human expenditure), and other versions that entail blindness to the real role of expenditure, thereby threatening man's, not to mention the planet's, survival." Against our own instincts (themselves encouraged by the ideologies embedded within modern political economy), conservation, frugality, maintenance, and homeostasis—whether of nature or our own bodies—"can lead only to mass destruction and the ultimate wasting of the world" (38). Our attention should instead be focused on how to discover and encourage those modes of expenditure that resonate with the macroeconomy of jealous hoarding, violent exchange, and explosive release.

On the face of it, this does not sound as if it would lead to a very peaceful society. But the argument is ever present: that the depressing jealousies, violence, and explosions we see in the news headlines every day would be far less harmful if they had a legitimate outlet, if they were organically interwoven into our interactions. The patient would therefore not be so quick to slash himself if he did not spend most of his life smothered by a libidinal straitjacket (a Freudian conclusion, despite being arrived at through a Marxist–Hegelian route). One would imagine that the concentrations of energy available from the earth's oil fields would have made Bataille's eyes glisten with erotic excitement, but Stoekl (2007, xv) believes otherwise, claiming that fossil fuels "entail a double humanism: they are burned to serve, to magnify, to glorify the human or (what amounts to the same thing) the human in the automobile ('freedom,' 'happiness,' etc.) as transcendental referent, and they are produced solely through the free exercise of the mind and will." (For this commentator, "no intimacy . . . can be envisaged through the mechanized expenditure of fossil fuels" [56]—which makes one wonder if he has ever read J. G. Ballard.)[36]

For Stoekl's Bataille, the privileged site for the ecstatic burn-off of surplus is the human body: the energy source of "libidinous and divine recycling, not the stockpiled, exploited, and dissipated energy of easily measured and used fossil fuels" (Stoekl 2007, xvii). After a century of species-supernova, the human star must retreat back to its humble origins. And yet, according to the general economy, the human is in essence no less powerful than a jet engine, at least on the level of subjective consciousness (a reading that puts Bataille perilously close to the humanists of our introduction: Frayn, Bloom, and Arendt).

Stoekl (2007, 41) admits that "*The Accursed Share* . . . presents us with a strange amalgam of awareness of the central role energy plays in relation to economics . . . and a willful ignorance concerning the socio-technological modes of energy delivery and use, which are far more than mere technical details." In other words, Bataille has no theory of depletion.[37] Stoekl redresses this shortcoming by updating his concepts for the looming, *literal* postindustrial age. This results in a vision clad in its own rather steam-punk aesthetic: not a return to premodern idylls (bucolic Amish farms tended by hand by people in hemp clothing) but rather a postmodern iteration (organic vegetable gardens inside the abandoned factories of Detroit, tended by hand-cranked robots and vinyl-clad goths)—not a full circle, but a spiral forward, retroprogress. Tomorrow's truly renewable society will be "one based on the glorious expenditure of unrefinable energy and not its obsessive and impossible conservation," which translates into "a muscle-based, human-powered" world. The key difference is between "energy as infinite *force* and profoundly limited available *resource"* (xx). Negotiating that difference is the human challenge of the twenty-first century.

Stoekl's (2007) case study is recycling.[38] In its current form, this practice fails the Bataille test for being too parsimonious (i.e., sub-scribing to the "austerity–authenticity–sustainability school of social commentary" [123]).[39] In contrast, the desire to reuse allegedly spent objects should be far less modest, "not merely a question of a new, slightly more benign form of maintaining a standing reserve... but the orgiastic movement of the parody of meaning, of the expenditure of the energy of meanings and of physical and social bodies, an eth-ics (and aesthetics) of filth" (xix). (One can smell the powerful whiff of Burning Man in these passages.) Orgiastic recycling works against "a cult of the self, jealous in its marshalling of all available resources" (142). Indeed, it will "tear us from our projects and project us into communication with others, with the void," and in doing so, expose "the lie of sheer utility" (175).[40]

There is a utopian impulse at work in Stoekl's ingenious ventril-oquism, operating somewhere between the Paris Commune and Situ-ationist *dérive*. It also extends the temporal limits of Hakim Bey's Temporary Autonomous Zone because the clocks themselves run slower after the oil well has run dry. "At the moment of the recognition of the finitude of fuel," writes Stoekl (2007, 185), "the space of the car opens out to another space, the space of another expenditure: that of the walker, dancer, or cyclist in the city; the *flâneur*, the voyeur, the exhibitionist." Moreover, "the city must be conceived as a topography of spectacular energy expenditure... rather than as a mere locus of energy use and conservation" (xix). Fusing an apocalyptic style with a pagan smile, the children of Bataille "refuse to take the downside of the bell curve as a simple and inevitable decline into feudalism, fun-damentalism, extinction" (205). This positive spin on the end-of-the-world-as-we-know-it is an important reclaiming of the dystopian tone as urgent forecasts of doom and gloom are often used by the powers that be (the elites) to blackmail the powers that become (the people) into further submission: to tighten the screws on an already screwed system (compare the War on Terror, financial bailouts, etc.—what Naomi Klein [2007] calls the "shock doctrine").

For Stoekl, the mantra of sustainability is a decoy word, pressuring potential transgressive energies to cap themselves according to an ideologically polluted, highly restricted economy: the libidinal equivalent of carbon trading ("I'll let you do this, only if I can do that, but let's not get carried away!"). The key questions are not usually asked, in the interest of pulling together for an unreflective greater good: "Sustainable for how long? At what level of consumption, decided upon by whom? Is a permanently sustainable economy even conceivable?" (Stoekl 2007, 119). Thus there is another species of anthropocentrism at work: the belief that climate change can be reverse engineered by human will and ingenuity and that natural cycles can be contained and maintained in a positive dynamic equilibrium. The universe, just as the stock market, may have other plans, beyond or indifferent to our well-being, whether humanity casts itself in the role of Dr. Frankenstein or the prodigal son. This is essentially why Stoekl insists that belief in a "completely sustainable (unchanging) world is . . . akin to believing in a coherent God" (140).

The issue that most thinkers would have with Stoekl's Bataillian solution to environmental crisis—other than the poetics of its dark romanticism—is that it is unintended. Survival is merely the blowback of an indifferent system and not the planned outcome of human resourcefulness. The commentator claims, "We inadvertently open the space of a *postsustainable world*. We no longer associate sustainability with a closed economy of production–consumption; rather, the economy of the world may be rendered sustainable so that the glory of expenditure can be projected into the indefinite future" (Stoekl 2007, 144; emphasis added). To put it another way, "survival is the unplanned aftereffect of the sacred rite; the gesture that risks the integrity of the human is also the one that assures it. . . . The hunter hunts to live so that he can practice the rite; he does not practice the rite only so that he can survive" (174–75). But this is to put great faith in something over which we have zero control, something that, for all their talk of trust in higher powers, humans have a lot of trouble actually doing.

PEAK LIBIDO

> Our epoch does not love itself.
> —Bernard Stiegler, "The Disaffected Individual"

> I don't know why, but I hate all comparisons involving oil.
> —Antonioni's *L'avventura*

Peak oil, of course, is not the only catastrophe facing our species today. However, one alternative scenario in particular commands our attention, and that is Bernard Stiegler's bleak belief that human libido has been tapped out by the rapacious hunger of capital.[41] For Stiegler, the socially constructive, life-affirming aspects of the libido have been overexploited to the extent that they no longer function, being replaced by sheer blind drive. That is to say, people will always *desire*, but the motivation behind that desire, and the objects toward which it reaches out, are severely debased and compromised by our political, economic, and technical arrangements.[42] Stiegler makes this claim— that positively charged libido has imploded into the negative spirals of drive—throughout his prolific works on the historical and ontological implications of technological evolution, though most clearly in the paper "Within the Limits of Capitalism, Economizing Means Taking Care."[43] Here he makes explicit the comparison between dwindling oil reserves and those of the libido.[44] To fully appreciate this provocative parallel, it is necessary to trace the complex complicities between the (symbolic) libidinal economy and the market, given how intimately intertwined they have become. (Indeed, it is most telling to type "libidinal economy" into Google, only to be asked the question, "Did you mean liberal economy"?)[45] After all, libido and oil are both forms of energy production—the former, theoretically infinitely renewable and sustainable, the latter, a materially finite resource. And yet the conditions of hypercapitalism have demanded so much from the intangible human resource of the libido that the marker line is falling lower and lower on the system's intrusive dipstick.[46]

Madison Avenue and Hollywood thus play the role of the Organization of Petroleum Exporting Countries (OPEC) in this little vignette, pumping the hearts and genitals of the world for crude desire, which can then be refined into pure profits. The higher the hem, the greater the margins. Adam Curtis's brilliant documentary series for the BBC, *The Century of the Self*, narrates an airtight conspiracy in which Freud's nephew, Edward Bernays, appropriates the scientific insights of his uncle and exploits their power to persuade the masses to do everything from dying for their country to smoking cigarettes (for this was the chronology in which it occurred: from governmental propaganda in the 1940s to commercial public relations in the postwar boom, before turning full circle to corporate-style politics in the 1980s to today).

The discovery and mapping of the topography of the human unconscious (i.e., capacity for irrationalism) is thus the equivalent of the discovery and drilling of the great oil fields beneath the planet's surface. One newsreel from the early 1950s, for instance, proudly announces, "More than any other country in the world, America is a nation on wheels. The automobile and the power behind it have been major factors in the growth of our country. We can drive anywhere we want to, at any time, for any reason ... including fun."[47] The narrative does not hesitate to equate the gross domestic product with the erotic thrill of mobility (and surely it is no coincidence that the new icon of irresponsible waste, the Hummer, is a car named after a sex act).[48] The lubrication of the wheels of industry, and the gears of commerce, is thus a job for both material and immaterial labor. Indeed, the more work is considered to be a means to buy desirable things and experiences, the more it is perceived as a labor of love, and the less those benefiting inequitably from this setup have to be concerned about uncomfortable questions (such as "why are *you* getting so much more access to desirable things and experiences than I am, when *I* work just as hard"?),[49] that is, until desire itself, as an organic resource, begins to dwindle. What then? What alternatives are there for libidinal energy? According to Stiegler, there is the inorganic soliciting and synthesizing of pure drive.

Stiegler's approach is a comprehensive and holistic one, complete with its own defamiliarizing vocabulary. His premise is based, once again, on human exceptionalism: "Humans die but their histories remain—this is the big difference between mankind and other life forms" (AE). Humans, however, are not essentialized *beings* but historical *becomings*: the ongoing extrusion of "tertiary retentions" (i.e., technical memories, from the flint to writing to the video camera). What we call "history"—or hominization—is therefore the specific and localized interactions "between the evolution of technical systems and that of other social systems" (AE). Beyond genetic memory, and beyond the psychological memory of the individual, there is *cultural memory*, which—for the sake of phenomenological rigor—Stiegler calls "epiphylogenetic." In other words, "it is the articulation between the nervous, technical, and social systems which constitutes the total human fact" (DI).

Humanity is, Stiegler claims, the first species to subdivide itself into the complex identity clusters of ethnicity, a process enabled by the objectification and externalization of collective memory.[50] To be German or Han Chinese or Iroquois means to be ontologically oriented by the tertiary retentions enabled by tools, techniques, and technologies that weave a particular world and a particular relationship to time and space. What is more, the habitus of the German (taken both spatially and temporally) is not commensurable with the Han Chinese or the Iroquois, and vice versa. What happens after the Second World War is "the transformation of the technical system into a planetary industrialized mnemotechnical system of retention. And with it *'consciousness' (as such) is challenged*" (AE). The homogenizing process initiated by colonialism intensifies in the age of postcolonial, liberal economic globalization, resulting in an "upheaval of the retentional systems that regulate common access to space and time (calendarity and cardinality)" (AE). From the 1950s onward, the entire constellation of cultures are subsumed into an ideological equivalent of Greenwich Mean Time, most significantly experienced as the absolute conflation of two intertwined but formerly distinct systems: the productive and the mnemotechnical.[51] The world becomes just that, "the world," engineered under the sign of a global mnemotechnical system, leading to a sudden drop in libidinal energy. Stiegler calls this "hypersynchronization," which leads to "a world consumed by the ever accelerating and engulfing synchronization of mass experience" (Ross 2006, 83).

For Stiegler, "the heart of cultures and societies is at stake; their most intimate relations to the world, their memories and their identities" (AE). Moreover, the standardization of the spirit is "experienced as a kind of *cultural entropy*, the *destruction of life*" (AE).[52] Globalization is thus held aloft as another name for hypermodernity, which in turn represents "imminent spiritual, civilisational and existential collapse" (AE). But what exactly is the source of such calamity? Is it not the case that our technologies allow greater progress in terms of hygiene, convenience, affluence, and thus happiness? Not according to thinkers who are still capable of making the distinction between a libidinal and a political economy. Profits in the latter do not necessarily lead to benefits in the former, especially since we humans—as fragile exemplars of singular and collective individuation—are milked by the media for every last drop of our erotic life force, like cows attached to industrial suction pumps.

Stiegler's dystopian vision rests on the key Freudian premise that the precious aspects of civilization are only possible because of sublimation: the productive channeling of the sexual instincts into more long-lasting, civic-minded, and beneficial projects than orgasm. (Of course, Stiegler's definition of *civilization* is not a naive Victorian one, although one could argue it has roots in such—which is not necessarily to critique it.) "If consummation is that which destroys its object," he writes, "libido is to the contrary that which, as desire and not as drive, that, as the sublimation intrinsic to desire, *takes care* of its object" (WLC).[53] The capacity to sublimate is thus the key to successful hominization and is what makes humanity, for Stiegler, the most fascinating of creatures. When we lose this capacity, however, the investments we make on a daily basis—financially, emotionally, intellectually—give way to the kind of short-term speculations that play havoc with the market system.[54] Hence "the gigantic financial crisis sending tremors all over the world is the disastrous result of the hegemony of the short term of which the destruction of attention is at once effect and cause" (WLC). Objects of desire—whether a lover, a house, a novel, a business, a performance, a farm, or any other project—require long-term investment, something we no longer have the ability to do, since libidinal cathexis has lost its stickiness through overuse. Transference becomes Teflon coated.

It was Bernays, and his marketing minions, who first figured out that *de*-sublimation, on a mass scale, makes for big business.[55] Through enticing us to crave instant soup and weight loss and designer lofts and fast cars and *jouissance* on tap, we lost the ability to orient ourselves in both the here and now and toward the future as a territory worth conceiving and constructing.[56] In having our senses continually teased and solicited, we live in a timeless and constant state of suspense (held forever between the menu and meal, in Adorno's metaphor).[57] The habitual reflexes around consumption (buying, using, regretting, reselling) are as cyclical and purposeless as the spasm of sphincters in accordance with bodily requirements. We are caught in the "bad repetition" of drive rather than in the good repetition of desire.[58] To desublimate is necessarily to demotivate. All the libidinal steam, accumulated during sleep and other downtime, is whistled off into the ether and not put to work inside the engine of existential, social momentum, hence the "tendency towards a decrease of libidinal energy, which is marked by a loss of individuation, destruction of the structures of primordial narcissism, loss of aesthetic and symbolic participation, and, finally, depression and demotivation" (CI). All the journalistic talk condemning our so-called individualistic culture in fact obscures the real issue: that Nietzsche's herd society is now grazing mindlessly all over the planet, "as if the efficacy of the lie was proportional to its enormity" (Stiegler 2009, 48). Far from the Ayn Rand style of valorization of the preformed, autonomous, heroic individual, Stiegler seeks to restore a symbiotic relationship between the *I* and the *We*, for without one, the other collapses.[59] Indeed, narcissism, in Stiegler's view, "is not a deafness or blindness to others, but the very condition of being-with-others" (Ross 2006, 82).[60]

All of this leads to the following question: what would constitute the equivalent of a stimulus package for a libido in free fall? In 2008, taxpayers in the United States were sent checks for six hundred dollars in the mail by George W. Bush to encourage them to spend more freely at a time defined by the credit crunch. While this may have resulted in an uptick in desire, this consumer-driven type of short-term investment would certainly not satisfy a libidinal economist, concerned by the evaporation of more vital currencies. How to counter peak libido then?

There are several pressing issues, according to Stiegler, in terms of the "liquidation of desire," which we can cluster into five interrelated categories, generally diffused throughout the culture: (1) desublimation, (2) attention-deficit disorder, (3) lack of shame, (4) loss of primordial narcissism, and (5) forgetting of *savoir-vivre* (ways of knowing/being and the eroticized ease these afford). Each issue aggravates the symptoms of the other, making manifest the increasing inability to "take care" (for oneself or for others). As a consequence, the solutions offered are restorative. First, we must learn to recanalize the libido toward the positively projected future.[61] Second, we must relearn to focus our attention and not become distracted by shrill solicitations

from all 360 degrees (of which Twitter is only the most recent exacerbating example). Third, we must rediscover a sense of shame (figured
as a negentropic relationship to processes of individuation).[62] Fourth,
we must reject the vulgar narcissism so prevalent on our screens and
in our behaviors to nurture the "primordial narcissism" that is the
precondition for all love (according to the principle that one must first
love oneself to then love another).[63] And finally, we must rewire and
recalibrate the global technical system so that it does not regulate our
cultural memories for us, so that we regain the opportunity to know
how to live in a mode of relative agency, so that life itself is understood
on a collectively symbolic level and is not approached according to
operating instructions delivered from an anonymous beyond, like a
giant, flimsy IKEA wardrobe.[64]

To force the matter into a nutshell: if contemporary citizen–consumers
manage to counter the predominant forces of the age (all gathered
today under the evocative name of "psychopower"), then the libido
has a chance of replenishing itself, of pulling itself out of the dried-up
oil well in which it disappeared, by its own greasy hair. For whomever
controls "*the future mechanisms of orientation will be [able] to control
the global imaginary*" (AE).

Readers familiar with Herbert Marcuse may be suffering from déjà
vu at this point in my exposition, for indeed there are a great number
of overlaps between this philosopher's critique of the "performance
principle" and Stiegler's moral call for an alternative to the "ideology
of performance" (CI).[65] Where Stiegler believes that the world has devolved into a place without perspective or true desire, Marcuse (1974,
xiii) also despairs that "freedom and satisfaction are transforming the
earth into hell."

Indeed, it is possible to play a game of "who said which" at times:

> As soon as the libidinal energy of individuals and groups is he-
> gemonically made to detour towards objects of consumption,
> all other objects of the libido—particularly those which permit
> the constitution of a civilization by supporting sublimation—are
> disinvested and seriously threatened. Thus the family and, more
> generally, education, schools, and knowledge in its totality are
> threatened, as are politics, law, and all the *sublimities of the mind*
> which are the fruit of what the Germans call *Bildung*. (CI)

Consider the preceding as (not) opposed to the following:

> The affluent society is in its own way . . . organizing "the desire for
> beauty and the hunger for community," the renewal of the "contact
> with nature," the enrichment of the mind, and honors for "creation
> for its own sake." The false ring of such proclamations is indicative
> of the fact that, within the established system, these aspirations
> are translated into administered cultural activities, sponsored by
> the government and the big corporations—an extension of their
> executive arm into the soul of the masses. (Marcuse 1974, xxiii)

Both object to the notion of quantifiable desire, just as both take
issue with the "mercantile organization of life" (DI) and the "scientific
management of instinctual needs" (Marcuse 1974, xii).[66]

For Marcuse as well, the various media machines that mushroom
around us are tampering with our species-being. The "repressive domina-
tion" necessary to create the economic conditions for late-stage industrial
civilization begins to create—via ever-more exquisite techniques of mass
manipulation of the libido—a "surplus repression" that warps the woof
of humanity.[67] "Where the high standard of living does not suffice for
reconciling the people with their life and their rulers," Marcuse writes,
"the 'social engineering' of the soul and the 'science of human relations'
provide the necessary libidinal cathexis" (xi). Moreover:

> The power to restrain and guide instinctual drives, to make bio-
> logical necessities into individual needs and desires, increases
> rather than reduces gratification: the "mediatization" of nature,
> the breaking of its compulsion, is the human form of the pleasure
> principle. Such restrictions of the instincts may first have been
> enforced by scarcity and by the protracted dependence of the hu-
> man animal, but they have become the privilege and distinction
> of man which enabled him to transform the blind necessity of the
> fulfillment of want into desired gratification. (38)

Thanks to the historically unprecedented strategy of making merchandise into objects of the libido, we moderns suffer from "repressive
affluence" (xiv). Thus "the erotic energy of the Life Instincts" (xxiii) are
wheeled out of the depths of our being, encouraging us to seize the

machinery of sublimation for fizzy, shallow, artificially sweetened instant gratification. Writing in the lead-up to, and during, the sexual revolution, Marcuse became a spokesman for Dionysian revivals of all kinds. And yet he was no fan of the neo-Bohemian, seeing in their alternative lifestyle a consumerist distortion of Eros as well as a capitulation to the one-dimensional society. ("The vamp . . . the beatnik . . . perform a function very different from and even contrary to that of their cultural predecessors. They are no longer images of another way of life but rather freaks or types of the same life, serving as an affirmation rather than negation of the established order" [Marcuse 2006, 62].) Indeed, many readers often failed to see the Marxist foundations of Marcuse's critique of contemporary society, mistaking it simply for a call to throw off the Man and indulge in polysexuality.[68] Marcuse would thus have been unmoved by Coca-Cola's famous appropriation of the flower power subculture in the late 1960s since Eros cannot find liberation within the "dehumanizing" conditions (an extremely presumptuous word, of course) of a world dictated by performance and profit. The personal may be political, but *economics* extends deep into the most intimate spaces and places of the person.

Marcuse insisted that he was not a utopian because this breed of thinker usually creates stagnant, rigid, ahistorical blueprints that never work in actuality. Rather he saw himself as a critical theorist who believed in the power of reason to guide civilization into less discontented territory. On one hand, he acknowledged that the "methodical sacrifice of libido, its rigidly enforced deflection to socially useful activities and expressions, *is* culture" (3), but on the other, he maintained that our pleasure-seeking organs need not be organized as teleologically as they are.

Marcuse notes the Freudian paradox that "culture demands continuous sublimation; it thereby weakens Eros, the builder of culture" (83). Foucault's hypothesis notwithstanding, the Victorians found it necessary to bifurcate their existence, working by day and debauching by night. But the answer is not simply to desublimate, for this leads either to partitioned schizophrenia (as exemplified by Dr. Jekyll and Mr. Hyde) or—as women enter the workforce and technics opens new fields of relations—an ubiquitous, alienated, and reified flaunting of sexuality.[69] This latter is what Marcuse calls "repressive desublimation," of which *Playboy* magazine is a clear example. Hugh Hefner's publication became a cultural icon by allegedly liberating the repressed life instincts, and yet it carefully stages this pseudo-liberation, simultaneously locking desires (as well as the object of those desires) into very limited and predictably profitable patterns. Women must be blonde and buxom, while sexuality must be heterosexual, phallocentric, and orgasmic. As for the scandalous stories of Nabokov and Tennessee Williams, "what happens is surely wild and obscene, virile and tasty, quite immoral—and, precisely because of that, perfectly harmless" (Marcuse 2006, 81). As a result, Marcuse writes, "sexual relations themselves have become much more closely assimilated with social relations; sexual liberty is harmonized with profitable conformity" (94). Indeed, "in their erotic relations, they 'keep their appointments'—with charm, with romance, with their favorite commercials" (95).

To strengthen his case, Marcuse quotes Jean-Paul Sartre, who observed, "Shortly after semi-automatic machines were introduced, investigations showed that female skilled workers would allow themselves to lapse while working into a sexual kind of daydream; they would recall the bedroom, the bed, the night and all that concerns only the person within the solitude of the couple alone with itself. But it was the machine in her which was dreaming of caresses" (quoted in Marcuse 2006, 29).[70] What Deleuze and Guattari might see as a potentially felicitous "desiring machine" Marcuse sees as a challenge to the human within Eros (or vice versa, which amounts to much the same thing). He writes, "The machine process in the technological universe breaks the innermost privacy of freedom and joins sexuality and labor in one unconscious, rhythmic automatism" (Marcuse 2006, 30).

As a consequence, the more flagrant the social signs of sexuality, the less Eros powering the common project of human existence. Hypersexualization equates to deeroticization. (The secret affinity between peak oil and peak libido can thus be traced between *Mad Max* and *Mad Men*.) Most significantly for us, perhaps, is that this situation is framed in terms of ecology: the erotic "landscape" is presented as "a medium of libidinal experience which no longer exists" (Marcuse 2006, 76). Furthermore, "the environment from which the individual could obtain pleasure—which he could cathect as gratifying almost as an extended zone of the body—has been rigidly reduced. Consequently, the 'universe' of libidinous cathexis is likewise reduced" (Marcuse 2006,

76), which is to say that the universe is not expanding but shrinking, rendering humanity claustrophobic in the process.

As evidence of his argument, Marcuse (2006, 76–77) invites us to compare making love in a field as opposed to in a car or on a Manhattan Street. The former allows an expansion of the libido, of which the environment itself "partakes" and "invites." In the latter two examples, the libido becomes localized and intensified, leading to the blockage of self-transcendence. One wonders, however, whether Marcuse should be so quick to denounce the erotic possibilities of the city. Could it not be the case that the libido is more resilient than he makes out and is not so inclined to make such a romantic and anachronistic distinction between natural and artificial environments?[71]

In any case, Marcuse's answer to this deceptive situation is, anticipating Stiegler, a nonrepressive form of sublimation. Rather than mistakenly claiming the adman's notion of sexuality as one's own, the truly empowering way to proceed is through a "polymorphous sexuality," unscripted by reproductive biology or repressive society. Hence, by eschewing *The Joy of [Commodified] Sex* as well as the missionary imperative, polymorphous people manage to "make the human body an instrument of pleasure rather than labor" (xv). Erotic life is thus no longer shrink-wrapped around the genitals and forced into the bedroom but—at least in theory—becomes omnipresent in both the human body and the body politic. One's libido can be just as engaged while attending a concert or constructing a table or tickling the elbow of one's neighbor with a specially selected feather. Thus "the free development of transformed libido within transformed institutions, while eroticizing previously tabooed zones, time, and relations, would *minimize* the manifestations of *mere* sexuality by integrating it into a far larger order" (202).[72] Marcuse even speaks of "the *ascendancy* of libido in sublimation," resulting "from an extension rather than from a constraining deflection of the libido" (169–70). Instead of a release or explosion, there is a spread and *transformation*.

This scenario is emphatically not a reversion to a more natural or animal state as Marcuse respects "the enduring truth value of the instinctual needs which must be 'broken' so that the human being can function in interpersonal relations" (274). In other words, we must be tamed like horses into our own species-being for culture to function.

The political animal must be broken in to harness the animal instincts for greater (i.e., nonanimalistic) purposes, even if we can still partially access them for holistic pleasures.[73] Sounding a lot like Stoekl, Marcuse observes that "in a genuinely humane civilization, the human existence will be play rather than toil, and man will live in display rather than need" (188).[74] However, such a statement fails to look beyond the horizon of satisfied needs to the era of scarcity. In other words, it has no notion of peak oil to supplement its theory of peak libido. "Non-repressive order is essentially an order of abundance: the necessary constraint is brought about by 'superfluity' rather than need. Only an order of abundance is compatible with freedom" (194). What happens, then, when Mother Earth refuses to provide dinner for her human progeny? Marcuse is mute on this point. And so, when he talks of the banishment of surplus repression and the introduction of a "libidinal rationality" (an oxymoron if ever there was one), we cannot help realizing that we are indeed in the presence of a utopian. Moreover, when he writes that "non-repressive order is possible only if the sex instincts can, by virtue of their own dynamic and under changed existential and societal conditions, generate lasting erotic relations among mature individuals" (199), the cynical Freudian in our heads can only reply, "Yeah, good luck with that."

But Marcuse has faith in what he calls the "Great Refusal": a diffuse resistance movement, led most visibly by heroic artists who do not squander or sacrifice their precious human resources on superficial comforts.[75] (It is this faith that dates him most, although it is still with us in various ways.) Despite this aesthetic disposition, he sets the stage for future post-Marxist thinkers such as Agamben and Žižek—and indeed echoes Marx himself—by foreseeing a systemic consummation of its own horrific conditions (a crucial point, where he parts ways with Stiegler). "The more complete the alienation of labor, the greater the potential of freedom: total automation would be the optimum" (156). Or to phrase it even more pithily, "the elimination of human potentialities from the world of (alienated) labor creates the preconditions for the elimination of labor from the world of human potentialities" (105). We see, therefore, one key difference between Marcuse and Stiegler, for the former believes in humanity, whereas the latter talks in terms of hominization.[76] But perhaps these are ultimately names for the same thing, one just burdened with a more naive ring to it than the other?

At any rate, neither seeks to go back to some bucolic time before the technocratic copyrighting of human experience; rather both intend to push forward to a more enlightened, less calculating relationship with the technologies that in turn created us. Marcuse makes the clarification that "what is retrogressive is not mechanization and standardization but their containment, not the universal co-ordination but its concealment under spurious liberties, choices, and individualities" (100). He thus looks forward to a "post-technological rationality, in which technics is itself the . . . organon of the 'art of life'" (Marcuse 2006, 242). Echoing such a neo-Hellenic fusion of technics and art, Stiegler hopes "to invent a new *industrial* model which is capable of interrupting the destructive process unleashed by the capture and unlimited exploitation of the libidinal energy of producers and consumers" (CI; emphasis added).

THE CALL GIRL OF BEING

> True civilization does not lie in gas, nor in steam, nor in turntables. It lies in the reduction of traces of original sin.
> —Baudelaire, "Mon Coeur Mis a Nu"

Yet we have only delayed the question of a stimulus package for the libido and what form it might take. Step 1 is to acknowledge the difference between a libidinal economy and a capitalist one, that is, between the general and the restricted. One clear symptom of the human capitulation to psychopower is the inability to tell them apart, even if they are always in tension (as when Woody Allen states in the taxicab, "She was so beautiful, I could barely keep my eyes on the meter"). Let us then consider the American film director Steven Soderbergh, who—while promoting his most recent film *The Girlfriend Experience* (which depicts the hyperalienated lives of contemporary New Yorkers[77])—stated that "the movie is about transactions. It sounds cold or clinical to say this, but . . . [life] is just a series of transactions. We all want something, whether it's emotional or monetary. Even if you're someone who says, 'I want to sit here and just be left alone.' You are going to have to negotiate on some level just to achieve that."[78] For the Dionysian and romantic–humanist alike, such sterile sentiments burn the ears, for they make no distinction between financial transactions and the symbolic exchanges that transcend, transgress, complicate, enhance, and/or negate them. Early on in Soderbergh's film, a generic Wall Street character tells his buddies, while drinking bottled beer in a private jet, "Obama is saying the bottom's up—we have a consumer economy. Seventy percent of the economy is a consumer economy. He's going to stimulate the entire economy by going after the seventy percent." "Let's talk about the stimulus of our *own* packages!" replies one of the frat-bankers, thereby making this most constitutive of innuendos explicit.

The Girlfriend Experience (2009) is possibly the first mainstream cinematic release to deal with the current global financial crisis. However, it gets caught up in the same set of logics that created the meltdown in the first place, thereby negating its own potential for insight or critique. Nevertheless, as a symptom, striving to be part of the diagnosis, it warrants a closer look. The protagonist, Chelsea, is a high-class prostitute who happens to be in a committed relationship with her boyfriend, Chris, a personal trainer. The parallel between their professions is structurally implicit: both are paid to be attentive in a one-on-one situation, activating the Marxist insight that under the alienated conditions of capital, we are all whores to differing degrees.[79] (Indeed, the contempt reserved by society for actual prostitutes is in ratio to the unconscious understanding that we are all the bitches of the pimp known as Capital—hence the progressivist push for the more economically honest name "sex workers.") In the case of the film, both characters have clients. The nature of the job is incidental.

Chelsea is not only a sexual outlet but also a psychological crutch for men who have become casualties of the credit crunch. These men are self-aware enough to realize that she is partly playing the role of shrink but admit that psychoanalysis is more pleasurable when the analyst is young and beautiful and the transference is understood and smiled on.[80] In contrast to the cautionary tale in which selling one's body is the fast track to a deadened soul, Chelsea's libido (or at least what passes for libido at this point in time) is responsive to certain clients, which complicates her relationship to Chris. She feels an emotional connection to some of the more sympathetic or attractive customers, but they all let her down, ultimately reminding her of her Janus status as commodity and/or dispensable worker. (The most extreme and disturbing case occurs when she is taken advantage of by the lewd proprietor of the

Erotic Connoisseur Web site, after giving him free sex in exchange for a glowing review: an arrangement he ignores in the nastiest of ways.) Chris, however, has similar dehumanizing experiences, as he attempts to work his way up the corporate food chain. Thus the bed and the bench are depicted as two exchangeable locations on the giant single plane of contemporary life. They are both markets that one can either master or be victimized by.

In Stiegler's terms, Chelsea's individuation occurs—as with all of us—on the three levels of the psychological, social, and technological. The narrative of her subjectivity is primarily framed by the brands of clothing she wears and the instruction manuals of her New Age "per-sonology"[81] books. Her days and nights are spent in the anonymous nonplaces of wine bars and hotel rooms and apartments, all of which look like each other. The inane conversations that pass for dialogue nevertheless speak eloquently of the alienated extrusion of language that Agamben (1993, 80) calls "linguistic being." (It is fortunate for the director that stilted acting translates well into disaffected mood.) Even the architect of the film is seduced by the flattening of affect of his own aesthetic, where questions of financial and emotional dependence are condensed into the mantra: "The economy is fucked." This observation would have been more interesting, however, had Soderbergh understood the reversal to be equally salient: "The fucked are the economy."

The Girlfriend Experience is thus *Pretty Woman* for the square-bespectacled set, differing only in its refusal to provide a fairy-tale happy ending (unless we are talking about the kind of "happy ending" in which Chelsea is so practiced; indeed, the final scene is unflinching in depicting just how *un*-happy such trivial terminal points can be, under current social conditions). For Stiegler, libidinal energy annihi-lates itself through the modern mirror-game of constant intersubjec-tive evaluation and calculation (DI). Any spark we may feel through our own eroticized objectification is thus superficial and fleeting: an instance of vulgar narcissism, which itself is but a shattered splinter of healthy, collective primordial narcissism.[82] After the daily anesthetic drip feed of the program industries (Stiegler's updating of Adorno's *culture industry*), individuals are numb to the possibility of meaning-ful participation, creating the perfect conditions to poach free-floating enthusiasm—when it flares up—for cults such as the People's Temple, the Yankees, and Amway. In such a world, intimacy just might be the rarest commodity of all, and so Chelsea's clients are mining her for it, hoping to get through the hardened emotional crust for a glimpse of something more precious than oil or gold because it is less tangible. A nonrepressive libidinal economy, as envisioned by Marcuse and Stiegler, would encourage and foster such intimacies, giving them the time and space to breathe and perhaps even flourish. But for the repressed society—in which the social contract is hammered out by lawyers and fixed with fine print—the libido is the residue of the Real: an industrial by-product that lubricates social and sexual intercourse in the same way that oil does for the financial wheels of the world. Whether in the bedroom or the boardroom, it is a matter of "getting down to business." Alas, the film is still too reflexively humanist to be capable of seeing the liberating potential in Leo Bersani's notion of "impersonal intimacy" (as discussed in chapter 2).

Chelsea is both flattered and disconcerted that a journalist (yet another middle-aged man) wants to get to know the real woman behind the self-branded persona. In her interview with him, she simply refuses the notion that men really want access to this supposedly real individual. "If they wanted you to be yourself," she tells him, "they wouldn't be paying you." And yet she does not deny the private–public split to herself—indeed, her psychic survival depends on it (despite the fact that the two become mingled when she gets too close to one client in particular). Chelsea recognizes her own subjectivity over and above her status as commodity, even if that recognition is afforded by the reflection she catches of herself in (other) objects of consumption (La Perla lingerie, Kiki de Montparnasse shoes, etc.). The existence of a true face behind the deployed mask is what the disoriented society puts into doubt, which in turn leads to strident but empty affirmations of the singular self. But where Nietzsche understood this essential anonymity of the human to be the route to overcoming the most sentimental and toxic of our species's self-deceptions, Soderbergh laments the loss of face in the name of neo-Darwinian triumph or survival (or as Marcuse put it, "the pain, frustration, impotence of the individual [which] derive from a highly productive and efficiently functioning system in which he makes a better living than ever before" [98]).

The meta-, extradiegetic twist provided by Soderbergh is the casting of a professional star of adult movies in the role of Chelsea, Sasha Grey. Critical commentary around the film presented her performance as something of a salvation story: lost woman found by progressively tolerant mainstream. Yet in evaluating her performance in the film, such critics only function as accomplices in the ongoing commodification of Sasha Grey, the actress.[83] Whether targeted toward the frat house or the art house, clothes off or on, Ms. Grey is now an avatar of whateverbeing—the figure of desire-without-libido,[84] a sports car with no torque after the gas pumps have run dry.

The most visible symptom of the destruction of libido, according to Stiegler, is not the hyperreification of all industries and private lives but the psychotic backlash of individuals who can no longer function without hope or purpose. "We live in a world where ugliness seeps out automatically," he writes. "We all know it, but no-one dares say it out loud: that would be reactionary. . . . The result is the destruction of ways of being and the vectors of sublimation which constitute them on the most intimate level of desire—as the origin itself of desire" (C). Where once we were threatened by saber-toothed tigers, we are now ravaged by television, the latter more disastrous because it takes away our ability to realize we are being ravaged or do anything about it. The stakes, then, teeter on the vertiginous precipice of the generation gap. While our culture preserves even the most trivial things for posterity (bottle cap collections, a museum dedicated to sneakers, etc.), we lack the knowledge to help the young to navigate between the authentic and algorithmic, the potentially productive and intrinsically foreclosed, the valuable and merely distracting, the human and shameless parodies of our species-being.[85]

According to this account, the all-important identificatory bond between children and parents is being broken by "industrial temporal objects": artifacts that capture the attention and channel it over a given block of time such as television shows, video games, and cell phones. Both love and life become poisoned by these new counteraffective relations, leading to a situation such as that of Emmanuel and Patricia Cartier, who—according to Stiegler—injected their five children with insulin in 2002, killing their daughter, in an attempt to save them from further anguish in adulthood. "Condemned to ten to fifteen years in prison, [the Cartiers] are as much victims as perpetrators. They were victims of the everyday despair of the intoxicated consumer, victims who suddenly, here, passed to the act, into this terrifying act of infanticide, because they were trapped by an economic misery engendering symbolic misery" (DI). The strong implication here is that the former would be tolerable if it were not reinforced by the latter. But if the symbolic economy collapses, then there is no form of compensation—material or spiritual—to catch those who find themselves in a debt spiral.

Indeed, Stiegler sees the same symptom at work in the case of Richard Durn, who, in the same year, walked into a council meeting in Nanterre and started shooting people to feel some kind of connection to the world other than blank insignificance.[86] Eric Harris and Dylan Klebold, the perpetrators of the Columbine massacre, are also infamous poster children for the socially disaffected. Among those just as likely to implode than explode are youngsters in Japan—the *hikikomori* and *otaku*—who do not communicate with anyone, least of all their parents, except via the Internet.[87] According to Stiegler, these represent merely the most extreme cases of what is happening to everyone because of the "constant industrial canalization of attention."[88] Were the Cartiers or the Columbine killers allowed to become individuals, within the empathic and coherent currents of a libidinal economy (so the argument goes), they would not have experienced the existential crisis to the degree that they did. Instead, with the libido made redundant—given the pink slip, as it were—the drive was the only thing left to guide them. However the drive has no driver: a role once played by that seemingly oxymoronic entity, responsible libido. And this sheer line of fright leads to explosions of aggression in daily life far more catastrophic than Freud (1989) could have anticipated in his gloomy *Civilization and Its Discontents* (which foresaw war and neuroses more than domestic psychosis).[89]

One obvious objection here is that terrible violence has occurred since day one, at least since hominids could pick up bones and use them as weapons. But for Stiegler, the issue is not a utilitarian one—not a matter of minimizing violence whenever or wherever it inevitably occurs—but an aestheticoethical one, concerning the texture of the quotidian. *Actual* violence is one thing, requiring a response on all sorts of discursive levels: interpersonal, psychological, sociological, juridical, communal, and so on. *Symbolic* violence—or rather, *the violence resulting from the destruction of the symbolic itself*—is beyond the pale, since there is no coherent way to respond, given that the discourses developed to do so have themselves succumbed to catastrophic stagflation. In such a situation, all bets are off—permanently. So while Stiegler could be criticized for exaggerating the deleterious effects of consumer lifestyles—and wasting his breath on lamenting the ongoing rot of the bourgeoisie rather than the truly abject plight of the excluded—he is in fact alerting us to an insidious assumption underlying the entire machine of globalization: a direct correlation between economic and spiritual prosperity.

On one fundamental level, illegal immigrants are seeking food and shelter. But if we subscribe to Maslow's hierarchy of needs—and rank basic subsistence more important than human values of happiness, hope, love, community, recognition, belonging, and so on—then we ignore the many ways that people value the latter over the former in their own lives. Humans are the animal that will refuse food for the sake of a belief or an idea or a statement. Many will give up the most fundamental things before losing face or shedding their prized dignity. And this is one of the most charged zones between the human and the nonhuman: the form of life that presumes to dwell in, and fashion for herself, an existential surplus beyond subsistence (from *zoë* to *bios*, in Agamben's vocabulary). But as soon as security is presumed to be about safeguarding the middle-class nuclear family, then there is no true security to be had. The penniless people scrambling to the West to make a living may find plenty of TVs and cars and cell phones but no life to speak of (hence the prevalence of zombie movies over the past decade or so).

New arrivals to the West represent new libidos to be tapped. But if they are already seduced by the Spectacle, if they seek the American dream—or some European analogue—then they have no libido to offer, only the cheap, unreliable energy of drives, the kind of energy that harms more than it helps.[90] Stiegler, in fact, is unflinching in pointing the finger across the Atlantic:

> The *American way of life* invented the figure of the consumer whose libido is systematically put to work to counter the problems of excess production, which is the social concretisation of this tendential drop in the rate of profit. This canalisation of the libido operated by the capture of attention ends up by liquidating the expertise in living *[savoir-vivre]* of consumers, by the massive development of societies of services which let them off the hook of their own existences, that is, of their diverse responsibilities as

adults having reached their majority. This is what ends up provoking the liquidation of their own desire, as well as the desire of their own children, to the strict extent that the latter can no longer identify with them, both because these parents no longer know anything, and are no longer responsible for anything, having become themselves big fat children, and because the process of primary identification is short-circuited by psychopower through the psychotechnologies. This destruction of desire (that is to say also the destruction of attention and of care) is a new limit encountered by capitalism, this time not only as mode of production, but also as mode of consumption, way of life, that is, as biopower become psychopower.[91] (WLC)

We are victims of cognitive and affective saturation. In fact, there is no *We* to speak of, only an anonymous *They,* of which the so-called individual cannot in fact find any points of recognition or distinction, no traction on which to experience the transductive relationship of being simultaneously an *I* and a *We.* (Capital's cogito is more a question than a statement: *they consume, therefore I am?*). So whereas films like King Vidor's *The Crowd* (1928) suggest that this type of alienation has afflicted humanity at least since the building of big cities, Stiegler would see it differently. For while the seeds of today were being sown at the beginning of the twentieth century, they had not yet reached this point of almost no return. He writes, "To love is to form the most exquisite *savoir-vivre*" (DI). But to live without love is to flounder. It is to remain mute and mouth breathing in front of that most ancient of questions: "what is to be done?"[92]

As one of Stiegler's most astute commentators and translators puts it:

About this we must be clear: it is *not* news that the techniques of consumerism and cultural capitalism tend to reduce the political to marketing, that is, to eliminate it; what *is* news is that this is also the elimination of my and our *economic* self, that is, the destruction of myself as a desiring being, as a motivated being. It is not a question of reducing political desire to the economic logic of marketing, but rather of the destruction of desire and motivation itself, which is the foundation of *all* economy. And, with this destruction of desire, what is thereby also destroyed is my knowledge of *others* as desiring beings, which is my knowledge of them as such, and thus what is destroyed in turn is the trust and confidence which determine the spirit without. (Ross 2007)

In the first decade of the new millennium, social networks (an a priori of the human) have devolved into social networking, an online caricature of such.[93] While life-affirming exchanges and relationships may indeed happen on Facebook, they are underwritten—"sponsored"— by the incredibly sophisticated info-harvesting engines spawned in the silicone valleys and alleys of the world. Users are either unaware of, or simply do not care about, the insidious architecture supporting their interactions. The text box has ears. Yet few would voice their support for social networking sites if the arrangement were realized offline and in real time, with marketing men pressed close, listening more intently, and with far more fine-grained filters than any Stasi agent ever had.[94] Where once big business smiled cheerfully as it went through your pockets, it now facelessly sifts through your deep packets with the aid of electronic arachnid familiars. Hence Stiegler's belief that "when everything becomes a service, transindividuation is completely short-circuited by marketing and advertising *[la publicité]*. Public life is, then, destroyed: *psychic and collective individuation become collective disindividuation*" (DI). This is not a nostalgic fable: that where once harmony reigned, now friction has its way; rather, the inability to effectively individuate ourselves means that there is no genuine basis of distinction on which to create the productive frictions known as culture or spirit. The tank has run out of gas.

LIBIDINAL ECOLOGY

The human, as the subject of prosthetic hominization, is an exceptional creature, by Stiegler's account. As allegorized in the myth of Epimetheus, Man is the result of not human but Titan error (specifically, the forgetting of the task to distribute qualities to *all* animals, including man). As a result, humans are the only animal that lacks an essential element: the species without qualities.[95] Thus there is no intrinsic human element, and we are "nothing outside our capacity to prostheticise ourselves" (Bradley 2006, 91). However, the enlisting of technics to compensate for this lack or default of origin establishes humanity as the exception to the natural rule.[96] (That chimps have recently been discovered to use a five-piece tool kit for extracting honey simply means that the higher primates are now one step closer to engaging in the same process of hominization.)[97]

For Stiegler, "knowledge is, strictly speaking, the experience of the sensible, which does not involve the animal world: the latter . . . *does not have experience*, for experience is what can be transmitted as the experience of the singularity of the sensible, that is to say, to the extent that experience is always itself singular and unexpected" (DK). "Nature," for Stiegler, functions bioalgorithmically, somewhat like Lovelock's Gaia, an acephalic system. So whereas humanity may not *have* an element proper to itself, it may very well *be* one. That is to say, taken as a species—both inside and outside the natural world—the human *is* the unstable catalytic element that gives sentience to life, even though it does not possess anything specific to it. Species-being is thus a matter of effect rather than essence. As Daniel Ross (2007) puts it, "with the human adventure something else begins, *another* negentropic process within and outside the already negentropic history of life, the history of the *exteriorisation* of memory in artifacts, tools, language and writing."

Deploying a sophisticated version of the anthropocentric double gesture, Stiegler (2009, 73) notes that "reality is conjunctive, a complex movement where each one tries to 'find one's place.' Without us, this complex is nothing. So *we* are the *dynamic inadequation* of this complex. . . . As such, we *exceed* this process, we are even the *exception* that can unsettle the process." Whether applied to nature or culture (as if any clear distinction could be made), humans themselves constitute the operating system of an autotelic machine, designed both to flatter and to disturb a species that needs to be disturbed to be truly flattered (via the pleasure received on responding to the disturbance). But in denying animals experience—along with culture or spirit[98]—Stiegler hitches his wagon to the entire philosophical tradition that Derrida put on trial not long before his death.[99] In equating technics with hominization, this tradition is blind to other ways nonhuman animals may engage with what Graham Harman calls "tool-being" and, indeed, the way technics itself may have its own ontological intentions, agency, or sentience.

Stiegler (2009, 72) notes that "even if technics is *constitutive* of anthropology, and, in that sense, man is a prosthetic life form, he is nevertheless not *only* technical. If one day he becomes *entirely* technical, then he will no longer be called man. . . . But then, for the process to continue, it would be necessary to find *another support for diachronicity and desire* other than man." This begs the question, what criteria would be used to distinguish this new support for hitherto exclusively human phenomena? If it quacks like a duck, and walks like a duck, is it not a duck? And is not even a mechanical duck a duck, if it can reproduce mechanical ducklings that do ducklike things?

But Stiegler finds a point of distinction: "Finally, the historical and political becoming of the human *is* this permanent social refunction-alisation, and nothing therein is understandable, in the final analysis, without being conceived as a genealogical apparatus of a libidinal economy" (DK). Animals do not have libido, according to this account (or at least not yet), because they have not developed a superego: a regulating principle that would authorize the necessary sublimation to create not only a sense of self but a sense of time, belonging, and collective projection. (Then again, the anguished expression on your dog's face when it is told that it cannot eat the cupcakes suggests that the acquisition of social restrictions—and the many "positives" this creates—is not an impossibility.) Once again, human sexuality, and the civility it affords when harnessed "properly"—rather than being squandered "like an animal"—is what distinguishes human libido from mere drive. The stark reality of civilization today is of the imminent spasm back into animal existence. Society becomes merely satiety. The question of posthuman or nonhuman libido is thus not only a fascinating question but a pressing one, especially for those who want to rescue the human from dissolving into what Leroi-Gourhan calls the "zoological flux."[100]

Yet even Stiegler and Derrida—the contemporary philosophers who did the most to offset latent and lazy humanism by emphasizing our "originary technicity"—succumb to "a residually anthropocentric dimension" (Bradley 2006, 79), at least according to Arthur Bradley. In an astute reading of technics in current Continental philosophy, Bradley (2006, 81) notes that larger questions fail to get asked, most notably, perhaps, "what form technology might take *outside* the—comparatively localized—process of human subject-constitution." In other words, approaches "intended to produce a de-anthropologising

of the human . . . [become] a new means of defining the *anthropos*"
(81).[101] Bradley also calls this conceptual zigzagging a "paradoxical
double gesture" in which "what starts as an attempt to *displace* the
human onto a non-human outside is folded back *into* the human as its
own 'proper' mode of being" (82). For Derrida, the human is an aporia,
produced by the asymptotic waltz between biology and technology:
"the expression of a logic of supplementation" (82), whereas Stiegler
takes this important—but essentially structural—idea and historicizes
it. But for Bradley, as for me, the intimacy between hominization and
technicity collapses into an exclusive relationship in Stiegler's system
and passes over the ways in which other biological beings have inter-
faced with technology and may do so in the future. The entire notion
of epiphylogenesis thus "risks *re-anthropologising* technics even in the
very act of insisting upon the originary technicity of the human"[102]
(95). Stiegler, however, anticipates such a critique, depicting the human
more as a genre than a species (97–98), one capable of incorporating
the greater apes. But this comes with its own set of problems, akin to
those of animal rights activists, who would merely widen the circle of
what counts as human rather than recompose the presumed zone of
inclusion.

At any rate, with the notion of a distributed technical milieu, generating a genus—*Homo sapiens*—from the generic gene pool, we have
traveled full circle back to Agamben's anthropological machine. Indeed,
we could consider this latter contraption a particular instantiation of
Stiegler's epiphylogenetic memory. The anthro-machine would certainly be impossible without externalized, technical memory supports.
But where Agamben's human recognizes himself in the mirror—in a
Linnaean extension of the mirror stage—Stiegler's human becomes so
disoriented that he can no longer recognize his own reflection in any
meaningful sense. Without a libidinal spit shine, there are no longer
any social surfaces reflective enough to make out the contours of an
I from among the *We*. "There are today," writes Stiegler, "disaffected
beings like there are re-purposed factories *[usines désaffectées]*: there
are *human wastelands* like there are industrial wastelands" (DI). What
is more:

> Those among us who still have the chance to live in the city cen-
> tre, and not in the outlying suburbs, try to survive spiritually by

assiduously frequenting museums, galleries, theatres, concert halls, art cinemas, etc. But such people suffer from another ill: that of cultural consumption, where one must absorb even more cultural merchandise, as if another form of addiction installs itself, without ever being able to re-establish the slow time of a true artistic experience, the time of the amateur, which has been replaced by the consumer suffering from a dazed cultural obesity.[103] (DI)

In other words, no one has the time anymore for authentic longing. For longing takes exactly that: a *long* time, if one is to do it properly. Despite the best attempts of the Long Now Foundation, the slow food movement, or Zen meditation centers, to bring back a mindfulness to our sense of time's passage, the hegemonic mode of media time (which is now global time) is that of breathless twenty-four-hour news cycles and just-in-time deliveries. As Franco Berardi's "Post-Futurist Manifesto" notes, "ideology and advertising have exalted the permanent mobilisation of the productive and nervous energies of humankind towards profit and war. We want to exalt tenderness, sleep and ecstasy, the frugality of needs and the pleasure of the senses."[104]

There is risk, however, embedded in such critiques: the risk is of sounding so "untimely" to the contemporary ear as to appear irrelevant, out of touch—noble but ignorable. Indeed, Stiegler does sound like a nostalgic aesthete when he calls television "the enemy of the beautiful" or laments the loss of "the primary affective solicitations of the greenery, of flowers, animals, the elements, solitude, of the village market, of silence and of slow time" (DI).[105] Yet to dismiss critics of compulsive multitasking, like Stiegler—to call them simply anachronistic romantics—may be just another type of reactionary reflex. Could not the greatest triumph of what Jodi Dean calls "communicative capitalism"[106] be the ironic contempt—from left, right, and center—for those who ask us to consider our own thoughts and actions with less distraction? Perhaps the boredom we fear will crush us, were we to actually unplug and stop juggling for several days, is in fact a bluff encouraged by the system. "The world would not be moving so fast," writes the Invisible Committee (2009, 60) in *The Coming Insurrection*, "if it didn't have to constantly outrun its own collapse." (Hence the power of the movie *Speed* [1994], which allegorized the fear that to slow down is to risk catastrophe.) What if Stiegler is right, and the green and tender shoots of resurgent libido are only possible if we scale down our plastic mouse clicking and turn instead to *actual* encounters with warm-blooded creatures (with no intended offense to reptiles)?[107]

The issue is an urgent one because any solution with a whiff of the Luddite is not going to work. Diatribes against the Internet may tap some retrohumanist reflex in the media for a week or two but then will sink like a stone, along with almost everything else. Stiegler (2009, 72), as Heidegger before him, knew that the answer was not to reject or resist but instead to recalibrate—to frame things differently, according to less "toxicomaniacal" priorities. "*It is a matter neither of adapting nor resisting*: it is a matter of *inventing*." As such, the environmental crisis brings with it something of a silver lining: an absolute material limit that serves to highlight the formerly invisible spiritual one. The fragility of the world's ecosystem reminds us of the fragility of the financial system, as well as that of society itself, as a contract between sublimating selves, hence the need to "reelaborate a politics of investment" in all three overlapping spheres.

Thus, it is

> necessary to combat the real problem, namely, *the ecological disorder of the spirit in the epoch of cultural and cognitive technologies*, monopolized by industrial populism, to which it would be necessary to oppose an industrial and political economy of the spirit, which is innovative, and capable of bearing a future, of inaugurating a new age of psychic and collective individuation. (DI; emphasis added)

Libidinal economy is thus revealed to be "a matter of an ecology of the milieus of the spirit" (Stiegler 2009, 75).[108]

It is revealing to step back briefly to Marcuse again here, for despite his inability to integrate environmental crisis into his system, he did comprehend the importance of libidinal ecology. Indeed, one of his key figures for this complex is—unsurprisingly perhaps, given the preceding—Narcissus. Again, sounding uncannily like Stiegler, Marcuse writes:

> The striking paradox that narcissism, usually understood as egotistic withdrawal from reality . . . is connected with oneness with

the universe, reveals the new depth of the conception: beyond all immature autoeroticism, narcissism denotes a fundamental relatedness to reality which may generate a comprehensive existential order. In other words, narcissism may contain the germ of a different reality principle: the libidinal cathexis of the ego (one's own body) may become the source and reservoir for a new libidinal cathexis of the objective world—transforming this world into a new mode of being. (169)

That is to say, "primary narcissism is more than autoeroticism; it engulfs the 'environment,' integrating the narcissistic ego with the objective world" (166).

Marcuse adds another mythological figure to the mix, that of Orpheus, whose lyre is a catalytic technology, seducing nature in a very literal sense so that it does not merely follow genetic paths but bends into more compassionate patterns: "The world of nature is a world of oppression, cruelty, and pain, as is the human world; like the latter, it awaits its liberation. This liberation is the work of Eros. The song of Orpheus breaks the petrification, moves the forests and the rocks—but moves them to partake in joy" (166). Further still, "trees and animals respond to Orpheus' language; the spring and the forest respond to Narcissus' desire. The Orphic and Narcissistic Eros awakens and liberates potentialities that are real in things animate and inanimate, in organic and inorganic nature—real but in the un-erotic reality suppressed" (165).[109] But isn't this merely the kind of anthropocentric projection we have been examining in detail throughout this book? Even if the "speculative realists" see a hint of their radically ahuman reading of the universe in such deference to the inanimate and inorganic, it cannot be denied that it is the human that considers itself the privileged element, triggering potential energy into the kinetic. Can a rock really *enjoy*? And let us say, for argument's sake, that it can; would it need a human to show it a good time? For Marcuse, "reality" is stark and unerotic without an Orpheus or Narcissus to bestow an objective *frisson* on it. Marcuse is in concert with Adorno and Horkheimer here, who baldly state that "nature does not know real pleasure but only satisfaction of want. All pleasure is societal—in the unsublimated no less than in the sublimated impulses. Pleasure originates in alienation" (quoted in Marcuse 1974, 227).[110] But this is a blatant case of explosive hubris and humanist self-inflation. That such a distinction sounds sensible to our ears attests to the ideological stranglehold anthropocentrism still has on our thoughts.

Were the profit motive and the performance principle removed from the libidinal equation, then—in a crude foreshadowing of Morton—the environment would no longer be quarantined, laminated, sentimentalized, and fetishized as the ultimate other but rather integrated in a cosmic *economy* that respects the similarities, as much as the differences, between humans, animals, and machines. This is what Stiegler (2009, 75) meant earlier when he stated that, henceforth, all economy is also "a matter of an ecology of the milieus of the spirit." That is to say, what Marcuse calls "the shaping of the environment, the transformation of nature" (xix) is inseparable from the libidinal policies of any political *dispositif*.[111]

To be clear, where Marcuse had a pronounced red streak (even if largely hidden under his linguistic vestments), Stiegler—despite having a great sympathy for Marx's writings—is no communist. He does not think capitalism is intrinsically evil but that its original "spirit" has been hijacked and redirected into dangerous territories. Under the guidance of heedless greed, capitalism is shooting itself in the foot. Where the Protestant spirit relied on the standing reserve of human sublimation, this potential power is now being annihilated by homogenizing marketing techniques, as if the passenger, during a seemingly endless road trip, is siphoning off gasoline from the driver but still expecting a smooth ride.

The alternative, for Stiegler, is a "new global capitalism," which "will not be able to renew its energies without inventing a new logic and new objects of investment—and here the word investment must be taken literally and in all its senses: both the sense it has in industrial economy and its sense within libidinal economy" (WLC). For "*libidinal energy is essentially sustainable*, except when it decomposes into drive-driven energy, which is on the contrary destructive of its objects" (WLC; emphasis added). Through his own writings, lectures, and Web site, Stiegler seeks to foster an *ars industrialis*, "an industrial politics of the technologies of spirit—that is, of sublimation—as the only sustainable libidinal economy" (WLC). Stoekl would no doubt shudder at such a concept, horrified that libidinal economists can be "conservative" too. But Stiegler's keep-it-in-your-pants program for social renewal is not necessarily prudish but rather a way of *protecting* the libido from extinction, a way of placing it on the endangered species list so that it may thrive under the right conditions in the future. No doubt Stoekl's counter to this strategy or argument is that tomorrow never comes and the libido can only survive by seizing the day—today.[112]

Nevertheless, Stiegler has stockpiled enough of his own libido to desire "a new politics of existence: a *noopolitics* susceptible of reversing and overcoming the deadly logic of psychopower" (WLC). And herein lies the stimulus package alluded to throughout this chapter—a nurturing of "*techniques* of life, what one could call the arts of living" (TC) (as opposed to the *technologization* of life—"bio-politics conceived at the level of the biosphere" [WLC]). And yet the catalytic object—the equivalent of the six-hundred-dollar check for taxpayers—remains very vague. Certainly priority one is "the relinquishment of a drive-driven economy and the reconstitution of a libidinal economy" (WLC), something even more urgent than kicking the addiction to fossil fuels.

As we have seen, Stiegler believes that "organisation based on consumption, and constituted by its opposition to production, is dangerous not only because it produces excess quantities of carbon dioxide, but because it destroys minds" (WLC). So though he acknowledges the reality of environmental crisis, and is willing to use it as evidence in a multilayered indictment against our misguided ways, he maintains that the primary affliction is on the scale of the human rather than the planet. "If there were no limit to this consumption," Stiegler writes, "and if fossil fuel were inexhaustible, the catastrophe would perhaps be even greater that [sic] the one resulting from the deplenishment of fossil fuels. Perhaps this deplenishment is finally a kind of stroke of luck: the opportunity to understand . . . the true question of energy" (WLC). And yet he does not believe that the crucial factor is the energy of subsistence but rather "an energy of existence."

Ultimately, the libido, for Stiegler, is closer to water than oil. It is a life source that encourages intimacy in the mode of the public well rather than the private derrick.

1929 / 1974 / 2008: LIBIDINAL SPECULATION
IN LYOTARD AND GUATTARI

> The vulva is jealous of the thoroughly kissed mouth, so is the
> mistress of the book her lover writes, the man of the young
> man's future, the sun of the closed shutters behind which
> your imagination lets itself go in adventures of reading.
> —Jean-François Lyotard, *Libidinal Economy*

Humans are the libidinal animal, and Eros embodies the potential of
Homo oeconomicus. This is what we learn from Stiegler, and Marcuse
before him. But between these two figures—in the symbolically potent
year of 1974—a book was published that presents a radically different
perspective on the situation. Seeking a third way of sorts between
economic reductionism and anticapitalist romanticism—and written
during the time of the OPEC crisis (a dry run for a world after oil as
well as during the peak of the sexual revolution), Lyotard's *Libidinal
Economy* presents a provocative challenge to any privileged link between
jouissance and humanity.

His central premise (as far as such an acephalic book has a center) is
that political economy *is* libidinal economy. As a result, any model that
distinguishes between them—as historical philosophers have presumed
to do for centuries—is a self-flattering humanist fable. Furthermore,
the libido is not something the subject *possesses* but rather a force that
provisionally assembles the subject-*effect* through its dynamic vacillations.[113] (To say that the subject is "possessed" by the erotic imperative is
still to give too much status or presence to the individual.) For Lyotard,
desire is "energetic, economic, non-representative" (Lyotard 1993, 22)
and "cannot be assumed, accepted, understood, [or] locked up in names"
(20). Were he still alive today, we imagine he would have little sympathy
with Stiegler's desire–drive distinction, since intensity overflows these
convenient sorting devices. In fact, it is just this kind of structural
division—embodied in the forward slash or bar—that authorizes, for
him, the most contemptible form of conceptual gatekeeping. To put it
somewhat differently, the grammatical and philosophical necessity of
making distinctions and grouping the world according to identities,
even on the most micro level, leads to more profound reification than

anything Capital could dream up. And like a hydroelectric megadam, taxonomy carves up the environment—physical or metaphysical—into discrete territories that can be drained but not sustained. The ongoing attempt to delineate (between ideas, objects, races, whatever) is thus an artificial attempt to police energies and exchanges, which are consistently blocked by the logic of the either–or: "The operator of disintensification is exclusion: either this, or not-this. Not both. The disjunctive bar. Every concept is therefore concomitant with negation, exteriorization" (14). Lyotard thus seeks to go *beyond the concept*—to remove this bar from its function, like a sword from its swallower, so that erogenous organs may not be punctured by the futile projects of men.

As may already be apparent, there is no room for people in this account, and thus we are in very disorienting territory (precisely because there is no *We* . . . except for the motley multitude of ironic, and vaguely smug, libidinal economists to whom Lyotard gestures throughout the twists and turns of his book). The challenge is thus to learn something from the vertigo of an equation from which the human has been removed, while still describing a recognizable world. (This is itself the pedagogic *jouissance* of poststructuralist thought as well as mathematics, biology, statistics, and systems theory.) To return to the rhetorical context of publication, Lyotard was responding to a prevalent Lacanian discourse of the time that desire is created through lack or absence. His writings thus share a connection with Deleuze and Guattari for translating their disillusion (with Marx, Freud, and the wake of 1968) into a positive reading of desire. From this angle, desire is not the expression of something one doesn't have (a breast, a beloved, a Nintendo Wii) but rather an affect that overflows the self in excess and subsequently looks for external connection points. Such a strategy leads to uncharted waters, including the exoneration—indeed, the celebration—of capitalism for its libidinal excesses, albeit from a left-wing trajectory.

Despite its wager on energy, Lyotard's book expresses a great fatigue: what I have elsewhere called "a politics of exhaustion."[114] He is moved to write against "the search for causes, responsibilities, the search for identity, the localization of desire, becoming conscious, masculinization, power, knowledge . . . analysis" (Lyotard 1993, 259). This characterization, however, would be too negative for his tastes. The issue is not to counter, negate, or resist, but to allow flows of intensities to occur, even at the expense of the self (which is only an illusion anyway). Lyotard notes, "There is the possibility of a pain through lack . . . only because it had been previously supposed that there was the presence of a mother, of *someone*" (22). So rather than lament some oedipal fall into the world, one should realize that there is no isolated self but merely an ongoing complication of the previous "lips–nipple connection" (25). To speak Deleuzian for a moment, it is a matter of the molecular, not the molar.

There is a strange kind of consolation to be found here, although Lyotard would no doubt bristle at such a palliative application of his ideas. For if there is no *me*, strictly speaking, to suffer, then much of the burden evaporates. There is suffering, but it is not *mine*. It belongs to the universe, an anticogito, which undoes much of the trouble Descartes unwittingly prepared for us.[115] But such a scenario is also profoundly troubling because—as we have just seen—it throws out the baby with the bathwater. Instead of the tragic reassurances of a story like *Romeo and Juliet*, Lyotard tells us, "great loves are not inscriptions on a spatio-temporal register, and continuity or fidelity play no part in them since there is nothing permanent from one encounter to another, only the singular intensity, opening its own labyrinth each time" (38). Most of us would prefer to die of poison—but certain of being loved for who we are—than to live in a world in which each separate encounter, even with the same lover, is in fact unique, isolated, and unconnected in any essential sense to the one before or the one to come (there is no potentially sentimental "fidelity to the event" here).

But what of the unfaithful husband, torn between duties and morality? "The cry which resounds in your helplessness, unfaithful one, is not your wife's, nor yours, it's true: it is the noise made on the band by the incompossibility of several co-present intensities" (41). Again, the silver lining is a form of theoretical relief, a tendency toward being "let off the hook." (One wonders how many flings Lyotard successfully justified to his wife by saying, "*Désolé, chéri. Mais ce bruit sur la bande était celui de l'incompatibilité de quelques intensités simultanées.*") But the entire political and judicial system collapses once we remove its structural support of subject–citizen, to say nothing of the romantic one. Where the law sees two married people (but not to each other) making love—and seeks to punish them for trespassing on private territories and extracting contraband *jouissance*—Lyotard does not even offer such a couple the emotional compensation of "forbidden love," or any communicational content whatsoever. Rather they are only connected by virtue of a certain species of proximity, sharing and conducting—albeit briefly—the same "pulsional surroundings."

To his credit, Lyotard admits that—as far as living in sync with this kind of existence—no one is up to such a task. "*Jouissance is unbearable*" (Lyotard 1993, 113). Indeed, "everyone seeks to flee these intensities and their undecidability in the direction of the system and its binary ideal" (31). Lyotard himself thus wavers between presenting himself as a posthuman desiring machine, meshing uncompromisingly with anonymous intensities, and as a tenured professor, speculating more modestly on the erotic options in an age of conflicting signals—on one hand, a giant Marshall-Stack-worth of sexual feedback, and on the other, an aggressively foreclosed libido.

And yet, though he admits the difficulties involved, Lyotard does not flinch in criticizing figures such as Marcuse for being reactionary, being resentful, and ignoring the reality of the hegemonic forces that regulate behavior (as well as the motivations behind them). Indeed, he goes so far as to say, "We do not speak as the liberators of desire: idiots with their little fraternities, their Fourieresque fantasies, their policy-holder's expectations over the libido" (Lyotard 1993, 42).[116] For Lyotard, Marcuse and other progressivist–moralists are simply in denial of the centripetal force of what he calls the "great Zero": a general term synthesizing "the Platonic world of forms, God, the authentic mode of production, the phallus, etc." (xiii)—that is to say, all those ideological trappings of a transcendent Truth. As a result, the great Zero is the nemesis of the libido: an ontological motif "imposed on desire, forever deferring, re-presenting and simulating everything in an endless postponement" (5).[117]

But a nemesis enables as much as it constrains. After all, what would Sherlock Holmes be without Moriarity, James Bond without Blofeld, or McNulty without Barksdale? It is the great Zero that allows singular and incommensurable experiences to be exchanged as a general equivalent, like the gold standard for extramonetary transactions. For instance, when Chelsea, in *The Girlfriend Experience*, felt a *frisson* for a client beyond the financial transaction, she was still assessing the value of her feelings and communications according to the great Zero, that is, according to the self-confirmation of sexual commerce—with or without money—mistaken for love.[118] In Stiegler's scheme, this is a travesty that should be refused or transcended; for Lyotard, it is an inescapable cultural reality that can compound unexpected intensities, even while trying to weaken them. "We, libidinal economists," the latter writes, ". . . must model ourselves an affirmative idea of the Zero" (5).

Not content with utopian images of reconciliation or redemption, Lyotard thus talks of a *permanent* revolution. The Dionysian genealogy of his ideas (inherited from Bataille, Sade, Klossowski, etc.) prompts him to create a centaur figure, inhabiting the labyrinth of his antisystem (a human–animal hybrid that embodies the immanent bestial aspect of sexuality). And yet "sexuality"—as something one *has*, or can consciously deploy—is nothing more than ideology for Lyotard. "To suggest to someone: let's fuck, would truly be to treat oneself as *representing* the sexual liberation movement" (Lyotard 1993, 29), a ludicrous position, no doubt leading to further delusions such as empowerment, justice, rights, and dignity. ("There is no dignity.")

No doubt, there is something disingenuous about the sleight of hand in which you are not being oppressed because, when viewed from the parallax view—ta da!—there is no you! It is a kind of venal Buddhism, of which Nietzsche would surely not approve, even though the target is the same: puffed-up human herd animals, bleating about their beautiful souls.[119] By insisting that there is the same potential for libidinal intensity in capitalist exchange as in symbolic exchange, Lyotard subverts some of the most cherished beliefs of radical philosophy, from Mauss to Baudrillard.[120] He thereby rather gleefully removes the ever-beckoning EXIT sign from the constantly burning movie palace of contemporary life. But in the same gesture, he grabs the microphone and announces, "Ladies and gentlemen, it's getting hot in here. So take off all your clothes."

The key thing to note is the absence of an Archimedean point in which to read desire in its purity. There is no position "where desire would be clearly legible, where its *proper economy* would not be scrambled" (Lyotard 1993, 108). For Lyotard, the belief in "an externalized region where desire would be sheltered from every treacherous transcription into production, labour and the law of value" (107) is nothing but a persistent fantasy. After all, the libido was hampered by many social factors long before capitalism came along. For desire, there are—and always have been—mediations, complications, and negotiations, to the extent where love itself is unthinkable without obstacles (and eroticism even more so without detours).[121] Moreover, "the pulsions are always in combat against themselves: it therefore has no need of capitalism in order to be 'inadequately' formulated" (93). The vain attempt to make a coherent subjectivity out of these competing pulsions is what we call the individual: a mythical creature, divided every moment by contradictory impressions, interpretations, decisions, solicitations, temptations, and obligations. The difference between Freud's libidinal economy and Lyotard's is whether there is any significant human presence in charge of the switching yard.

In any case, for Lyotard, the desires created by Capital are neither better nor worse—nor less or more authentic—than any other kind. (Indeed, if Lubitsch's *Ninotchka* [1939] is anything to go by, capitalism is more human and erotically appealing than communism.) "Capital is not the denaturation of relations between man and man," he writes:

> nor between man and woman, it is the wavering of the (imaginary?) primacy of genitality, of reproduction and sexual difference, it is the displacement of what was in place, it is the unbinding of the most insane pulsions, since money is the sole justification or bond, and money being able to justify anything, it deresponsibilizes and *raves* absolutely, it is the sophistics of the passions and at the same time, their energetic prosthetics. (Lyotard 1993, 138)[122]

Capital is presented as the buster of myths (divine authority, the permanence of institutions) and thus as the liberator of libido, which finds itself with new, unexpected options and opportunities. From this perspective, Marx made the common human error of positing something like a species-being in the first place, unsullied by machines and technical mediations. According to Lyotard, the task Marx set himself was "to discover an object of love, a hidden priceless thing, forgotten in the subversion of prices, a beyond-value in the trade fair of values, something like a nature in denaturation. To rediscover a natural *dependence*, a We, a dialectic of the You and the I, in the sordid solitude of pornographic independence to which the capitalist function of money and labour condemns all affective expenditure" (138–39). In such a task—or fantasy, rather—Lyotard also describes Stiegler: insisting we must "put a stop to the critique of capital, stop accusing it of libidinal coldness or pulsional monovalence"; rather "we must take note of, examine, exalt the incredible, unspeakable pulsional possibilities that it sets rolling, and so understand that *there has never been* an organic body, an immediate relation, nor a nature in the sense of an *established site of affects*" (140).[123]

Capitalism finally tears off that human mask that has allowed so much hypocritical and inhumane behavior up to this point in history. What's more, it teaches us the hard lesson that there is no face beneath the mask, no back-stage behind the theatrics, and no meaning beneath the metaphor. Instead of value, there is only price. And flying in the face of Freud, "there are no holes, only invaginations of surfaces" (Lyotard 1993, 21). Deeper significance evaporates as a comforting mirage in the desert of the Signification (as opposed to the desert of the Real). Certainly this is one way to reconcile the reality principle and the pleasure principle: by fusing them onto the same surface. But this approach is also a hard sell. Who among us would want to live in "the sordid solitude of pornographic independence"? For Lyotard, the English working class "enjoyed" their exploitation, decomposition, dissolution, and so on. What is more, "one can enjoy swallowing the shit of capital, its materials, its metal bars, its polystyrene, its books, its sausage pâtés, swallowing tonnes of it till you burst" (116)—just as the prostitute allegedly gets off on her own abjectness. These rather despicable claims have their own logic, however, and as with Baudrillard—advocating the capital punishment of animals—it is important not simply to turn away in disgust because there is an irritating grain of truth at work, deep within Hume's oyster.

Consider two libidinal commands that have no doubt been voiced under very different socioeconomic conditions. The first is "use me," which Lyotard (1993, 63) translates as meaning "there is no me." This conceit is something with which we are already familiar and certainly has its literary and cinematic precedents. Yet in the Homeland Security era, it seems naive in the extreme to revile what he calls "the dull, odious, inept organic body of the *habeas corpus*" (73). Dull it may be, but Lyotard may lose the courage of his hypothetical convictions when such a constitutional right is withdrawn, leading to imprisonment, even torture. (How to *live* Continental theory?—always the impossible question.) As for "don't come yet," this is presented as "simply another modality of *jouissance*, which is found in the libidinal *dispositif* of capital" (99). Here we return to issues of not only peak libido but also peak oil.

Though the organism tends to seek the intensity of discharge, it also realizes that certain modes of energetic accumulation create a different kind of intensity: one based on inhibition, deferral, investment, or "putting into reserve." Capitalism—or rather capitali-*zation*—can thus be found in unlikely places such as in the ancient Taoist practice of postponing orgasm. Lyotard seizes on traditional Chinese erotic physiology—which encourages the man to excite the woman and resist his own climax so as to steal the woman's yin energy for himself—to demonstrate that it is more than simply a "saving" of energy but rather also comes with a compounding of interest. That is to say, when correctly managed, bodily fluids create their own revenue stream. A surplus force is created. Moreover, the imagery Lyotard uses to depict this primal scene of sorts is a Hobbesian or Darwinian libidinal ecology:

> Not only is emission, that is expenditure, suspended, which is the saving; but the *augmentation* of forces, for which the penis no longer operates as an escape route for the over-full, but, in the opposite sense, as a drilling channel through which the energetic substances dormant in the folds of the body (of the earth-woman) are gathered-up, stock-piled (genitals, spine, head; pumping stations, pipe-line, reservoirs), and subsequently put back into circulation as means of production (fertilizing emission of semen; combustion of hydrocarbons for so-called reproductive goals). . . . [But] the analogy is insufficient: the mining must be imagined, by itself, through the excitement it provokes in the layers which contact and open onto the enormous reamed glans promised to them, which already multiplies the energy that they contain. Something that is not true of mining itself (of the intromission of the penis into the vagina), but of cracking, something like the erotic manoeuvres surrounding penetration. (Lyotard 1993, 209–10)

Yet, as we saw with Conan Doyle's sadistic fantasy of probing the earth until it shrieks, the analogy may be sufficient after all, if not indeed necessary. The screaming of the world and the reaming of Gaia are fatefully intertwined. (It is worth noting here that in the 1960s, one in forty-four oil wells paid for themselves, and one in one thousand made a good profit.[124] The promise of profit alone is not enough to account for such a frenzy, at least for the libidinal economist, fully attuned to the subtext of the 2008 Republican National Convention's frat house–style slogan "Drill Baby Drill."[125])

Indeed, the pulsions created by exploration, conquest, and pillage—what we could call the vidi, vici, veni principle—only gives a foretaste of the vicious *jouissance* of capital as it migrates into the virtual:

> strata of Yin dormant in the receptacles of femininity, that come to arouse the works of masculine erotics; masses of natural ener-gies (coal, water, petrol, nuclear) or human energies (artisans, unemployed farmers), which lie dormant in the fringes of capital and which the latter comes to seize and exploit. So the intensities of which capitalism is capable are not exclusively associated with inhibition and reservation, but they necessarily are with *conquest* and agitation. (Lyotard 1993, 222)

There is something like a dialectic at work between the sexual sparks created by hitting the brakes and going full-steam ahead. Lyotard (1993, 227) notes that the stock exchange "is not an investment at all, it is a battlefield and a field of conquest by means of buying and selling."[126] Moreover, the crash of 1929 proves that the so-called social body is nothing but a patchwork of rags that can be taken to pieces by frenzied and jealous impulsions. (But in Lyotard's system, no one is to blame for this. *It is what it is.* Greed happens.)[127]

As I write, in 2009, the world is lurching from a tragically farcical repetition of 1929, in which speculators created an entire arsenal of "financial instruments" and other abstract technologies to mimic the yin-stealing bedroom technique of Lyotard's archetypal Chinaman. (After all, it is no coincidence that vernacular language conflates the sex act with losing or being exploited: "you're fucked/screwed.") The expert commentary on this most recent crash focused on the seemingly systemwide irrationality of personal short-term gain at the expense of collective medium-term disaster. But for Lyotard, even writing in the early 1970s, risky investments in securities over commodities "is no more explicable than the fact that the libido lodged in the genital zone moves towards the anus or the ear" (Lyotard 1993, 236). It is a matter of tapping the collective ass. He notes, "There is a slow, cosmic time there, that of the seed *[semence]* and its fruit, of the chicken and the egg, of gestation, and of dripping honey. With monetary 'signs,' we get away from this time and its space. We go crazy in signs" (239–40).

The temptation to resist here, however (according to Lyotard), is the appeal to an abstract Big Other who would regulate the libidinal–political economy, whether this be a purportedly socialist-leaning president or the free market itself. *"There is no one* to keep the accounts of suffering and *jouissance"* (Lyotard 1993, 100). In line with his previous swipe against Marcuse, there is no insurance policy for the libido: no guarantee that whatever erotic excitation you just endured or enjoyed means anything beyond its taking place. The good news is that there is no taxman, no audit. The bad news is that there is no pretence of justice, no tax return.[128] Hence:

> Fucking ought not to be guaranteed, in either sense, neither as proof of love nor as the security of indifferent exchangeability; love, that is to say intensity, should slip in in an aleatory fashion, and conversely intensities may withdraw from the skin of bodies (you didn't come?), and pass onto the skins of words, sounds, colours, culinary tastes, animal smells and perfumes, this is the dissimulation we will not escape, this is the anxiety and this is what we must *will.* (256)

The libido must go through a refining process, much like oil, not for the purposes of utility but for the further lubrication of exchanges. (Once again, Lyotard admits that within such a scenario, "there is no question of rendering it pleasant" [256].) After all, petroleum jelly greases not only the moving parts of our industrial machinery but also our own organs and sphincters. It is a matter of minimizing friction. Contrast such a position to the guardians of the great Zero, who maintain that "only love should erect the penis, only truth should erect the word! Such was Plato's demand, and so it remains, even in apparently cyni-cal, but in fact very religious, modern discourse" (257). Think here of the distress unleashed by those all-too-rare passionate encounters and how the psychic architecture of the self threatens to collapse. Where prostitution is relatively bound by the financial strings attached, the unspoken contract of an affair necessitates an overcompensatory discourse to keep erotic anarchy at bay. "In prostitution," writes Lyotard, "one goes from intensity to order; in adultery, from order to intensity" (81). But such intensity must be reordered. Hair must be rebrushed and buttons resewn if life is to continue in the established mode. Even more important, vows must be remade, no matter how illicit. "'We must operate penises, vaginas, arses and skins so that love becomes the condition of orgasm.' That is what the lover, the mistress, dreams about, so as to escape the terrifying duplicity of surfaces pervaded with pulsions" (256).

All of this is to say that—pace Marx, Freud, Marcuse, and (to a lesser extent) Stiegler—there is no contradiction within capitalistic civilization, which may destroy it (152).[129] There are only tensions, tensors, pulsions, voluptuousness, vacillations, and incandescences, which contribute to the ever-proliferating machinations of money, bodies, objects, and affects.

In the same year that Lyotard was writing *Libidinal Economy*, another French theorist—Félix Guattari—was being tried for committing an "outrage to public decency" in publishing an issue of *Recherches* titled "Three Billion Perverts: The Great Encyclopedia of Homosexualities" (Guattari 2000, xii). Eight years earlier, at the comparatively late age of thirty-five, his life changed dramatically when he received his driving license: "I became more independent, which eventually led, among other things, to a divorce" (10). Thus Guattari enjoyed an oil-based event (a car-based line of flight) that led to the liberation—or rather "deterritorialization"—of his libido. Guattari would then connect with Deleuze to write two of the classic touchstones of contemporary theory, valorizing the schizophrenic desiring machines enabled by contemporary capitalism.

Later still, in another watershed year—1989—Guattari published *The Three Ecologies*, which avoids explicitly discussing the political revolutions occurring in eastern Europe, preferring instead to further unpack his notion of micropolitics and molecular revolution. That is to say, Guattari seeks a revolution that will "also take into account molecular domains of sensibility, intelligence and desire" (Guattari 2000, 28)—change on a level both above and below the citizen, the monad, the individual. Such a micropolitics would equate to "a politics of desire that questions all situations" (83), beyond the traditional preoccupation with institutional structures that constitutes political thought or action. In the fifteen years or so separating *A Thousand Plateaus* from this book, however, Guattari seems to be taking a position, vis-à-vis capitalism, that sounds closer to Marcuse and Stiegler than Lyotard's uncompromising affirmation of exploitation. "What condemns the capitalist value system," he writes, "is that it is characterized by general equivalence, which flattens out all other forms of value, alienating them in its hegemony" (65). No matter if we are dealing with "material assets, cultural assets, wildlife areas, etc." (29), they are all bargained with on the same two-dimensional tabletop. And against the surprisingly monolithic adversary of what he calls "integrated world capitalism," Guattari hopes to deploy a "resingularization" of values that cannot be measured against the great Zero (to translate it back into Lyotard's terms). Thus Guattari writes against what he calls "the seductive efficiency of economic competition" (68) (aka the performance principle).

Anticipating Stiegler, Guattari (2000) believes that "mass-media manufacture...is synonymous with distress and despair" (34) and that one of the key problems we face as a species is "the introjection of repressive power by the oppressed" (49).[130] Despite the poststructuralist poetics, then, we are in relatively stable post-Marxist territory. Speaking with an eye toward the nascent Internet, and the political potential of narrowcasting, Guattari states, "An essential programmatic point for social ecology will be to encourage capitalist societies to make the transition from the mass-media era to a *post-media age*, in which the media will be reappropriated by a multitude of subject-groups capable of directing its resingularization" (61).[131] Moreover, "the information and telematic revolutions are supporting new 'stock exchanges' of value" as well as encouraging "dissensual enterprises" (65).[132] So far, so familiar.

Yet Guattari's rhizomatic project to avoid capitalistic foreclosure was ahead of many of his peers in contextualizing matters in ecological rather than economic terms. For Guattari, allowing what we might call "desirable desire" to thrive is emphatically a concern for libidinal ecology and depends on three different ecological registers: environment, social relations, and human subjectivity. Of these three, the latter is probably the most elusive, given Guattari's sophisticated conception of the forces that constitute it in flux. "Rather than speak of the 'subject,'" he writes, "we should perhaps speak of *components of subjectification*, each working more or less on its own." In other words, "vectors of subjectification do not necessarily pass through the individual, which in reality appears to be something like a 'terminal' for processes that involve human groups, socio-economic ensembles, data-processing machines, etc." (Guattari 2000, 36)—another notion that should be familiar to us, under the alternative name of "epiphylogenetic memory."

For Guattari (2000, 34), the question of desirable subjectification, which itself enables the nurturing of the three ecological registers, is an "ecosophical problematic." Given the inextricability of nature and culture, we must learn to think "transversally" between "eco-systems, the mechanosphere and the social and individual Universes of reference" (43). It is a matter of creating "dissident vectors" as well as "experiments in the suspension of meaning" (45) to detoxify the collective sphere: currently a fractured mass of media-addled opiate addicts, existing inside an amniotic sense of "pseudo-eternity." As a result, Guattari insists that "ecology must stop being associated with the image of a small nature-loving minority or with qualified specialists" (52) and become a concern for all those who comprehend the stakes of protecting "the environment": whether natural, cultural, social, or personal.[133] Like Marcuse and Stiegler, then, Guattari seeks "to reevaluate the purpose of work and of human activities according to different criteria than those of profit and yield" (57). And also like these thinkers, the human seems to be the privileged (potential) revolutionary subject.

"It is not only species that are becoming extinct," writes Guattari (2000, 44), "but also the words, phrases, and gestures of human solidarity." Furthermore, micropolitics should be "working for humanity and not simply for a permanent reequilibration of the capitalist semiotic Universe" (51). At one point, he even evokes that worm-ridden albatross, the "destiny of humanity" (67). One certainly wonders about Guattari's position here, given his previous attempts to become-animal and escape this congealed and compromised taxonomic metacategory. Perhaps the most powerful seduction is not economic competition but Linnaean organization. Yet if Guattari is a latent humanist, he is certainly one who eschews the liberal individual on whom classical humanism traditionally rests—an antiliberal humanist, if you will.

"Natural equilibriums," notes Guattari (2000, 66),

> will be increasingly reliant upon human intervention, and time
> will come when vast programmes will need to be set up in order
> to regulate the relationship between oxygen, ozone and carbon
> dioxide in the Earth's atmosphere. We might just as well rename
> environmental ecology *machinic ecology*, because Cosmic and
> human praxis has only ever been a question of machines, even,
> dare I say it, of war machines. From time immemorial "nature"
> has been at war with life! The pursuit of mastery over the mecha-
> nosphere will have to begin immediately if the acceleration of
> techno-scientific progress and the pressure of huge population
> increases are to be dealt with.

The human is less an essential element (as with John Conner's
strong heart in *Terminator 4*)[134] than a machinic effect of meshing
vectors of intelligence, desire, vitality, and so on.[135] "The creation of
new living species—animal and vegetable—looms inevitably on the
horizon," hence the need for "an ecosophical ethics adapted to this
terrifying and fascinating situation" (67). But as an aesthete, Guattari
is not only concerned with cloning and biotechnology but with the
future of creativity and expression. As he writes three years later in
a different text, "how do we reinvent social practices that would give
back to humanity—if it ever had it—a sense of responsibility, not only
for its own survival, but equally for the future of life on the planet, for
animal and vegetable species, likewise for *incorporeal species* such as
music, the arts, cinema, the relation with time, love and compassion
for others, the feeling of fusion at the heart of the Cosmos?" (Guattari
2000, 71; emphasis added).[136] Guattari would thus expand, even explode,
the Linnaean legacy of classifying only "living" creatures, thereby identifying a potentially infinite number of species that themselves thrive
to different degrees on the three ecological registers.

That human subjectivity is one of the three modes, however, demonstrates the weedlike tenacity of anthropocentrism in critical discourse.
Once again, the double gesture proves itself to be one of those rhetorical
species that is in no way endangered, except insofar as humans themselves are endangered, at the beginning of the twenty-first century.
Guattari (2000, 61) does, however, acknowledge that the difference

between "living autopoietic machines" and "machines of empty repetition" is "not so clear cut." Humans can behave according to exceedingly predictable patterns, and machines can delight and surprise (as anyone at MIT will attest), hence the angst with which the line of demarcation is drawn and redrawn on a daily basis.

In *A Crude Awakening*—the peak oil documentary discussed earlier in the chapter—an Amish man riding in a horse-powered buggy muses on the difference between a horse and an automobile. He notes that the former is a living thing, and thus "a certain amount of affection develops." (We have previously seen just how far this affection can go.) Yet one need only possess a passing familiarity with everyday car culture to appreciate the affectionate—even erotic—rapport that can happen between people and their enabling machines. After all, many a gearhead would sooner keep his vehicle than his spouse.

After the oil wells run dry, Stoekl, Stiegler, Guattari, and many others hope that a new kind of intimacy will develop between men, women, and animals, one prefigured in the millennia preceding Henry Ford but that will be forever inflected with the fact of the automobile having been. The different brand names rusting on the carcasses of cars abandoned by the side of the road will silently speak of the different species of dinosaurs that live on not only in fossils but also in the memory of fossil fuels. Cities will be transfigured, and life will unfold on a more human scale. But it need not be considered diminished for all that. The emerging "green Detroit," for all its gentrified tensions, points to heartening possibilities, not only for urban renewal, but for interspecies renewal as well.[137] Turning full circle to the *truly* postindustrial age, humans will be forced to rethink what it is that makes them human. And it is hoped that the answer will not be "resilience," or "courage," or "innovation" but rather a recognition that what makes them human also makes horses horses, gardens gardens, books books, music music, computers computers, and life—organic or inorganic—vital. That is to say, at any given moment, we may be in the presence of an elusive human element, yet to bring it into being, and to identify it, we *need* natural or cultural technics. We need the horse to take us to the town meeting or the guitar to sing the blues.[138] As nature's prosthesis, humans tend to forget this humbling fact. We have grown accustomed to the idea that we are "the shepherds of Being" (to quote Heidegger). Yet, as Morton states, the idea of the environment "is about being-*with*"—not, of course, the kind of being-with that simply assimilates otherness to ourselves, as with the Orphic or Narcissistic inclusion, but the kind in a mode that is just as attentive to the specific "excellences" of humans, animals, and machines as to the many and varied overlaps and points of connection.[139] So after the fall from a fossil-fueled economy—which allowed an exponential sense of immortality and hubris—we may just learn to base our actions, and transactions, on a forward-looking libidinal ecology. In the meantime, however, Gaia will not be holding her breath.

Conclusion

Human Remains

Experience is the name everyone gives to their mistakes.
    —Oscar Wilde, *Lady Windermere's Fan*

I have learned so much from my mistakes that I'm thinking
of making several more.
    —Anonymous

To err is human . . .

But why are we so quick to embrace this ostensible fallibility? This fallacy? After all, animals miscalculate, too (and get gobbled up by other animals in the process). Computers are seemingly nothing but the furtive, chattering activity connecting error after error. As Erol Morris's film *Fast, Cheap, and Out of Control* (1997) demonstrates, animals, humans, and machines all "fail." But rather than being an ontological flaw, it may in fact be a *capacity*: the key to adaptation, survival, and—yes— learning.[1] Without error, we could not function, or rather, we would *merely* function.[2] Freud once said that America was a mistake but a "tremendous" one.[3] I would venture the same about humanity (without getting too carried away by that which makes us so). After all, as soon as a group fetishizes its own achievements, to project it competitively with others, that unit congeals into chauvinism or nationalism, thereby neutralizing the phenomenon worth celebrating.

In terms of humanity itself, the imperfection is largely systemic, that is to say, moralistic. Inconstancy—to give only one example of thousands—is a systemic conflict, not a character flaw, even if it is experienced as such. Thus the infidelity of Bette Davis in *The Letter* (1940) is akin to a child stealing a loaf of bread because she is hungry, a crime that in historical hindsight seems anything but. (Of course, to the censors, a dead woman is preferable to an unfaithful one.) Flaws are as much aesthetic or ideological as they are ethical, as embodied in the purity of a diamond. The lesson, therefore, may be in fact not to *avoid* mistakes, since this is impossible, but to consciously cultivate more *interesting* ones: mistakes not based on the us-and-them principle of the anthropological machine but according to the infinitely more promising potential of contingent and makeshift zoological devices[4]— not to proceed in terms of redemption or salvation—whether figured personally, politically, or theologically—but to take seriously Lacan's insistence that "there is no Big Other" (for this is a by-product of the Big Self, or vice versa). How much more fascinating, more vital, more seductive to inhabit a world of events and encounters that are not structured and limited by fixed taxonomy, by defensive or aggressive sovereignty, by the intense need to invent one's own spotlight and then stay within its beam (like a manic-depressive Liza Minnelli). It is a testament to the ideological hold of the Right Path, however, that such a suggestion sounds somewhat facetious.

But why, at this late stage, come to the defense of mistakes? Have I not—throughout this book—been holding humanity to task for mistaking its own reflection in the mirror of its manifold media machines? Have I not been arguing that it should "see the error of its ways" in terms of its own relationship to itself? Well, yes, but there is not necessarily an inconsistency here. For the human, to be unthinkingly sure that it is a human (and therefore decidedly not an animal or a machine) is not an interesting mistake to make. In fact, it is secular Scripture (and is increasingly zealous at that, as scientific and philosophical evidence mounts to the contrary).

So let me be completely clear, for those who may mistake what I am trying to say. I am not antihuman, in the sense that, say, deep ecologists or Klingons are. After all, some of my best friends are humans. I am often one myself—among other things. Indeed, I catch myself saying things like "I feel human again" after a good sleep. Certainly this is not an entirely meaningless statement. Even Daft Punk admits (in robotic voices, to be sure) that they are "human after all."[5] And of course, there is *something* that I respond to as worth recognizing and cherishing—a gesture, a caress, a song, a poem, an expression, and so on. But I am not convinced that this something is adequately—or even accurately— described exclusively in terms of humanity. More appropriate words might be *singularity, haecceity,*[6] *dividuality,*[7] *event, intelligence, communication, intersubjectivity, interobjectivity,* or even *beauty*—words that are not irredeemably contaminated by the radioactive half-life of puritanical moralism. Indeed, *human* is the least scrutinized term in the lexicon. It is the word that remains unexamined so that the others may be de- and reconstructed from a patch of solid conceptual ground. However, on those rare occasions when we *do* zoom in to the properties and qualities of such a term, the edifice on which it is based soon evaporates. The content of the human becomes so transparent as to be invisible, or so opaque as to create the same effect: as when a photograph is magnified to the degree where the dots or pixels mean nothing to the eye.[8]

Which is not to deny its efficacy outright. The human certainly "exists." But it does not belong (exclusively) to humanity. It is a vector, splashed across the cosmos and the species like water. We may *think* we see the human—in movies, in books, in compassionate or humorous exchanges between people—but on closer inspection, it reveals itself to be a special effect of the anthropological machine: an apparatus that uses smoke and mirrors to activate the overlapping zone of the Venn diagram between technics and animality. Thus the human can, in fact, only be glimpsed out of the corner of the eye. As soon as we try to fix our gaze on it, whether as image or reflection, it becomes something else: the effect of technology; the warm reassurance of instinct.

The catalyst of these qualities, of these resources, depends on the context, on the scenario itself. It cannot be isolated within *Homo sapiens.* So rather than considering humans as animals with invisible halos— or as animals with an especially demonic capacity for evil (merely the same gesture, in reverse)—it is incumbent to wrench the narcissistic gaze from our own image and begin taking note of the machine that projects this image. (If this statement sounds a little Platonic, we must be careful not to attribute a light of Truth outside the cave or movie theater but understand that any knowledge to be gleaned from seizing the projector is allied with the need to come up with new uses for the machine and not merely to sabotage it. That would indeed be noth-ing short of a neo-Luddite reaction.[9] Better instead to refashion the equipment as *détourned* "machineries of rejoinder."[10])

No doubt, for every anthropocentrism I denounce, several have slipped into my thinking without my even noticing. It is not a matter, then, of transcending our humanity, or of successfully becoming some-thing else, but of trying the best we can to acknowledge our persistent errors for what they are: a somewhat expedient category mistake, an often productive delusion. Disenchanting our sense of species-being is not a part of being a killjoy; rather it is to counterbalance the rampant sense of entitlement, individually and collectively. It is to reframe the entire relationship to each other, to other life-forms, and to the rap-idly retreating world, in which the human is no longer the ideological fulcrum for the rest.

"What is wrong with human exceptionalism?" asked a very intel-ligent interlocutor, playing the devil's advocate (a question I should have been more prepared to answer on the spot). Well, let us start with its presumption, and thus its condescension. It is just plain rude and inhospitable. Like the British Empire, the more confident we are in our own benevolence and stewardship, the less in evidence those qualities are in our behavior when viewed from the perspective of other existential stakeholders. By the same token, human exceptionalism can be seen as analogous to American exceptionalism. America *is* exceptional, of course, but those who choose to wallow in this fact are often blind to all the other national and cultural exceptionalisms around the globe. Yes, we have achieved great things that other species have not. But as thinkers understood many centuries ago, we cannot do those things without nonhuman assistance, especially through technology. Birds can fly unassisted, so what makes us so smug as we wait to be herded into a cut-price airline carrier?[11] We may sometimes feel divine but are in fact only prosthetic gods. To emphasize human frailty, fallibility, and failure, however, is simply to reverse the same coin. It is to presume a covenant with God, or some abstract alternative, to which we cannot live up. It is to be trapped in a masochistic and melancholy circuit from which other life-forms are given a free pass, but only because they are not significant enough to suffer so. They are cast as innocents, whereas our fault is an original sin: a mark of the accursed but one that comes with its own perverse pride—the stain of the exceptional.

Even the most progressive philosophies of the past few years—those that acknowledge that "the history of human beings is perhaps nothing other than the hand-to-hand confrontation with the apparatuses they have produced" (Agamben 2007, 72)—are caught up in this double gesture. To take away the human element, or the essence of Man, merely creates another exceptionalism: "What *defines* the human is paradoxically a radical, singular and exclusive indefinability" (Bradley 2006, 92). In other words, what seems from one angle to be a disadvantage is turned into a boon. We play the role of Adam, naming and sorting all the other creatures and not allowing anything else to label us, a state of affairs that leads to "the same vulgar ingratitude of men who will not admit their non-human origin" (Arendt 2007, 155; writing somewhat against type).

Thus species-being has largely become a matter of specious-being. Yes, we are exceptional, but we are not alone in this. *Every* animal, indeed *every* machine, is exceptional in its own way. To trumpet our own form of exceptionalism is to be trapped like Narcissus. Indeed, this is the danger of all centric thinking: imagining identity radiating out from a core (e.g., the heart or the soul) rather than as being distributed, overlapping, intertwined, *between.* The actual situation on the ground is much more akin to human *becoming* than human *being.* So in case it isn't clear yet, *we* are the anthro-machine, and our error is to disavow the machinic part of ourselves as well as the animal aspect.

Timothy Morton (2007, 180) assures us that "one cannot help anthropomorphism. A completely 'flat' approach, one that never anthropomorphized and thus kept mind and matter separate altogether, would be worse." On the other hand, "*must* we anthropomorphize in order to love" our various nonhuman neighbors? The challenge is thus to love (or at least respect) entities that do not resemble or remind us of ourselves, not to enfold them in our clammy embrace but to let them both *be* and *become* according to their own sense of time and place. Morton writes, "If we try to get rid of distance too fast, in our rush to join the nonhuman, we will end up caught in our prejudice, our concept of distance, our concept of 'them.' Hanging out in the distance may be the surest way of relating to the nonhuman" (204–5).

I must confess that in my more misanthropic moments, I believe that humanity (or hominization) is the chrysalis for something else—not necessarily something "better" because that would be too optimistic and teleological, as if we were intelligently designed for a pregiven purpose, an absurd and self-flattering fantasy. But just as certain conditions exist that, in retrospect, serve as an incubator for something that transcends it, humanity may have been ushered into being to act as the womb for magnificent pulses, striking geochemical art,[12] creative worlds and environments, or a whimsically nurturing version of Skynet. For just as we had to suffer the dull party to lock eyes with the seductive stranger across the room, humanity may be the necessary evil that gives rise to an unexpected blessing. How else can we account for the occasionally inspiring tracings, noises, frequencies, excursions, extrusions, and materialized delusions that are fashioned in the name of our species? Our literature, music, art, architecture, politics, and projects may be the husk from which an objectively interesting artifact, process, subspecies, or by-product emerges. And I'm not talking about the kind of H+ model so beloved by Stelarc and other posthumanists, which is just a way to magnify the human into something hard and immortal. ("The trouble with posthumanism," writes Morton [2006, 195], "is that we have not yet achieved humanity, and that humanity and posthumanity have no time for what Derrida calls the animal that therefore I am.")[13] No. This *something* would be our wake—the sublime slime we leave behind. (Or is that, too, just a melancholic and narcissistic wish? It is impossible to tell, alas, from the inverse vanishing point of the present.)

In *Capital,* Marx (1992, 311; emphasis added) noted, "The *mortal remains of machines,* tools, workshops etc., always continue to lead an existence distinct from that of the product they helped turn out. . . . The instrument suffers the same fate as the man." In this prelude to Bruno Latour's (2004, 181) actor network theory—which seeks to do away with "the tyranny of the dichotomy between objects and subjects"—the human is asked to take off the crown and consort with the ontological proletariat.[14] The more civilized the culture, according to Latour, the less it will make value distinctions between, say, hands and hammers, since both need each other to create such a civilization.[15] Instead, we should look forward to "imbroglios of humans and nonhumans on an ever increasing scale" (180). "Do they mediate our actions?" he asks. "No, they are us" (190). And yet, as we have seen, Latour cannot help but conceive of this enlightened and extended form of belonging as a Parliament of Things.

Not so for Graham Harman (2002), who pushes the agency of objects, tools, and technologies to its extreme point, delivering possibly the most sophisticated and uncompromising blow yet to humanity's seemingly indestructible superiority complex. For Harman, everything under the sun partakes of the same mode of being, that is, "tool-being." Every entity—whether it be moonbeams, toucans, puppets, wishes, numbers, jewelry, the word *Cuba,* or humans—are all examples of what (following Heidegger) he calls "equipment." In other words, any distinction made by humans between themselves and animals (or plants or machines) is nothing more than a case of "the narcissism of small differences." Like myself, and a growing list of others, Harman seeks to dissolve "the common-sense prejudice that there is some sort of golden schism between the human and nonhuman realms" (38), preferring instead to emphasize "vectors of relation" (79). By insisting that "the world is an infrastructure of equipment already at work, of tool-beings unleashing their forces upon us just as savagely or flirtatiously as they duel with one another" (20), Harman encourages us to appreciate "the drama at work in the heart of tools themselves" (35).[16] "The interplay of dust and cinder blocks and shafts of sunlight," he writes, "is haunted by the drama of presence and withdrawal no less than are language or lurid human moods" (16). According to this approach (which has since been dubbed "speculative realism"[17]), there are no valid criteria to distinguish the natural from the artificial, the organic from the inorganic, and the human from the nonhuman. All are types of essentially technical existence. But far from collapsing everything into one giant blob, like a philosophical game of Katamari Damacy, such a switch of perspective requires a new, "diligent taxonomy" (77). That is to say, each encounter between existents should take careful note of the singular qualities that compose any such relationship.

The good news is that "we are finally in a position to oppose the long dictatorship of human beings in philosophy," giving way to "a ghostly cosmos in which humans, dogs, oak trees, and tobacco are on precisely the same footing as glass bottles, pitchforks, windmills, comets, ice cubes, magnets, and atoms" (Harman 2002, 2).[18] Such a radical shift necessitates a new respect for absolutely everything we encounter, as loving thy neighbor expands to beyond the horizon. So in contrast to the inherited assumption that a stone has no world, it might even be the case that, like the menacing toys prowling in some depraved Gepetto's workshop, objects truly flourish only in that midnight reality that shields them from our view. Perhaps entities are actually rendered bland or uni-dimensional only *through* their contact with humans. Perhaps instead of *liberating* the objects into a clearing, Dasein is actually guilty of *chloroforming* the things, of pinning them down like the exterminated moths that bulk up an amateur's private collection. (92)

One imagines Harman's response, then, to the old riddle that asks "if a tree falls in the forest, and no one is there to hear it, does it make a sound?" as "Of course! What a stupid question!" Where George Berkeley believed that "to be is to be perceived" *(esse est percipi),* the thinker attuned to tool-being sees the world as functioning perfectly smoothly without humans to hear it, feel it, smell it, taste it, or see it.

To do all this, to recognize the profound agency or presence of nonhuman existents, is thus to address (quoting Derrida) all those "betrayals of repressed human possibilities, of other powers of reason, of a more comprehensive logic of argument, of a more demanding responsibility concerning the power of questioning and response" (Harman 2002, 105). Similarly, for Gary Steiner (2005, 17), the task is to forge "a conception of cosmic holism," that is, "the notion of an essential commonality between human beings and animals, [that] might provide the necessary background for the emergence of a revised virtue ethics." The very word *virtue,* however, should set off alarm bells, however muffled it may be. The trick, instead, is to cultivate the "*inessential* commonality" that, when approached according to the preceding paths, allows the emergence of an interspecies "community of those who have nothing in common."[19]

We have attempted to cobble together such a loose community throughout this book as well as keeping tabs on those forces and discourses that would prefer that such unlikely solidarities lie dormant. We began with televised nature documentaries and the corporations that funded them while continuing to plunder the environment. In the slogans celebrating the "human network" (Cisco), "human energy" (Chevron), and the "human element" (Dow), we came face-to-face with the kind of xenosentimentalism that has forever fueled the anthropological machine, whose primary task is to *identify* and thus promote *identification.* Various definitions of "the human" were then paraded before us, some positive (Frayn, Arendt, Bloom) and some negative (Gray), but all agreeing that a certain exceptionalism can be taken for granted. We then met Timothy Treadwell, who wanted desperately to become-animal but only managed to finally do so by being literally digested by a grizzly bear (recorded by the video camera's microphone). After this, we were introduced to a whole host of zoophiles who refused to keep Eros on one side of the fence separating species and—with the exception of Haraway, who approached this trespass with more lucidity than most—duly paid the price. We then explored the elasticity of human law, some instances of which demanded that animals be responsible for their actions (as with Topsy the elephant), while others considered them innocent of such attention (and thus expendable, in a different way). Bersani's notion of "impersonal intimacy" was then floated as a useful concept to avoid simply anthropomorphizing animals into the role of lover or best friend but to keep their alterity intact and the encounter ecstatic. J. A. Baker's book *The Peregrine* was proferred as an admirable example of this mode of approach. Another potential member of the community was then introduced: the anonymous woman who left a distressed message on the answering machine of a musician. Her call was considered alongside the SOS signal sent into space by NASA in the hope of extraterrestrial recognition. Santner's notion of "creaturely life" was subsequently raised as a possible escape route from human narcissism—acknowledging the nonhuman aspect that both haunts and constitutes us—yet this was shown to lead to the very same metaphysical patch of ground from which we were attempting to get away (albeit from below rather than from above). Finally, we came across Nature itself, as the shape-shifting material metaphor enabling a complex history of cultural mandates. We saw humans torture her sexually in Doyle's short story and also more literally (and only slightly less allegorically) in Lovelock's Gaia and Hubbert's peak. The creative, communal force of libido was proposed by Stiegler and Marcuse as the human transcendence of mere instinct or drive, while Lyotard (and to a lesser extent Guattari) insisted that *all* economies or ecologies are libidinal and accordingly argued that this is no criterion on which to base species distinctions. In almost all these instances, the human error is a mistaken identity—or better yet, the mistake *of* identity.

SCREEN / MEMORY / MIRROR / FANTASY

> Man is a unique case only in his own eyes.
> —Roger Caillois, "The Praying Mantis"

> Only humans can be inhuman.
> —*Revenge of the Nerds*

There is a temptation, even a danger, in talking of the anthropological machine: one into which Agamben himself falls, namely, a form of metanarcissism in which criticism, aimed at disarming a certain form of self-fascination, serves to further that very same self-fascination. This methodological flaw parallels that of ethnocentrism, whereby the most ingenious exposure of, for instance, Eurocentric thinking (myopia, presumption, pretention, ignorance, etc.) is rendered moot by the failure to incorporate insights from anywhere other than the West. Using the tools of one's culture to dismantle one's house because the original architectural plans were inadequate is not the most sincere way to proceed, even if it seems the most efficient. There is a *jouissance* in being confronted by our limitations. We can be mesmerized by our own capacity to be captivated. Sadly, this seldom leads to politically enabling insights regarding theories of relativity, or transitivity, or transduction.

Anticipating this train of thought, Derrida (2008, 58) refers to the scenario, common on *America's Funniest Home Videos,* in which animals watch themselves on TV, sometimes barking or squawking or hissing in response to images of their own kind. Such a nonhuman, televised mirror stage opens the possibility of "the zoological machine" operating diagonally across the contraption with which we have been tinkering thus far. Moreover, such an alternative to Agamben's device is supplemented by what may be termed "the medialogical machine": the technological apparatus that turns the recording device on itself. Cinema, in fact, does this at the very moment of its own birth with *La Sortie des Usines Lumière (Workers Leaving the Lumière Factory).* The remarkable event here is this mise en abyme effect. The first motion picture features the primal scene of the first motion picture. We see the midwives of this new medium exiting the first dream factory of the dawning century (and indeed the majority featured are women), and with this gesture—only partially a "decision" of the human element or director—*the machine itself* is revealed as narcissistic; it is an autodesiring machine, as it were.

Thus, to drain the residual anthropocentrism from Agamben's machinic anthropology (anthro-apology?), it would be necessary to do more than deconstruct the ways in which the machine itself sorts and renders nonhumans as either zoological or technical. The task would rather be to see the functional meshing, as well as profound incompatibilities, of these three machines, created by the cybernetic triangle (just as the cybernetic triangle is created by them). Crudely put, "the world" is no more and no less than the "objective" interaction of the anthropological machine, the zoological machine, and the mediaological machine (as opposed to the first framing and determining the other two).

As Deleuze and Guattari have indicated before, there are as many machines as there are potential points of intersection. In this book, I have not really considered vegetal machines,[20] viral machines, crystalline machines, dust machines,[21] and so on, because of the practical need to focus one's subject. The anthro-machine has programmed languages for dealing with all these. The question is how a human (i.e., the creature self-consciously involved in hominization) can possibly approach or conceive of these other machines without processing them through such self-referential languages. Anthropocentrism is inevitable as long as the sentient supports of human symbolic structures (i.e., "people") comprehend the world through such species-specific grids. But as with all things, there are degrees, and the reasons for sabotaging one over the other can be reduced to a simple preference for an open mind over a closed one.

The dynamics of identification or recognition are both enabled and complicated by the interaction—and indeed, interchangeability—of the screen, memory, mirror, and fantasy. As Freud understood, a screen can both hide and expose, depending on whether it is used to obscure something or to project an image to make it visible. Screens can thus function as mirrors, if the image is morphically recognizable, inviting a subjective kind of projection from subject to object, self to alter ego. This, in turn, influences the constant push and pull between memory and fantasy, as any image—mediated or not—solicits both faculties from different angles. But this trick of virtual teleportation into the space of the other is not necessarily uniquely human. In 2003, for example, *New Scientist* published an article that suggested that "fish can be turned on by an aquatic equivalent of pornography" (Pearson 2003). It is unlikely that anyone or anything can be "turned on" unless there is an empathic connection with the trigger image (whether this be described as instinctive or not).

The article explains matter-of-factly:

> Swiss scientists have discovered that male sticklebacks ejaculate more sperm if first stimulated by a "soft porn" film featuring "virtual" flirting fish. The University of Fribourg researchers believe the fish porn simulates conditions in the wild where mating male sticklebacks ejaculate more if they are threatened by other finned Romeos swimming nearby. . . . Researchers showed 17 male sticklebacks (in separate tanks) two films using computer-animated fish: one a "sexy" courting film; the other of a male caring for his brood. After each stickleback had watched one film for a couple of minutes, a female was put in the tank to spawn. Each fish ejaculated more sperm over the eggs if they had seen the fish "porn" film. (Pearson 2003)

One cannot help but wonder about the relation here between simulation and stimulation. Does mediation or artificiality enhance the positive feedback effect of desire, beyond its biological quota? Could we speak of a specific apparatus or *dispositif* of arousal that does not go beyond the human but rather incorporates it? (Pandas, too, let it be noted, are also encouraged to mate by watching videos of their own species having sex.)

The question is essentially about captivation and the extent to which any life-form is blinded by the dance of its own forms, a blindness only enhanced by so-called instruments of revelation. Heidegger would no doubt say so. Instead of "the Open," our technologies, more often than not, bypass the human realm and capture the instinctual, the compulsive, the repetitious. Modern-day humans are most comfortable when drip-fed hot pink pixels, unthinkingly ensconced in "the Closed" (and somewhat disconcertingly, so it seems, are some animals). It is conceivable, then, that we could restage the infamous experiment in which a bee's abdomen is slit open to show how it continues to suck honey despite the injury, only this time with a gambling addict. Need we look for an exceptional form of captivation in the latter? Is not the oblivious mesmerism of the honey-sucking bee and the lever-pulling human the same, on some existential plane beyond natural instinct, figured in opposition to cultural addiction?

Through such distinctions, the anthro-machine is shown to be not only powerful but seductive. Very few of its children really want to deprogram that from whence they came, and those that do tend to replicate its effects by rejecting it within the confines of its own coding. Even Baudrillard (2010, 44), an expert spotter of naked emperors, looks for a singular perversity in the human, stating in one of his final pieces of writing that "the human species is doubtless the only one to have invented a specific mode of disappearance that has nothing to do with nature's law. Perhaps even an art of disappearance. . . . This entire electronic, cybernetic revolution is perhaps merely a piece of animal cunning that humanity has found in order to escape itself."[22] Yet he poetically complicates things at the end there, as the point considered to be at the top of the cybernetic triangle is spun into a dizzying blur. The human is rendered as an animal trying to escape itself via technology. And the effect is not unlike that Victorian toy, the thaumatrope: a spinning disc on a piece of string, animating and blending the two pictures painted on either side because of persistence of vision. On one side we have the human, or the other the animal. Thanks to the technology of the toy, we see one single, yet hybrid, image—triangular coevolution in action.

As it happens, the very first video uploaded to YouTube depicted the cofounder of the company, Jawed Karim, on a day trip to the San Diego Zoo (Alleyne 2008). For nineteen seconds, Karim stands in front of some incarcerated elephants and meditates aloud on how "cool" they are because they have "really, really long trunks . . . and that's about all there is to say." As with the first Lumière film, this could not be more perfect, especially in terms of the metamechanics of the machine. No matter what change in paradigm occurs from broadcast media to "narrowcast" platforms, the *anthropos* continues to assert its privileged role of reassuring the observer that he or she is human and not bestial. "Man is the only animal that laughs and weeps," wrote William Hazlitt (1889, 269), "for he is the only animal that is struck with the difference between what things are and what they ought to be." But as we have seen—with electronically transfixed fish, engineering insects, aesthetically minded birds, and tool-making primates—the recognition of the gap between status quo and desired future, or imagined alternative, may not be the exclusive preserve of humanity. Indeed, this may be yet another disjunction that, paradoxically, reveals those remarkable continuities between entities that have been deliberately left outside the human frame—until now, that is.

ASTRONOMY DOMINE

> Two things fill the mind with ever new and increasing admiration and awe . . . the starry heavens above and the moral law within.
> —Immanuel Kant, *The Critique of Practical Reason*

> Two things are infinite: the universe and human stupidity; and I'm not sure about the universe.
> —Albert Einstein

Let us finish, then, as we began: with a humanist fable. This one is memetic and apocryphal, credited to several different people, and tells of the public opening of a great telescope. In one version, it is Kant himself in attendance, listening to a lecture on the topic of man's place in the universe.[23] "So you see," concludes the astronomer, "that astronomically speaking, man is utterly insignificant," to which the sage of Königsberg replies, "Professor, you forgot the most important thing. *Man* is the astronomer."[24] Throughout this book, we have seen several variations on this theme, in which humanity is the supreme secular subject, validating the cosmos's very existence by virtue of bearing witness to it. The more science pushes humanity from the center of the universal diagram, the more the figure doing the pushing—the Scientist—serves as an emblem of our ongoing relevance, even centrality. A clearer example of the double gesture would be difficult to find, and the astronomer is certainly a key engineer of the anthropological machine. Indeed, we should not be surprised that the Vatican has its own observatory and that many so-called hard scientists believe in a higher power that listens to their prayers. Seeking to understand the mechanics of the universe's quantum whims is akin—from such a perspective—to tracing the infinite edge of the divine font of God's Word. But even if we are dealing with confirmed atheists, the paradox remains: humans are magnified by their very capacity to magnify that which dwarves them.

As I write, in 2009, the world is officially observing the International Year of Astronomy by celebrating the four hundredth anniversary of Galileo's telescopic experiments as well as the publication of Kepler's *Astronomia Nova*. The tagline for this ongoing event is "The Universe Is Yours to Discover," encouraging young and curious minds to claim ownership of the seemingly endless firmament. One can only hope that the general undercurrent of related events does not rely on the preceding moral fable but encourages a more reflective relationship to ourselves, our cosmic neighbors, and the instruments that allow unprecedented access into the dark depths. As part of the promotion, portable "Galileoscopes"—described as "simple and sophisticated"—are hoped to help in this initiative so that a new generation can celebrate the moment when the instrument's namesake redefined humanity's place in the cosmos while also leaving it firmly in place. This kind of cosmic curiosity can only be a good thing. However, were I fortunate enough to be a consultant for the International Year of Astronomy, I would have also raised awareness of Tycho Brahe, the gold-nosed cyborg and last of the great astronomers to make his observations without a telescope (but with many ingenious optical instruments leading to such a device).

Tycho was allegedly the first figure to propose "mapping the heavens conducted from a single location over a period of several years," thereby setting the stage for the scientific revolution (Nardo 2008, 26–27). He lost his nose in a duel and replaced it with several different prosthetic ones he crafted for different occasions: sometimes silver, sometimes gold, but also copper. Tycho's untimely death is said by some to have been induced by poisoning at the hands of his assistant, Kepler, who then stole his work; others blame his alchemical experiments; while the most popular account is that he refused to urinate at a dinner party for fear of offending his host, putting etiquette above personal health, and paid the ultimate price. Before his unfortunate end, Tycho kept an elk as a pet, as well as a dwarf named "Jepp," who performed simultaneous duties as a clairvoyant and court jester, sitting under the table during mealtimes. It is this alloyed sense of existence that is Tycho's legacy, as much as his quest for an astronomic Archimedean point. It should remind us to turn the lens on ourselves as much as the heavens, to magnify our errors as much as our finer points, and to further appreciate the strange ensembles that constitute us as much as we do them.

New instruments themselves, however—divorced from mundane, sensual realities—do little for our intimate understanding of Being, at least for someone like Hannah Arendt. In *The Human Condition*, she writes:

> The modern astrophysical world view, which began with Galileo, and its challenge to the adequacy of the senses to reveal reality, have left us a universe of whose qualities we know no more than the way they affect our measuring instruments, and—in the words of Eddington—"the former have as much resemblance to the latter as a telephone number has to a subscriber." Instead of objective qualities, in other words, we find instruments, and instead of nature or the universe—in the words of Heisenberg—man encounters only himself. (Arendt 1998, 261)

Thus "in the [astronomical] experiment man realized his newly won freedom from the shackles of earth-bound experience; instead of observing natural phenomena as they were given to him, he placed nature under the conditions of his own mind, that is, under conditions won from a universal, astrophysical viewpoint, a cosmic standpoint outside nature itself" (265).

But this is ultimately to blame our tools: not only telescopes and astrolabes but also the abstract equations of algebra, theories of relativity, and the God-like mobilities of virtual perspective. Arendt's argument—erudite and nuanced as it is—rehearses the now-standard narrative of human falling and failing. Once upon a time, we had an organic connection to the surround, it suggests, readable and relatable through the data of our perceptions. But this has since been lost after our own complicity with the exile from Eden. From this perspective, the more exquisite our models of interpretation, the more divorced from reality they become, and the more we require crutches fashioned from the forbidden Tree of Knowledge to make any progress on the level of Humanity (figured as the collective subject of ethical evolution).

And yet, the more sensitive our instruments, the more we have the capacity to divine elusive presences through astronomic inference rather than through the kind of identification allowed by the naked eye and rudimentary lenses. That is to say—several centuries after Tycho's calculations—we can hypothesize the existence of an entity by the shadow effect it creates in the data rather than by any positive sign of appearance (a process akin to saying that "love exists because my heart feels broken" rather than because of any verifiable identification of the offender). So, too, with ourselves. Humanity must exist, so this logic goes, because the world behaves as if we do. Dogs jump to our call. Sliding doors open at our approach. Magazine headlines solicit our attention. And other humans wish us a nice day (if we are buying the magazine).

For someone like Jakob von Uexküll, however, the mystery *is* this mute *ballet metaphysique* between subjective entities, for according to him, each creature dwells exclusively within its own existential soap bubble. The tick, for instance, lives in a world entirely tailored to its perceptive faculties. So, too, the cow on which the tick drops is likewise living in a completely divorced subjective reality. Space and time are radically different for each, and "all animals, from the simplest to the most complex, are fitted into their unique worlds with equal completeness. A simple world corresponds to a simple animal, a well-articulated world to a complex one" (von Uexküll 1959, 11). There are no "ontological overlaps" in Uexküll's system, and any communication between species occurs through elaborate, ultimately solipsistic mistranslations. Subjects use other subjects as objects within their respective realities—as food, as tools, as shelter—which is why something like an oak tree is a completely different encounter to a forester, fox, owl, or little girl playing in its branches. Such a vision of the ecosphere is a useful reminder of radical difference, but it goes too far in carving up the cosmos into untied molar units. And yet the notion of soap bubbles has its efficacy. Humans may flatter themselves that they have the most complex of such bubbles in which to live, but this should not dupe us into thinking that we have true ontological access to others.

To emphasize this point, Uexküll himself finishes his hypothesis with a brief discussion of "the *Umwelt* of an astronomer" (von Uexküll 1959, 76–77):

> High on his tower, as far as possible from the earth, sits a human being. He has so transformed his eyes, with the aid of gigantic optical instruments, that they have become fit to penetrate the universe up to its most distant stars. In his *Umwelt,* suns and planets circle in festive procession.... And yet this whole *Umwelt* is only a tiny sector of nature, tailored to the faculties of a human subject.[25]

We should thus be somewhat wary of our ability to compensate for the ego bruises to our species-being—inflicted by Copernicus, Darwin, Freud, Trump, and so on—by gesticulating toward ourselves as the falsely modest Astronomer. Of course, neither should we feel so traumatized by our celestial dethroning that we end up shivering in the corner like Hermann Broch's Virgil, who suffered from "the horrible fear of the animal, which recognizes the utterly amorphous animalhood of its own non-being, oh, the stifling horror of the universe!" (Broch 1995, 168). Such are the Scylla and Charybdis of our journey: the hubris of self-bequeathed entitlement on one side and the paralysis of a naked and meaningless mortality on the other.

Long before speculators plundered the earth for short-term gain, "speculation" meant to look at the stars with the aid of a mirror to more profoundly orient the observer not only geographically but philosophically. Once again, the significance of the enabling technology (in this case, the mirror) should itself be acknowledged in the equation. We humans place great stock in those extremely rare species that can recognize themselves in a mirror because that capacity (some might say flaw) is the signature of sentience.[26] The so-called mirror test relies on a supremely narcissistic notion of self-awareness, at once literal and symbolic. Such recognition *of* reflection, and reflection *on* recognition, induced by the splitting and doubling of oneself, constitutes all further conscious parsing of the world—or so it is assumed.[27] But judging animals according to their fidelity to the anthropological machine is a tautological and self-confirming process.[28] As per usual, Man casts himself as *metron*: the measure of all things. But what the scientists conducting the mirror tests don't register is that the same is occurring on a metalevel: not only between animal and reflecting surface but between researcher and subject. The scientist unconsciously reads the animal's response according to his or her own assumptions, expectations, and behavior. The cybernetic triangle is thus in full effect on the shiny polished surfaces that compose (and compromise) the human environment.[29] Monkey see, monkey do—or the man-monkey sees other monkeys making do.

But this emphasis on optics, figured as the privileged route to metaphysical comprehension, is at least as old as the ancients, who declared—in not so many words—that "the eye is the window to the soul."[30] The historical relationship between lens, mirror, and retina is therefore a crucial one, allowing humans to complicate their soap bubble to the extent where they englobe the universe with their own subjective reality. (As Adorno [2005, 50] once noted, "the splinter in your eye is the best magnifying glass.") Moreover, as David Hockney has suggested, some of the most prominent painterly masterworks of the Renaissance would be unthinkable without the camera obscura and various other optical techniques for projecting traceable images. The human element is demoted in such a scenario, as the artist is rendered a glorified tracer of materialized Euclidean lines, instead of the familiar genius, or divine medium, of autochthonous Platonic forms. Art, the very apex of human endeavor and expression, is also revealed to be a matter of smoke and mirrors. *But should it be any less impressive for that?* Should we feel only disappointment that we have—from the very beginning—outsourced our resourcefulness to objects? Must it leave a bad taste in the mouth to even consider the possibility that we have been inspired by these very same objects, to the degree where *they* are outsourcing their noumenal secrets to *us?*

In essence, the anthropological machine—powered by "the media" or "the Spectacle"—is an ongoing mirror test, on the scale and register of the species[31] (the species that *it itself* enables and shapes). As the bear was said to lick its young into the correct form, the anthro-machine does the same. It is an audiovisual echo of our originary mirror stage, in which our recognition is a splitting and our identity becomes also a mistaken identity. And though the history of philosophy insists on the (r)evolutionary importance of the autodesignatory gesture—the turning of the thumb to indicate oneself as both subject and object—this figurative operation is always occurring on the metalevel of self-surveillance and reflection. In other words, we are *that* creature over *there* that mimics *this* one *here,* that is *responding* to that *same one* there. What's more, this operation occurs every second in every anthropological encounter, whether one is ordering a milkshake or discovering the theory of relativity—a constant process of bringing into being complicated by the existence of "mirror neurons." Me Tarzan, you Jane—except when Jane laughs or winces in pain. Then Tarzan is simultaneously Tarzan *and* Jane, speaking in terms of phenomenology and neurophysiology. To say nothing of Cheeta . . .

Notes

INTRODUCTION

1   The *New York Times* takes note of the subsequent popularity of this show (over three million copies sold) as well as some of the subcultural rituals that have sprung up around it. Journalist Alex Williams (2009) quotes one female fan, who said, "I love making out when planet earth *[sic]* is in the background . . . it's so natural."

2   For the official Dow "human element" Web site, see http://www.dow.com/hu/.

3   See http://news.dow.com/corporate/2006/20060619c.htm (accessed May 2007). For a sobering critique of Dow's corporate strategy, media activists have reedited this commercial and uploaded it to YouTube using the same voice-over but with images of the Bhopal disaster, environmental pollution, the effects of napalm and agent orange, etc. See also Doyle and Environmental Health Fund (2004).

4   In the 1957 film *Desk Set,* Spencer Tracy—playing a kind of proto-Google executive—talks of "the human element" when introducing the new supercomputer to board members, in reference to the part of the system that can skew information.

5   For the official Cisco "human network site," see http://www.cisco.com/web/thehumannetwork/.

6   See Agamben's (2000) "Notes on Gesture" in *Means without End.*

7   See http://blogs.cisco.com/wireless/mobilizing_the_human_network_part_1/.

8   Jumping on the same bandwagon, although not shown during the *Planet*

Earth screenings, is Chevron, which currently claims that it relies on "human energy." The company's recent series of commercials could have been commissioned by Dow or Cisco and also leverage the sublime within the global quotidian: "Humans have always reached for what seems impossible, because it is then that we find a way. Tell us what can be done, then watch as we tap the greatest source of energy in the world: ourselves. This is the power of human energy."

9   From the DVD *Beautiful World* (2006), directed by Mieke Gerritzen, screenplay by Geert Lovink.

10   Though I have settled on the triangle for this project, there are indeed many other possible points, and thus geometric shapes, with which to work. The virus, for instance, troubles any neat division between organic and ontological categories—even between life and nonlife. Likewise, the monster and the alien could very well lead us to a pentagon or beyond (in more ways than one). As Žižek notes in *The Pervert's Guide to Cinema,* "humanity means the aliens are controlling our animal bodies."

11   For a sustained discussion of both the overlaps and the divergences between the three points of the cybernetic triangle, see Mazis (2008, 21): "It is a mistake to define humans, animals, and machines as three separate kinds of entities, for there are mechanistic dimensions of animals and humans, as well as animal dimensions of humans and, in some ways, even of machines." In other words, it is possible "that we ourselves as humans could be encountered as 'open systems' that are partially machine and animal, even if something unique emerges in our distinctive human activity" (17).

12   *Hominization* is the evolutionary and cultural process of "becoming human," mapped by disciplines such as sociobiology, anthropology, archaeology, paleontology, and linguistics. For Bernard Stiegler, hominization begins with the appearance of "an epiphylogenetic memory," that is to say, the externalization of thought in traces, tools, and objects. When I use the term throughout this book, I intend the phrase to have a crypto-Deleuzian resonance, whereby *Homo sapiens* are always already de- and reterritorializing the elusive element that *would potentially* make us human, were it not for the fact that humanity is the embodiment of an asymptote. In other words, those creatures concerned and involved with hominization are forever pre- or posthuman, depending on the context. (It is not necessarily an issue of chronology.) As such, these creatures do not in fact represent something both philosophers and scientists once called "Man," for this would be the principal human error:

to (mis)-recognize oneself as coinciding exactly with the humanized image of oneself. Alas, we do not have the Neanderthal around today to appreciate how hominization may conceivably have occurred in a species other than *Homo sapiens,* that is, because the latter wiped out the former. Ergo genocide—on the level of species—is part of hominization.

13   As with most cultural categories, definition is provided negatively, that is to say, by what it is *not.* Understanding of the human is hinted at through constant references to "inhuman" or "inhumane" behavior, leaving the positive definition as a kind of charged vacuum.

14   Bruce Mazlish (1993, 60) writes, "For Thomas Carlyle, in *Sartor Resartus,* clothes became the symbol for human culture, the artificial skin, if you like, taking the place of natural skin. It was only fitting, then, that the first industry to start the profound continuing change in human culture that we refer to as the Industrial Revolution should have been the textile industry." In other words, clothes maketh the Man, literally.

15   In his book *Dorsality,* David Wills (2008, 3) begins with the premise that "there is technology as soon as there are limbs, as soon as there is bending of those limbs, as soon as there is any articulation at all." As a consequence, it is prudent to acknowledge "the originary mechanics at work in the evolution of the species. This is not to replace the organic with the mechanical but to argue against any rigorous purity of either" (5–6). The "originary technicity" of the human is a substantial and growing field, mapped by Simondon, Leroi-Gourhan, Derrida, Stiegler, etc., and I will not rehearse their compelling conclusions here but rather presume the existence of a Möbius strip for "natural" and "human" technologies, together referred to as *technics.* See also chapter 7 in my book *Love and Other Technologies* (Pettman 2006) for a more developed discussion of this crucial issue.

16   "Kynicism and Legality" (Sloterdijk 2005).

17   One could add a more positively inflected list here, including the shaman, the priest, the king, the queen, the star, the celebrity, the hero, the superhero, etc.

18   Agamben's (2004) paradigm is crying out for the injection of gender dynamics.

19   See Stiegler (1998, 1:114ff.).

20   I refer the reader to Agamben's (2004) book for the more intricate Heideggerian aspects of his argument, especially in relation to captivation, revelation, and *Dasein,* esp. chapters 10–14.

21   A useful analogy might be that of the border town, which is often

ironically more "patriotic" than the capital of any given nation since the latter is nestled in the bosom of secure identity. That is to say, identity reinforcement occurs and radiates more vigorously from the threatened edge rather than emanating outward from a perceived geopolitical center. Of course, it is also the place where blending and promiscuity are likely to occur.

22   For the infinitely more sophisticated original treatment of this difference, see Agamben (2004, 37–38) as well as one of the best commentaries thus far, Laura Hudson's (2008) "The Political Animal: Species-Being and Bare Life."

23   See Galloway and Thacker's (2007) *The Exploit.*

24   E.g., we are being interpellated by the machine more obviously when watching a Hollywood film than lying eyes closed next to a babbling brook. But the thoughts circulating in our minds during the latter scenario are highly likely to be running anthropological routines, even as we hope momentarily to escape the shackles of our species.

25   For those "professional resenters" (9) who would dare bring Marxist or feminist or structuralist concepts to bear on Shakespeare, Bloom (1998, 719) has an unequivocal warning: "His universality will defeat you; his plays know more than you do, and your knowingness consequently will be in danger of dwindling into ignorance. [So don't even try—bitch!]." (Admittedly, the last line of this quotation is not found in the original, but it is strongly implied.)

26   Characters written by Shakespeare's contemporaries are dismissed as "cartoons" or "ideograms" by Bloom (1998, 5).

27   Bloom (1998, 714) writes, "Shakespeare is the original psychologist, and Freud the belated rhetorician."

28   The foundational study is Humberto Maturana and Francisco Varela's (1980) *Autopoiesis and Cognition: The Realization of the Living,* which has since been adopted and adapted by Niklas Luhmann's systems theory (see esp. Luhmann 1990).

29   Bloom (1998, 741) rather reluctantly acknowledges that others have dated "the birth of the inner self" to 1520, two generations before Hamlet, with Martin Luther's "Christian Freedom."

30   The exact quote is from *The Order of Things* (Foucault 1973, 387) and reads, "Man is an invention of recent date. And one perhaps nearing its end. If those arrangements were to disappear as they appeared, if some event of which we can at the moment do no more than sense the possibility—without knowing either what its form will be or what it

promises—were to cause them to crumble, as the ground of classical thought did, at the end of the eighteenth century, then one can certainly wager that man would be erased, like a face drawn in sand at the edge of the sea."

31   There are three "official" Humanist Manifestos, penned in 1933, 1973, and 2003, as approved by the American Humanist Association. The first has a decidedly religious tone and theme to it, whereas the more recent ones are at pains to earn their secular credentials.

32   To cite one example that gave me pause, Francis S. Collins, the director of the Human Genome Project, is a practicing Christian and author of *The Language of God: A Scientist Presents Evidence for Belief* (Collins 2006). Collins posted a message to the CNN Web site in 2007 that began with the following statement: "As the director of the Human Genome Project, I have led a consortium of scientists to read out the 3.1 billion letters of the human genome, our own DNA instruction book. As a believer, I see DNA, the information molecule of all living things, as God's language, and the elegance and complexity of our own bodies and the rest of nature as a reflection of God's plan." http://www.cnn.com/2007/US/04/03/collins.commentary/index.html.

33   If we go further back into Deep Blue's family tree, we find "The Turk"— aka, "The Mechanical Turk"—constructed in 1770 by Wolfgang von Kempelen for the delight of the Empress Maria Theresa. This putative chess-playing automaton, which was exhibited throughout Europe for nearly a century, defeating opponents as exulted as Napoleon and Benjamin Franklin, turned out to be a hoax. The Oriental(ist) exterior actually hid a human chess champion, who mimicked the robotic movements of a mechanical man. For a lively history on this fascinating phenomenon, see Standage (2003), and for its genealogical relationship to Deep Blue, see Hsu (2002).

34   Marking the tenth anniversary of this historic ego bruise to humanity, William Salen (2007) wrote, "When the cosmic game between humans and computers is complete, here's how the sequence of moves will read. In the opening, humans evolved through engagement with nature. In the middle game, we projected our intelligence onto computers and co-evolved through engagement with them. In the endgame, we merged computers with our minds and bodies, bringing that projected intelligence back into ourselves. The distinction between human and artificial intelligence turns out to have been artificial."

35   In contrast to this long-held belief about limited, rational computers,

some TV commentators, during the financial meltdown of October 2008, stated outright that "the computers themselves are panicking" (meaning that they were selling off stocks automatically, and in exponentially accelerated loops, once these stocks dipped below a certain level).

36   Once again exploiting the double gesture, Frayn (2006, 108) enlists the notion of error itself as another mark of (paradoxical) mortal superiority: "The perfection of living forms that so astonishes us arises from the imperfection that they embody—from random error in the transmission of genetic information upon which the precise and brutal mechanisms of natural selection operate. . . . If genetic material always reproduced itself without error there would be—well, no genetic material, for a start. . . . Fallible material is improvable material; infallible material remains unchanged."

37   Arendt preferred the title *Vita Activa* for her book, a wish that only her German publisher granted. See Stephan Kampowski's (2008, 7) *Arendt, Augustine, and the New Beginning*.

38   Internal quotations are by Albert Camus. All subsequent Arendt quotations in this section are from *Reflections on Literature and Culture* (Arendt 2007).

39   The modifier *mere* is often used to make an anthropocentric point without flagging the conceptual pecking order explicitly.

40   When Arendt (1998, 190) writes, "I have no idea whether or not it is part of human nature to be a worldly or world-making being. There are worldless peoples, just as there are worldless individuals. . . . The earthly home becomes a world only when objects as a whole are produced and organized in such a way that they may withstand the consumptive life-process of human beings," she seems to be leaving the door open for a reassessment of Heidegger's rendition of the cybernetic triangle (replacing *stone* for *machine*). However, her broader argument and orientation do not consider the prospect of worldly animals and proceeds under the assumption that only humans have the potential to become so. This becomes clear when she states that "the things of the world produced by man, insofar as he is a worldly and not just a natural being, do not renew themselves" (182). The question remains, however, how far does the "insofar" extend?

41   "Culture and Politics," originally delivered as part of the commemoration of the eight hundredth anniversary of the city of Munich and published in 1959.

42   I have been less inclined to agree with such statements since discovering

that Greek marble statues were originally painted in Day-Glo colors and that they were since stripped to the material itself to make them less gaudy. Such epochal changes in taste weaken Arendt's claim to the auratic durability of artworks through time, even while she insists that "taste is the political faculty by means of which culture is humanized" (201).

43   The human capacity for error is itself something that Arendt (2007, 201–2) reserves the right to cherish because we should not be held hostage by objective facts or truths. To do so is both "apolitical" and "inhuman" since doing so does not take into account the perversities of affinity, taste, and friendship that constitute our milieu and condition.

44   Gray (2007, 9) writes, "Our bodies are bacterial communities, linked indissolubly with a largely bacterial biosphere. Epidemiology and microbiology are better guides to our future than any of our hopes or plans."

45   A term used by E. O. Wilson (1998) in his book *Consilience: The Unity of Knowledge.*

46   Gray (2007, 144) makes special note of the Extropians, who "seek to make the thin trickle of consciousness—our shallowest fleeting sensation—everlasting," yet forget that "we are not embrained phantoms encased in mortal flesh. Being embodied is our nature as earth-born creatures."

47   The internal quote is from pioneer roboticist Hans Moravec.

48   Witness how Gray is willing to gesture toward "humanity" when it suits him.

49   A monastery inside a zoo is not such a bad idea, although it may turn out something like the surreal English TV show *The Mighty Boosh.*

50   See Norman Geras (1983).

51   In *The Poverty of Philosophy* (1847), Marx (2008, 160) writes that "all history is nothing but a continuous transformation of human nature." Elsewhere, three years earlier, he utilizes a sweeping possessive pronoun: "my true nature, my *human* nature, my *communal nature*" (Marx 1986, 34).

52   In "Estranged Labor" (1844), Marx (2002, 123) reveals his anthropocentric bias, noting that "animals produce only according to the standards and needs of the species to which they belong, while man is capable of producing according to the standards of every species and of applying to each object its inherent standard; hence, man also produces in accordance with the laws of beauty." Marx has somewhat more affinity with the machinic edge of the cybernetic triangle, believing that further mechanization was necessary, albeit organized differently. For instance, in *Capital* (Marx 1992), he writes, "The relics of the instruments of labor are of no less importance in the study of vanished socioeconomic forms,

than fossil bones are in the study of the organization of extinct species" (from Mazlish 1993, 5). Furthermore, "Darwin has aroused our interest in the history of natural technology, that is to say in the origin of the organs of plants and animals as productive instruments utilized for the life purposes of those creatures. Does not the history of the origin of the productive organs of men in society, the organs which form the material basis of every kind of organization, deserve equal attention?" (Mazlish 1993, 6).

1. BEAR LIFE

1   Thereby finding a much wider audience than in the previous year of its release in art house cinemas.

2   Strangely, the lead character in the B movie *Cherry 2000* is named "Sam Treadwell." This film is also about a man who prefers the eroticized company of nonhumans, albeit a cyborg female rather than grizzly bears. See "The Virtual Apocalypse" in my book *After the Orgy* (Pettman 2002) for a discussion of this schlock humanist text.

3   It is tempting, albeit rather uncharitable, to see in Herzog's title a sly pun, in which the "grizzly man" refers to the protagonist's tendency to grizzle or whine.

4   "According to psychologist Paul Horton, teddy bears are so similar to the human configuration that they have greater comforting potential: 'The bear is enough like a human for the child to relate to it, but different enough to distinguish it. . . . It's ideally situated in psychological space'" (Bieder 2005, 129).

5   In the accumulating secondary literature on *Grizzly Man,* I have yet to see any mention of an intriguing companion film, *Project Grizzly* (1996). Together they make a perfect double feature concerning the symptomology of cross-species interaction and intergenerational (sexual?) trauma. This lesser known film is also a documentary; however, the protagonist, Troy Hurtubise, is thankfully still alive (if spiritually scarred from his near-death experience with a grizzly bear). For Hurtubise, the question is not "will it kill me?" but "why didn't it kill me?" and indeed there are several clues that the trauma may be linked to sexual abuse. All the bears he encounters are called "the old man," and he notes that, for him at least, "all bears have the same eyes." Hurtubise is monomaniacal, spending his life savings and every spare second on crafting a bear-proof suit, which looks like something an astronaut gladiator might wear. This

ludicrously heavy suit, the Ursus Mark VI, is a perfect emblem—and amazing condensation—of human folly, fear, and tenacity in terms of responding to trauma. It represents an extruded and damaged psyche, allowing Hurtubise possibly to withstand another attack, but freezes him in one place, immobile. It is a panic room for one and a perfect emblem for an epoch obsessed with "security" at any cost.

6   Yet another dark irony of the film is that Treadwell met Jewel while they were both working at a prime rib restaurant. The film notes that Treadwell's own rib cage is the most visible remains of the attack.

7   See my piece "Look at the Bunny: What Roger Rabbit Can Tell Us about the Second Gulf War," in *Avoiding the Subject* (Clemens and Pettman 2004).

8   Not to mention the Chinese poachers and harvesters who cruelly and systematically milk live bears of their bile for ostensible medical and status reasons.

9   Lest we forget, the "distinguished" philosopher, Thomas Taylor, wrote the satirical essay *A Vindication of the Rights of Brutes* in response to Mary Wollstonecraft's 1792 call for the rights of woman. For Taylor—and many of his peers besides—it seemed equally preposterous that women and animals should have the same rights as men.

10 As I write, in April 2007, Germany is in the grip of "Knut fever," referring to a polar bear cub born in the Berlin Zoo and rejected by its mother. Barely five months into its life, Knut has been adopted by the German minister for the environment, registered as a trademark by the Berlin Zoo (resulting in a swift doubling of its stocks), the beneficiary of his own online media center (updated every few minutes, around the clock), and—astonishingly—photographed by Annie Liebowitz for the cover of *Vanity Fair*. (However, as I *re*-write, two years later, Knut is now large and in no way, shape, or form cute. One wonders if he is relieved to be abandoned by the spotlight or whether he suffers the same kind of posttraumatic stress disorder as child actors, neglected by the public in their adult years.)

11 Bullfighting is, of course, the most obvious surviving example of spectacular interspecies antagonism. This, however, comes with its own established bibliography, so I shall respectfully leave this case to the experts.

12 As late as 1939, Cornell University's Big Red football team was using a live bear as its mascot who was known as Touchdown. This has since been replaced by an undergraduate dressed in a bear suit (doing little to quell allegations of cruelty to animals).

13   All Deleuze and Guattari quotes are from *A Thousand Plateaus* (Deleuze and Guattari 1987), unless a different citation is given to indicate otherwise.

14   Deleuze and Guattari's reading of early evolutionist theory as producing "kinematic entities" (255) provides something of a missing link between the materialism of biology and the more spectral qualities of cinema, which, since Muybridge and his ilk, has injected an uncanny and inherently technological "creaturely" element into the ongoing regulation of species-being. In other words, the shift from perceiving all animals, and thus ourselves, as kinematic entities invites us to take the next step and see ourselves as intrinsic cinematic entities. A ten-minute walk around the streets of New York City should make this abundantly clear.

15   One wonders if Björk is aware of the Kwakwaka'wakw transformation bear mask of the Kwakiutl Indians of British Columbia, which opens to show the human within (see Bieder 2005, 100). The chances are slight, if not impossible. However, her Scandinavian heritage may well have brought her in contact with something similar.

16   Deleuze and Guattari write, "The becoming-animal of the human being is real, even if the animal the human being becomes is not" (238).

17   The reservations inhabited by Native Americans or Aborigines expose the projected status of indigenous peoples, caught between the chthonic and the cultivated.

18   Taken from *The Ister* (2004), directed by David Barison and Daniel Ross.

19   See *Commercial Advertiser* (1903). I shall talk further in the following chapter about the recent rash of delinquent and murderous elephants in Africa and India.

20   The definitive popular books concerning human–animal empathy have become those by Temple Grandin, who claims that her autism has given her a special affinity with other creatures. See Grandin (2009) and Grandin and Johnson (2005).

21   I am, of course, simplifying here. Agamben (2004, 37) discusses the different logics involved in the ancient anthropological machine and the modern model. For Sam Eastern's Critter-Cam (in which animals are becoming-camera), see http://www.anivegvideo.com/AVV.html (accessed October 2007). For a less high-concept version, see http://news.nationalgeographic.com/news/2006/03/0328_060328_bears_video.html?source=rss. Donna Haraway (2008) discusses these in her book *When Species Meet*.

22   For a now classical piece of cinematic self-reflection on the human–ape continuum, see Barbet Schroeder's *Koko: A Talking Gorilla* (1978). Once

again, the camera–screen complex is a crucial component of the events, not only capturing Koko's interactions with Dr. Francis "Penny" Patterson but also preempting them. In one scene, we see Koko engrossed in the images provided by a ViewMaster and also becoming excited when she recognizes herself on the TV news. We also see her putting on makeup in front of a mirror (albeit without the finesse of her keeper) and kissing photographs of other animals, including an alligator and ducks. Before arriving at thorny ethological questions concerning Koko's parsing of human-produced media, we are already involved in the meshing of the ancient and modern anthro-machines: one that humanizes animals and the other that animalizes humans.

23 Pets, of course, are the great liminal species, prompting Deleuze to dismiss them in theory (although not in practice) as oedipal animals, guilty of submitting to disciplinary mechanisms. Derrida, for his part, gave more ontological latitude to his cat, whereas Perry Farrell, of the band Porno for Pyros, claimed that humans would "make great pets" for Martians.

24 In 1906, the Congolese pygmy Ota Benga was exhibited in the Bronx Zoo, alongside an orangutan. We should not only be troubled by the dehumanization of Ota Benga but also by the enduring incarceration of so-called exotic animals for neo-Victorian entertainment.

2. ZOOICIDE

1 According to Xenophanes, "Pythagoras implored a man to stop whipping a dog because "Tis a friend, a human soul; / I knew him straight whenas I heard him yelp!'" (quoted in Steiner 2005, 46). This instance of compassion was based on a theory of reincarnation, or metempsychosis, rather than on a more abstract circulation of empathy.

2 Lesley Chamberlain (1996, 209) writes that Nietzsche's dramatic gesture— his "ecstasy of pity"—stemmed from "some ultimate autobiographical urge," neatly anticipating Derrida's insistence that our relationship with animals unfolds within the auspices of autobiography, i.e., the tracing of selfhood via signs, whether these be created by ink on paper or urine on fire hydrant.

3 Despite his keen critique of anthropocentrism, Derrida (2008, 35) seems to take the charitable view of Nietzsche in Turin: "Sometimes I think I see him call that horse as a witness, and primarily in order to call it as a witness to his compassion, I think I see him take its head in his hands." The motif of human–horse compassion, of course, both predates

Nietzsche and continues to echo into the present as a specific mode of affective intersection. In his article "Forbidden Foods," e.g., Peter Garnsey (1999, 84) notes that in some classical societies, horses were not eaten because "they are so close to man they become quasi-human." Though the animated film *Waltz with Bashir* (2008) depends on this same theme for a dramatic release of repressed horror during the 1982 Israel-Lebanon war, the narration states, "[One particular soldier] saw a huge number of carcasses . . . of slaughtered Arabian horses. 'It broke my heart,' he said. 'What had those horses done . . . to deserve such suffering?' He couldn't handle seeing those dead and wounded horses. He had used a mechanism to remain outside events . . . as if watching the war on film instead of participating. This protected him. Once pulled into the events he could no longer deny reality. Horror surrounded him and he freaked out."

4　Jacqueline Goldsby's (2006) book *A Spectacular Secret* contextualizes Topsy's death as an attempted lynching, in which the racist and persecutory logic of the American South was extended to include an anthropomorphized elephant, noting that the creature's name was "no doubt named after the unruly black girl-child of Harriet Beecher Stowe's *Uncle Tom's Cabin*" (225). Goldsby's account differs from some others' accounts, stating that the original plan was called off because Topsy was too heavy for the wooden scaffolding.

5　The first Society for Prevention of Cruelty to Animals was founded in coffee shop in London in 1824. Tellingly, in more recent times, "when the Society for the Prevention of Cruelty to Animals asked the Pope for his support, he refused it, on the ground that human beings owe no duty to lower animals, and that ill-treating animals is not sinful. This is because animals have no soul" (Bertrand Russell, as quoted in Marcuse 2002, 242).

6　For a sophisticated treatment of early cinema's strategies for coping with the "embarrassment of contingency" as well as its "orchestration of guilt and punishment," see May Ann Doane's (1997) piece "Screening Time." This essay also includes a sustained discussion of *Electrocution of an Elephant*.

7　Freud writes, "Children who distinguish themselves by special cruelty towards animals and playmates usually give rise to a just suspicion of an intense and precocious sexual activity arising from erotogenic zones" (quoted in Bersani 1986, 36).

8   A representative place to start for this coalescing field is Stanley Cavell et al. (2008).

9   The Universal Declaration of Animal Rights comprised ten articles made public in 1989 by the International League of Animal Rights (see Derrida 2008, 87, 169–70). The execution of Topsy would not have been tolerated by this declaration as number 4 of Article 5 reads, "Exhibitions, shows, and films involving animals must also respect their dignity and must not include any violence whatsoever." But Derrida asks, "Must we pose the question of our relations with [animals] . . . in terms of 'rights'?" (88).

10   The only other aspect of the test shown in the film is the instruction to "describe in single words only the good things that come into your mind about your mother"—which, of course, sends the subject into a homicidal rage.

11   Ursula K. Heise's (2003) essay "From Extinction to Electronics: Dead Frogs, Live Dinosaurs, and Electric Sheep" conducts an astute reading of the latent humanist thrust of the book, as opposed to the more ambivalent ontological suspensions of the movie. She also notes how much of a more significant role animals—both organic and electric—play in Dick's universe rather than in Scott's.

12   Swimming, as is his wont, against the current of common wisdom, Nietzsche finds the origins of "justice" in the animal kingdom and not in the world of men. "The beginnings of justice, as of prudence, moderation, bravery—in short, of all that we designate as the *Socratic virtues*—are *animal*: a consequence of that drive which teaches us to seek food and elude enemies. Now if we consider that even the highest human being has only become more elevated and subtle in the nature of his food and in his conception of what is inimical to him, it is not improper to describe the entire phenomenon of morality as animal" (quoted in Gray 2007, 111).

13   The expression *kangaroo court* derives not from Australia but from California in the mid-nineteenth century, most probably because of the way in which proceedings leapt from one fixed stage to the next.

14   For Baudrillard, humanity is "haunted" by its Others: madmen, criminals, children, animals, etc.

15   The year 1980 was clearly a nadir for animals in cinema.

16   The exact quote from Bentham (1907) is as follows: "What else is it that should trace the insuperable line? Is it the faculty of reason, or, perhaps, the faculty of discourse? But a full-grown horse or dog is

beyond comparison a more rational, as well as more conversable animal, than an infant of a day, or a week, or even a month, old. But suppose the case were otherwise, what would it avail? the question is not, Can they *reason?*, nor, Can they *talk?* but, Can they *suffer?*" (311).

17   As I write, the *New York Times* hilariously, tautologically, and rather embarrassingly published an article (Parker-Pope 2008) announcing the scientific discovery—allegedly confirmed by neurological imaging—that bullies enjoy bullying.

18   Entertainment, medicine, and profit were similarly inscribed into the fleshy folds of Joseph Merrick (aka the Elephant Man) two decades earlier.

19   The well-known Lacanian Jacques-Alain Miller (2009, n.p.) goes so far as to claim that Eve "had rivals" in the form of Edenic animals, especially in the time period before her sacred fashioning from Adam's rib. "For [medieval rabbi] Rashi it means that Adam, our common human father, had sexual intercourse with animals, domesticated and wild, but was not satisfied with those relationships. He did not know they were *contra natura*. There is no reason to believe that the coupling of Adam with the animals was *contra natura* before the appearance of Eve."

20   Derrida (2008, 55) actually conflates Western and Middle Eastern attitudes toward the animal by referring to the Greco-Judeo-Christiano-Islamic tradition.

21   Again, anticipating the theme of interspecies sexual congress, the mule laments the crudity of those human masters who feel it necessary to curse their animal by yelling out to anyone who might listen, "This ass' prick up the ass of the dealer's wife!" (Ikhwān al-Ṣafāʾ 1978, 62).

22   On the political ontology of this kind of nesting motif, see Louis Dumont's (1974) *Homo Hierarchicus: The Caste System and Its Implications.*

23   Later in the trial, the parrot backs up this point made by the bee, protesting that humans are not the only artisans or possessors of a craft: "Bees are swarming creatures, but they make homes and hamlets more cunningly and more skillfully than do your artisans, builders and architects . . . not needing any compass . . . any plumb line to let down or any builder's angle against which to gauge their corners" (Ikhwān al-Ṣafāʾ 1978, 171).

24   Or, if you prefer, from Caliban to the Taliban.

25   The Brown Dog Affair is considered one of the earliest watershed moments for modern animal rights and was sparked when female Swedish activists stormed the University of London's medical lectures to protest

the dissection and vivisection of animals (most notably a brown terrier that sparked the initial occupation). Battles and even riots between protestors and medical students raged for seven years and centered around a memorial statue to the dog in Battersea. For more information, see Peter Mason's (1997) *The Brown Dog Affair* as well as Richard Ryder's (2000) *Animal Revolution: Changing Attitudes toward Speciesism.*

26   That this case took place in Freud's hometown is something of an added bonus, given the responsibility to redefine the tenets of human nature.

27   See "In Austria, Hiasl, the Chimpanzee, Has Been Denied a Legal Guardian," April 28, 2007, http://primatology.net/2007/04/28/in-austria-hiasl-the-chimpanzee-denied-legal-guardian/.

28   It must be noted, however, that there is a sinister side to the granting of such rights, should they be increasingly extended to animals over time under the current ideological conditions. As Laura Hudson (2008, 99) warns, "the increase in animal legislation may be less a cause for celebration of our increased enlightenment than an omen of things to come: *the inclusion of animals in the political realm marks the extent to which human beings have themselves been reduced to bare life.*"

29   Steiner (2005, 57) notes that Aristotle's remarks on animals are very different in his biological works, such as the *History of Animals* and *Parts of Animals,* than in his more metaphysical and ethical texts, implying capacities, such as belief, in the former but denying them in the latter.

30   Perhaps we should burn less mental wattage on dilemmas such as whom to kill or torture—as moral analytic philosophers seem to love to do—than on examining the intellectual *jouissance* that underwrites such activities in the first place, since philosophers clearly get some kind of kick out of putting their fellow creatures in mortal peril and moral mercy.

31   In "What Is Man?" Mark Twain (1919, 84) writes, "It is just like man's vanity and impertinence to call an animal dumb because it is dumb to his dull perceptions."

32   There is an irony here in that this "obligation" to recognize the nonhuman Other via ethical projection into its virtual subjecthood is itself anthropocentric, assuming—as it does—that we are the only ones capable of doing so.

33   While Esther Perel's (2007) book *Mating in Captivity: Unlocking Erotic Intelligence* sounds like it is taking a refreshingly nonanthropocentric approach to domestic issues, it unfortunately does not really treat married couples as if they were pandas.

34   In his book *On Creaturely Life,* Eric Santner (2006) makes particular note of "Freud's crucial distinction between animal and human sexuality, between *instinct* and *drive.*" He goes on to say that "one of Freud's great insights was that human sexuality, precisely that dimension of human life where we seem to be utterly reduced to animality, is actually the point at which our difference from animals is in some ways most radical" (30–31). In chapter 4, we shall see a slightly different use of *drive,* when Bernard Stiegler contrasts this still somewhat *inhuman* notion with the more ontologically advanced *libido.*

35   Prior to his death, Pinyan kept a plaster cast of this horse's penis in his office.

36   This disturbing footage also comprises the structuring absence of the narrative, in parallel with Timothy Treadwell's last screams, captured on audiotape. The voyeuristic compression of repulsion–fascination, elicited by any such extreme artifact, is displaced in this case—as with Herzog—onto diegetic surrogates for the audience: people who take on the burden of watching, or listening to, the horror of the trace. So we see H.'s boss (a member of the National Horse Association), along with his wife, weeping stoically as they watch their beloved horse in an inadvertent snuff-porn film, just as Herzog himself endures the terrified shouts of Treadwell before instructing the latter's friend never to do as he just did. One should be careful not to stare such violent, primal deaths in the face, these films suggest. And yet they tease the audience with the scopophilia encouraged by the medium itself, by *showing* that which they refuse to show (as Hitchcock and Powell did with such sadistic virtuosity in the classical cinematic mode).

37   The specific examples being the Greek myth of Leda and the Swan; the sculpture of a man engaging in sexual congress with a horse on the wall of a Hindu temple in Khajuraho devoted to the deity Lakshmana; *The Dream of the Fisherman's Wife,* an 1820 Hokusai woodcut depicting a woman's erotic–oneiric encounter with two tenticular creatures; Comte de Lautréamont's (1994) *Maldoror,* in which a man has frenetic frottage with a shark; and more recently, the collected grassroots female erotica edited by Nancy Friday, which sometimes involves bears and other wild animals. Peter Shaffer's play *Equus* is also notable in this context.

38   See *Marie-Claire UK,* June 2001. That this is the most authoritative source, despite being plastered over countless blogs, should mean we digest such information with a good deal more than a grain of salt. However, its memetic reach alone is significant in terms of human squeamishness

toward interspecies sex and the ways in which both race and gender complicate the transgression.

39 While all the voice-overs are those of the actual participants, H. and the Happy Horseman are played by actors, for the sake of anonymity.

40 In her study of Victorian treatments for hysteria, *The Technology of Orgasm,* Rachel P. Maines (1998, 8) writes, "When the patient was single, a widow, unhappily married, or a nun, the cure was effected by [among other things] vigorous horseback exercise." Horseback riding was thus one of those accepted forms of "social camouflage" for the release of female orgasm, considered potentially pathological if left uncoaxed and unexperienced—much like the gym is today.

41 Or more accurately, *kenotype,* meaning a relatively recent recognizable character set.

42 Perhaps it is this scene that disqualifies director Robinson Devor from citing the usual disclaimer at the end of the movie: "No animals were harmed in the making of this motion picture."

43 For any potential readers from the far-flung future, in which distinctions between animals, machines, and humans have dissolved, let it be known that the Fox Network was a channel for the latter category, not foxes per se.

44 During this voice-over, at the point of the hyphen, there is some obvious sound editing. Only the filmmakers know what was cut to make this comment as stark and confronting as it is.

45 Her push was successful, now making bestiality in Washington State a class C felony, meaning up to ten years in prison. The film tells us that one man has already been prosecuted under this law when photos of him sodomizing the family dog were found on his wife's cell phone.

46 Current trends in ethology tend to view animal sexual behavior as opportunistic or "promiscuous" rather than simply as instinctually hardwired (or, conversely, *so* hardwired as to create unexpected strategies and couplings). For one recent example, see Matt Walker's (2008) piece for *BBC News Online,* "'Sex Pest' Seal Attacks Penguin." For an inventory of such stories, see the same author's book, *Fish That Fake Orgasms: And Other Zoological Curiosities* (Walker 2007). It is also worth mentioning Isabella Rossellini's rather unique educational television show, *Green Porno* (2008), in which the venerable actress rather fearlessly impersonates insects and other critters to reenact their intriguing sex lives. One wonders, however, if this is a cultural symptom of a significant anti- or posthuman project, or if it is merely the cross-species version

of blackface: a "playing" at/of the Other, a simultaneous exoticization and domestication of alterity.

47   I am particularly struck by the pronoun *what* rather than *who* here, pertaining to the ahuman immortality of such historical figures in their works. Keats is well known for his attempts to transcend his individual mortality as the "chameleon poet" (of which some more later). And Tolstoy (2006, 182), writing on the subject of human commerce with horses in *Anna Karenina*, describes Vronsky admiring his ride, Frou-Frou: "In her whole figure and especially in her head there was a distinctly energetic and at the same time tender expression. She was one of those animals who, it seems, do not talk only because the mechanism of their mouths does not permit it." (This is an interesting intertext with the theme song for the television show *Mister Ed*: "A horse is a horse, of course, of course, / And no one can talk to a horse of course, / That is, of course, unless the horse is the famous Mister Ed.")

48   The same cannot be said of Walerian Borowczyk's exploitational fairy tale *The Beast* (1975), which begins with a mercilessly lingering shot of a pulsating mare's vagina: possibly the most confronting "opening" in the history of cinema and one that sent a high percentage of the Hampstead Cinema, in which I saw it, scurrying for the exits. (For a more subtle but no less eroticized depiction of such "horseplay," see Gustav Machatý's *Ecstasy* [1933], the same film that gained Hedy Lamarr fame and notoriety for the first simulated orgasm on screen.) Borowczyk returned to this theme a few years later in *Immoral Women* (1979), in the vignette about a young woman's amorous relationship with her pet rabbit. However, for arguably the most elliptical, poetic, and metaphysically haunting portrait of a woman's sexual relationship with an animal, it is necessary to turn to literature (perhaps due to the different register of mind's eye, as opposed to actual eye). See Robert Musil's (1999b) "The Temptations of Quiet Veronica."

49   The preference of primates for blonde human females has become over the years something of a pseudoscientific truism. Nevertheless, it is sometimes reflected in actual cases. See Charles Siebert Scribner's (2009, 153) *The Wauchula Woods Accord: Toward a New Understanding of Animals.*

50   One subculture that flirts with this sexual form of becoming-animal is "the furries": mostly young urbanites who like to dress up as animals or monsters for erotic purposes and who have also been known to arrange "human petting zoos" in various underground venues. I cannot help

thinking that this may be the aftershocks of Jim Henson's contribution to popular culture, as we see a generation weaned on *Sesame Street* and *The Muppets* acting out their fetishes and complexes in an age when TV shows are as likely to be the target of displacement and cathexis as the more traditional Freudian domestic stage props. See, in particular, Marianne Shaneen's documentary film *American Furry* (2009), whose tagline is "life, liberty, and the fursuit of happiness." Along somewhat similar lines, see also Hugh Raffles's (2010) remarkable exploration of "crush freaks"—men who sexually identify with bugs or worms being crushed by theatrical femme fatales—in his book *Insectopedia*. Here Freud is subtextually supplemented with Kafka, Bataille, Masoch, Mulvey, and Caillois.

51 We might pause for a moment, however, to face the unpleasant fact that humans have sometimes been the greater victim, as was the case in Rome's blood-spattered Colosseum. Martial's (1993) *Book of Spectacles,* written in A.D. 80 for Emperor Titus, tells of the reenactment of exulted myths, such as Pasiphaë and the Bull, for popular entertainment. As historians Marguerite Johnson and Terry Ryan (2005, 151) write, "a woman, presumably a slave or a criminal, was joined to a real bull before the massive crowd in attendance." A possibly apocryphal paper titled "Prehistory of Bestiality," by an author by the name of Masters, notes that "a surprising range of creatures was used for such purposes—bulls, giraffes, leopards, cheetahs, wild boar, zebras, stallions, jackasses, huge dogs, apes, etc." (Wikipedia).

52 Newkirk also states, "If you French kiss your dog and he or she thinks it's great, is it wrong? We believe all exploitation and abuse is wrong. If it isn't exploitation and abuse, it may not be wrong" (quoted in Donnan and Magowan 2009, 105). On a related note, a survey conducted by the Times Square Alliance in 2007 revealed that "more people will kiss their pet at midnight [on New Year's Eve] than will kiss a friend" (Harper 2008).

53 We can only be grateful that Haraway will not suffer the fate of Amy, the protagonist of Bob Goldthwait's indie film *Stay* (aka *Sleeping Dogs*; 2006), which tells the pathetic story of a young, bored, and lonely college woman who, in a moment of curious "petophilia," drunkenly performs oral sex on her dog. Amy's ill-advised decision, several years later, to tell of this encounter to her new boyfriend leads to revulsion and rejection as well as an abject lesson in the benefits of letting sleeping dogs lie. There is no reason, however, to assume that Haraway's relationship to

her "Klingon warrior princess" goes beyond light petting. And even if it did, her circle of friends and fellow dog lovers seem to be far more accepting of the physical intimacies that can occur when species meet than are Amy's.

54   Lacan states that "love . . . never makes any one go out of himself" (quoted in Bersani and Phillips 2008, 74). Love is thus equated with "narcissistic extravagance" (76). Later in the same book, Bersani and Phillips write, "To love what is other is to love what cannot be loved; it is like being force fed" (101). Though this statement seems rather blunt, and even obnoxious, taken out of context—i.e., stripped of the extremely sophisticated psychoanalytic logic leading up to it—it warrants serious consideration. However, I still find this conclusion too remote from Haraway's polar opposite interpretation of love. Thus I attempt to stake my own middle ground in more detail, a little further into the chapter.

55   Haraway is relying on Isabelle Stengers's definition of this term, but one wonders to what degree it is haunted by Kant's cosmopolitanism, "in which human beings stand alone among earthly beings as capable of perfecting their natures and achieving the status of 'lord[s] of nature'" (Steiner 2005, 1).

56   Haraway sidesteps this objection by stating that she loves not only the individual Cayenne but entire kinds such as the red merle Australian shepherd. However, her chapter on woman–dog sport agility displays the same kind of sulkiness and ecstasy that accompanies common garden love, so perhaps her worldliness comes and goes and can be replaced by falling back to earth.

57   A wonderful, subtle moment of "cognitive dissonance"—prompted by the exceptional objects that challenge our criteria for automated classification—comes in Pixar's WALL-E. The eponymous, detritus-collecting robot hesitates between his separated collection of spoons and forks when wishing to add a spork to his collection. His compromise is to place it between the two, thereby recognizing a new type of cutlery-based being.

58   If we use the Oxford English Dictionary definition of dogmatic to mean "proceeding upon a priori principles accepted as true, instead of being founded upon experience or induction," then Haraway is not a dogmatic thinker. Then again, if we choose the definition "of assured opinion, convinced," then perhaps she is.

59 Phie Ambo's fascinating documentary *Mechanical Love* (2007) intro-
    duces us to an old woman in a care facility who is given a robotic seal
    for companionship and comfort. The woman is delighted, and they are
    soon inseparable, much to the disgust of some of the other residents,
    who suggest she has succumbed to senility. However, the woman's
    comments make it clear that she understands that the animal is not
    "real" but that this trivial technicality makes no difference at all to
    her affection for it and attachment to it. Indeed, the robo-seal is utterly
    "schön."

60 Haraway (2008, 330) notes, "I use the term critter to mean a motley
    crowd of lively beings including microbes, fungi, humans, plants, ani-
    mals, cyborgs, and aliens," as opposed to taxonomically neat *creature,*
    with its theological undertones.

61 Haraway (2008, 73) writes, "My suspicion is that we might nurture re-
    sponsibility with and for other animals better by plumbing the category
    of labor more than the category of rights, with its inevitable preoccupa-
    tion with similarity, analogy, calculation, and honorary membership in
    the expanded abstraction of the Human."

62 See Steve Baker's (2000, 184, 203) *The Postmodern Animal.*

63 *When Species Meet* (Haraway 2008, 17) provides the timely reminder that
    the "Latin *specere* links to the issue of the gaze, and the ocular will-to-
    mastery, with its tones of 'to look' and 'to behold'." The Linnean legacy
    is very much a scopophilic phenomenon, based on visual elements of
    morphology, as is the anthropological submachine that he invented to
    plug into the existing conceptual contraption (a moment equivalent to
    Gutenberg's invention of the printing press, based as it was on modified
    weaving looms). As we saw in the previous chapter, Linneaus was a com-
    plex case, for on one hand, he is the father of modern taxonomy, which
    insists that "there is a place for everything, and everything in its place."
    Yet on the other, he refused to grant *Homo sapiens* a privileged throne
    on which to perch. And yet, as Bourdieu famously states, classification
    classifies the classifier, or, as Goodman puts it, "the argument that no
    one species represents the head of the food chain but that all depend
    on one another was used by Linnaeus to show that the interdependence
    of all living things is far more symmetrical a system than it may appear
    when viewed from the anthropocentric perspective of human ends and
    intentions" (Ikhwān al-Ṣafā' 1978, 17).

64 See the work of 1930s Soviet psychologist Lev Vygotsky, who wrote that

"the child's and the adult's words coincide in their referents but not in their meanings" (quoted in Steiner 2005, 30).

65   Derrida (2008, 26) writes, "Everybody knows what terrifying and intolerable pictures a realist painting could give to the industrial, mechanical, chemical, hormonal, and genetic violence to which man has been submitting animal life for the past two centuries." Two initial questions spring to mind here: first, to what degree is the violence done to humans by humans an extension of this broadly biopolitical scandal, or an exception to it? And second, why does Derrida use the rhetorical device here of a realist painting rather than the (theoretically) direct knowledge of unrepresented experience (as if a painting of an abattoir by necessity has the same moral freight or impact as a *visit* to an abattoir)? Anticipating the grander claims of the present book, it seems that the technology of depiction—at one remove, as it were, from what it attempts to depict—is an important component of the anthropological machine, which itself created the biopolitical conditions of modernity and beyond.

66   For Haraway, *autremondialization* essentially means a hitherto untried alternative to collective modes of worlding—a concept she borrows from Isabelle Stengers.

67   No mention either of Clarissa Pinkola Estés's (1992) feminist kitsch classic *Women Who Run with the Wolves,* nor of http://www.marryyourpet.com/.

68   Lacan believes that animals cannot "pretend to pretend": "Nor does an animal cover up its tracks which would be tantamount to making itself the subject of the signifier" (quoted in Derrida 2008, 129–30). See Derrida's critique of this formula in "And Say the Animal Responded: To Jacques Lacan," in *The Animal That Therefore I Am* (Derrida 2008).

69   *Delicious* is a loaded word here, given the omnipresent shackle of the food chain.

70   Which is not to say that there is no romanticization going on within these pages at all. Wherever there is enthusiasm, I would venture, there is such a legacy. (Indeed, one wonders if the human could function in an atmosphere entirely purged of the romantic gesture, not in terms of a flower or a sonnet, necessarily, but in the sense of finding meaning or hope in the forsaken or unsalvagable. Alas, pursuing this topic would require another book.) Baker, however, could be cast as the J. G. Ballard of the countryside, romanticizing desolation in a style stripped of traditionally romantic trappings.

71   *Entertain,* from the Old French *entretenir,* "to be held mutually; to

hold intertwined." Flipping to the other side of the coin, the threat of boredom is also important here, for Baker (2005, 109) notes, "You can almost feel the boredom of a hawk that has bathed and preened and is neither hungry nor sleepy. It seems to lounge about, stirring up trouble, just for the sake of something to do." This is in stark contrast to Agamben (2004, 63–70), who follows Heidegger in reserving boredom as a uniquely human curse and/or privilege. (As Goethe [1998, 120] himself once noted, "if monkeys could reach the point of being bored, they could turn into human beings.") That is to say, for Agamben, boredom is "the metaphysical operator in which the passage from poverty in world to world, from animal environment to human world, is realized." For Agamben, "at issue here is nothing less than anthropogenesis" (68). One suspects that the philosopher would thus accuse the bird-watcher of anthropomorphism: projecting his own boredom onto the peregrine. If Baker is right, however, and animals *are* capable of boredom (as the Dog Whisperer—and countless zookeepers—will no doubt also attest), then Heidegger's ontological hierarchy is not so clear-cut.

72 For a discussion of the assumed differences between (human) language and (animal) codes, see Derrida (2008, 123ff.).

73 Which, according to the etymology of project, is to "throw forth" or "cast away." The question of "animal art"—for instance, the painting elephants of the Asian Elephant Art and Conservation Project (http://www.elephantart.com/)—draws attention to the anthropological stakes lodged deep within the concept of a "project," in the humanistic heroic mode of devising or designing the future, or *for* the future. But as the etymology provocatively suggests, a human sense of linear time need not be the condition for a project but merely a type of action (which may or may not be deemed "aesthetic"). See also Amir Bar-Lev's documentary film *My Kid Could Paint That* (2007), which deals with such questions as tested by the liminal case of childhood, implicitly framed as that suspended state between animality and full human consciousness.

74 *Twitcher* is British slang for "bird-watcher." I use the term *whatever* here in Agamben's sense of whatever-being, as sketched in *The Coming Community* (Agamben 1993) and as I *détourn* in *Love and Other Technologies* (Pettman 2006). The primary notion here is of a being blessed with no essential identity—an ornithologist without qualities, as it were.

75 Baker (2000, 73) continues, "All morning, birds were huddled together in fear of the hawk, but I could not find him again. If I too were afraid I am sure I should see him more often. Fear releases power. Man might be more

tolerable, less fractious and smug, if he had more to fear. I do not mean fear of the intangible, the suffocation of the introvert, but physical fear, cold sweating fear for one's life, fear of the unseen menacing beast, imminent, bristly, tusked and terrible, ravening for one's own hot saline blood."

76 This descriptive phrase is lifted from Jacques Khalip, who is drawing on the famous passage from Keats's letters that reads, "As to the Poetical Character itself, (I mean that sort of which, if I am any thing, I am a Member; that sort distinguished from the wordsworthian or egotistical sublime; which is a thing per se and stands alone) it is not itself—it has no self—it is every thing and nothing—It has no character.... A Poet is the most unpoetical of any thing in existence; because he has no Identity—he is continually in for—and filling some other Body—The Sun, the Moon, the Sea and Men and Women who are creatures of impulse are poetical and have about them an unchangeable attribute—the poet has none; no identity—he is certainly the most unpoetical of all God's Creatures" (Keats and Rollins 1958, 1:386–87).

77 A cinematic companion to Baker's book is Jacques Perrin's *Winged Migration (Le peuple migrateur),* a documentary film that uses pioneering camera techniques to teleport the viewer inside the flocks of dozens of different birds as they fly around the globe. It is an extremely effective instance of technologically enabled subjective projection, as the spectator vicariously experiences the gravity-defying thrill of flight. The director, however, like Baker, does not sentimentalize, including several graphic scenes of birds meeting their demise at the hands of predators such as other birds or humans. Even more disturbing, however, is the 1970s Tolkien folk music that keeps inexplicably intruding into the sound track.

78 An elegant inversion of Heidegger's claim that "animal behavior is encircled by a disinhibiting ring" (quoted in Derrida 2008, 176).

79 Baker (2000, 171) is not so entranced by the hawk that he neglects to notice other creatures: "It is a good life, a seal's, here in these shallow waters. Like the lives of so many air and water creatures, it seems a better one than ours. We have no element. Nothing sustains us when we fall." The observation that "we have no element" is a direct echo of the animals stating their case in Ikhwān's fable.

80 Steve Baker (2000, 121) reminds us of a crucial clarification when it comes to Deleuze and Guattari's "becoming-animal" to avoid a common misreading of the concept: "Becoming is not, therefore, a matter of moving from one distinct state into another, from a point of origin to a point of arrival, both of which must have their independent realities."

Or in their own words, "the becoming-animal of the human being is real, even if the animal the human being becomes is not. . . . This is the point to clarify: that a becoming lacks a subject distinct from itself" (Deleuze and Guattari 1987, 238).

81 See Emmanuel Levinas (1990), "The Name of a Dog, or Natural Rights."

82 As fate would have it, I myself recently experienced "this strange bondage of the eyes" with an eagle, while walking to the gym on the Lower East Side of Manhattan. No doubt, it was the dawn prospect of rodents that summoned such a surprising creature to an environment that hosts little other than humans, rats, pigeons, and cockroaches. In any case, it was an enchanted moment for a city dweller like myself, but I would be hard-pressed to render it in words as evocative as Baker's.

83 It is possible, from Baker's (2000) perspective, to consider the peregrine as an "ideogram" in Roger Caillois's (2003) sense since it is something that contains "objective lyrical value" (79), thus making it capable of two important interventions: (1) acting directly on the emotions and (2) revealing "the systematic overdetermination of the universe" (76). For Caillois, it is "preferable" to seek the origin of psychoanalytic complexes (oedipal desires, castration anxiety, etc.) "in comparative biology, rather than in the human mind alone" (81). That is to say, any given neurosis or phobia or philia should be viewed in a larger context than human psychology. For instance, the brutal poetics of the praying mantis affects men not because they are prone to castration anxiety; rather men suffer castration anxiety because they are afraid of being eaten. Baker's book conducts his own form of ethnographic experiment in comparative biology, whereby the ideogram of the peregrine incites "passional virtualities" (80) and "lyrical force" (69) as well as imaginative synthesis. Such phrases are utilized by Caillois to describe a profound, yet ultimately immanent, cosmic–mimetic machine, itself producing emotional clusters and correspondences (81).

84 For Derrida (2008, 7), "thinking concerning the animal, if there is such a thing, derives from poetry."

85 In the introduction to the *New York Review of Books* edition, Robert Macfarlane (2005) states, "As an account of a human obsession with a creature, it is peerless." I'm inclined to agree, with the possible exception of Nabokov's *Lolita* (which itself is said to have been inspired by the news report of an ape that was given the means of artistic expression, only to draw the bars of his own cage; see *The Annotated Lolita* [Nabokov and Appel 1991, 432]).

86   Baker (2005, 118) observes, "They were sea falcons now; there was nothing to keep them to the land. Foul poison burned within them like a burrowing fuse. Their life was lonely death, and would not be renewed. All they could do was take their glory to the sky. They were the last of their race."

87   All Bersani quotes in this section are from *Intimacies* (Bersani and Phillips 2008), unless indicated otherwise.

88   In *Forget Foucault,* Baudrillard (1987, 97) writes, "Women, children, animals—we must not be afraid of assimilations [!]—do not just have a subject consciousness, they have a kind of objective ironic presentiment that the category into which they have been placed does not exist. Which allows them at any given moment to make use of a double strategy. It isn't psychology, it's strategy."

89   Freud's original term, *das Es,* is more accurately translated as "it" than Strachey's now-established "id."

90   In his earlier book, *The Freudian Body,* Bersani (1986, 29–30) writes, "Sex is, in a sense, nothing more than the strategic implementation of a more fundamental effort to control the definition of the human itself." Furthermore, "human sexuality, as distinct from those experiences of bodily contacts which we share with animals, is a kind of *functional aberration of the species*" (40; emphasis added).

91   In his book *Profanations,* Agamben (2007) gives a name to the impersonal element: "Genius," the name used by the Latinate ancients for the god who becomes each man's guardian at the moment of birth. Thereafter, and into our own time, "each person's character is engendered by the way he attempts to turn away from Genius, to flee from him" (17). In an observation that took my breath away when I first read it, Agamben writes, "that is why when we love someone we actually love neither his genius nor his character (and even less his ego) but his special manner of evading both of these poles, his rapid back-and-forth" (Agamben 2007, 17). Look no further for the reason why it is possible to love someone we do not actually like.

92   Elsewhere I have answered similar questions with Agamben's phrase *inessential commonality.*

93   For a sustained exploration of these themes, see the forthcoming book from Alphonso Lingis, *Violence and Splendor.*

94   Saint Thomas Aquinas believes animals to be "*non agunt sed magis aguntur*—they do not act, but are instead acted upon" (quoted in Steiner 2005, 27). Werner Herzog again provides us with an interesting case, this

time in *Encounters at the End of the World* (2007), in which a seemingly deranged penguin appears to reject his instinctual fate of moving between the Antarctic ocean's feeding grounds and the designated breeding grounds. Instead, he "chooses" to wander toward the icy peaks, directly perpendicular to nature's path, and toward "certain death." Moreover, who among us humans can say with a straight face that he or she is not "acted upon" leading up to and/or during the sex act itself?

95   "Christian" is an ironic name for a lion, given the Roman history between this religious sect and the great cats. In any case, it is interesting to note that a proverbial precursor to this tale of interspecies respect appears in the eighteenth-century writings of de la Mettrie (1996): "History offers us a famous example of a lion which would not devour a man abandoned to its fury, because it recognized him as its benefactor" (quoted in Mazlish 1993, 28). For a full account of the more recent version of the story, see Anthony Bourke and John Rendall's (2009) *A Lion Called Christian*.

96   Odysseus's dog Argus wags his tail in recognition of his former master, despite many years passing in the interim. Because Odysseus is trying to conceal his identity, he cannot reciprocate but instead sheds a silent tear of gratitude and love.

97   Of course, Siegfried and Roy did not get away with such a happy ending. One of the more entertaining burlesque shows I have seen reenacted this infamous Las Vegas attack, humorously homoeroticizing the violent encounter between man and beast.

98   Underlining this point, Haraway (2008, 206) reminds us that human exceptionalism has always relied on the conceit that "to be animal is exactly not to be human and vice versa."

3. AFTER THE BEEP

1   E.g., Peter Singer argues that it is more ethical to experiment "on low-functioning ('marginal') humans than on high-functioning nonhumans such as apes" (Steiner 2005, 7). One wonders, however, what scale is being used to measure different levels of function. The suspicion is, as usual, that Man is the *metron*. For her part, Donna Haraway is not as antiexperimentation as one might presume and performs a very delicate balancing act between her belief in the need to harvest scientific knowledge and the right of animals to avoid being subjected to unnecessary pain. See "Sharing Suffering: Instrumental Relations between Laboratory Animals and Their People," in *When Species Meet* (Haraway 2008).

2   La Mettrie is credited with prying the soul from the Man-machine in the eighteenth century, thereby ushering in an unprecedented form of materialism to the question of the human. And yet this author still viewed his own species as superior because of its being the most perfect incarnation of the one type of organization in the universe: "He is to the ape, and to the most intelligent animals, as the planetary pendulum of Huyghens is to a watch of Julien Leroy" (i.e., more instruments, more springs, more wheels) (quoted in Mazlish 1993, 29). This is the "double gesture" in full effect, whereby a black eye to humanity is twisted into the sign of a hero. Similarly, in Descartes's eyes, "human error" is proof of our species's agency and free will. As Bruce Mazlish explains, human superiority is "saved in a most paradoxical fashion: according to Descartes, Man is a machine that, unlike the animals, has reason (or soul), and can therefore err. . . . It is as if, denying Man the perfection of the animal-machine on one level, he wished to endow him with this 'inhuman condition' on another, higher level" (20). Indeed, in his private notebooks, Descartes wrote, "From the very perfection of animal actions we suspect that they do not have free will" (quoted in Mazlish 1993, 20–21)—once again, the double gesture.

3   For Scarry (1985), pain is the limit threshold of human language and communication. This inexpressibility, however, and loss of world can be recovered posttrauma through modes of creativity.

4   Mme. de Sévigné, in 1672, two decades after Descartes's death, wrote, "Regarding machines that love, machines that have an affinity for someone, machines that are jealous, machines that fear! Come on, come on, you're making fun; Descartes never intended to make us believe so" (quoted in Mazlish 1993, 25). Another critic of the venerable philosopher—taken aback by his conflation of animals and clocks—asked rhetorically, "But do we caress our watches?" (quoted in Mazlish 1993, 22). In the age of Rolex and iPhone fetishism, the answer can no longer be presumed to be in the negative.

5   The strong possibility that Descartes was devoted to a custom-made automaton doll of his deceased daughter Francine certainly raises the specter of an intriguing disjuncture between his public philosophy and his private comportment toward the nonhuman. Unfortunately, without the benefit of a time machine, we can only speculate whether he attributed a soul to this mechanical doppelgänger of his flesh-and-blood or whether she was elevated to the status of a real girl.

6   Descartes acknowledges the capacity to communicate between birds and

insects, for example, but he believes this to be—in Derrida's words—"a language that doesn't *respond* because it is fixed or stuck in the mechanicity of its programming, and finally lack, defect, deficit, or deprivation" (Derrida 2008, 87; emphasis added). Regarding the preceding example of the spouse-as-answering-machine, Derrida goes on to make an important observation concerning "the question of how an iterability that is essential to every response, and to the ideality of every response, can and cannot fail to introduce nonresponse, automatic reaction, mechanical reaction into the most alive, most 'authentic,' and most responsible response" (112).

7   Far closer in both time and geography—and lurking in the foreground of Spielberg's sadistic spectacle—are the lynchings that took place in the United States, especially those that were committed under the auspices of entertainment. One such example was the murder of Will Porter, who was hung by an entrepreneurial mob in the Opera House of Livermore, Kentucky, in spring 1911. White locals bought tickets for the opportunity to shoot at the swinging body from the orchestra seats (Goldsby 2006, 227).

8   In his blurb featured on the back cover of the *New York Review of Books* version of Carlo Collodi's (2008) *Pinocchio,* Benedetto Croce writes, "The wood from which Pinocchio is carved is humanity itself." Such a narcissistic view of a tale that so profoundly troubles the ontology of this category of supreme convenience is a knee-jerk one, no less a thoughtless reflex for originating in the brain. Giorgio Agamben (2007, 31), more sensitive to the ways in which the fabulistic in particular, and writing more generally, troubles the literary critic's comfortable criteria of "humanity," writes that Collodi's Pinocchio embodies the "eternal archetype of . . . the *grace of the inhuman.*"

9   The cyborg's self-sacrifice at the end of *Terminator 2* (1991) is staged for maximum audience concern for machinic mortality, as is the operatic finale of *Blade Runner* (1982). See also the uncannily disturbing viral videos of the children's toy Tickle Me Elmo laughing hysterically while writhing on the ground in flames. As journalist Daniel Roth (2009) has noted, perhaps the time has come for humans to think about *their own* moral obligations in response to Asimov's self-serving Laws of Robotics.

10   As witnessed by the utterly depressing Fox reality show (if that's not too redundant) *When Good Times Go Bad.*

11   Derrida was not the first philosopher to become entranced by his cat. For Martin Buber (1996, 145) in *I and Thou,* e.g., the eyes of his house cat express a certain "I-less self-reference that we lack."

244 NOTES TO CHAPTER 3

12 A gesture offstage to Foucault, who did the most to promote the notion of biopolitics as a regime of knowledge, classification, and action that simultaneously frees the subject, indeed *creates* the subject as we know her today, via a series of interlocking and horizontally repressive mechanisms. See esp. *Discipline and Punish* (Foucault 1995).

13 In his lush coffee-table book *Creatures,* photographer Andrew Zuckerman (2007) creates a series of hyperrealistic portraits of animals on a stark white background. In the epilogue, he writes, "The images you see in this book are the product of a journey of discovery and of learning how to connect with the soul and essence of all creatures. In animals, as in humans, the eye connects the creature to the outside world and centers our focus to see deeper into the heart and very nature of the creature. The goal of these images is to intensify the viewer's connection to the animals and inspire new perspectives on the familiar and immediate linkage to creatures we have never seen before" (n.p.). Beyond the usual unthinking art-world self-justifications and self-publicity (only a certain percentage of animals have eyes, to cite only one instance of lazy logic), Zuckerman's pictures eloquently attest to John Berger's (1980) argument concerning the troubling correspondence between an explosion of animal images at the very moment of a mass implosion of actual species: "Zoos, realistic animal toys and the widespread commercial diffusion of animal imagery, all began as animals started to be withdrawn from daily life. One could suppose that such innovations were compensatory. Yet in reality the innovations themselves belonged to the same remorseless movement as was dispersing the animals. The zoos, with their theatrical décor for display, were in fact demonstrations of how animals had been rendered absolutely marginal" (24). As Zuckerman himself notes, "I wanted these images to feel like the taxidermy I was so drawn to in the natural history museums: stoic, frozen, and engaged in singular thought" (n.p.).

14 See *Totem and Taboo* (Freud 1950) as well as *Moses and Monotheism* (Freud 1955) for Freud's controversial but influential view that religion is to be understood through the prism of primordial family dynamics, specifically the power struggle between fathers and sons (in which the murdered or deposed patriarch becomes more powerful—as a structuring absence—after the deed is done).

15 It may be worth noting in passing that, in the seventeenth century, *Ventriloquie* could refer to "divination by the inwards of beasts." See

Henry Cockeram, *The English dictionarie, or an interpreter of hard English words* (1623), via the *Oxford English Dictionary.*

16   In an interview with Hugh Raffles (2007), titled "The Language of Bees," the anthropologist opines: "The question is, why would language be taken as the index of some kind of interior life at all? And why does that interior life have to be on the model of our own? If we imagine our intelligence as being language-based, why do we ask other beings to demonstrate that particular capacity as a sign of intelligence? It just points to how our dependence on language has limited our imaginative capacity. I'm struck in all this by our constant impulse to interpret in terms that are already intelligible to us. Of course, this raises the question of what other terms are possible for us to think in anyway. But let's start from the position that we have certain limitations in our capacity to understand, rather than that these other beings have limitations in their capacity to become us. Then maybe we can begin to think productively about our relationships with them based around some kinds of difference which aren't—like language, at least as we define it—distinctively human" (n.p.).

17   See Hauser, Chomsky, and Fitch (2002), in which the authors argue that the only factor that distinguishes between human and animal language vocalization is recursion (as opposed to the evolutionary hard-wiring theory of universal grammar).

18   According to Kittler's Lacanian scheme, the gramophone encodes the Real, the cinema inscribes the Imaginary, and the typewriter engenders the Symbolic. Being a poststructuralist at heart, however, Kittler does not allow his cultural history of technology (or rather technological history of culture) to be graphed quite so neatly on every occasion.

19   Kittler's (2001) *Discourse Networks* tells of a perhaps apocryphal attempt to capture the voice of Goethe, several generations after his death, spurred by the assumption that particles of sound continue to reverberate around any given room for centuries after the source has been silenced (230–31). The trick is to find ghost-busting instruments sensitive enough to detect them. It was perhaps this tall tale that inspired associates of Kittler himself to experiment with the acoustic reach of siren songs off the Amalfi Coast, a fascinating folly whereby members of Humboldt University Berlin, as well as the Center for Media Arts and Technology Karlsruhe, "demonstrated" that Odysseus could indeed have actually heard the enchanting sounds over the noise of the

wind and ocean. In short, the experiment was designed to answer the question, "can the acoustic phenomenon of the Siren songs be located media-archaeologically, traced by measurements (analytic rather than performative) and thus verified?" (Ernst 2005, 1). In doing so, Kittler and company created "a GPS system for ancient Greece" (T. Elsaesser, pers. comm.). See Wolfgang Ernst (2005).

20   See Jody Rosen's (2008) *Slate* posting "The Best Music of 2008 Was the Oldest." Also see the First Sounds project: http://www.firstsounds.org/sounds/index.php.

21   For a brilliant "provisional archaeology" of "postally transmitted acoustic inscriptions"—including the mechanics of de Martinville's invention, prior to this posthumous feat of reverse engineering—see Thomas Levin's (1995) "Before the Beep: A Short History of Voice Mail."

22   At the time of writing, the scientific jury was still out concerning whether this ghostly voice belonged to a woman or whether it is the trace of a man played back at the wrong speed so as to make the voice sound higher than the original source.

23   In Mark Neale's film *No Maps for These Territories* (2000), William Gibson discusses an English country priest who wrote of his first experience with a phonograph during a picnic in the early days of the twentieth century. This man of the cloth was so disconcerted by the sound of a human voice coming out of a mechanical contraption that he could only explain it as the devil's work. Gibson's point, however, was to conjecture that the priest was probably less and less perturbed each time he subsequently heard the phonograph, illustrating how quickly we repress or absorb the shock of technological "amputation" (to borrow a term from McLuhan). From this perspective, much of contemporary culture can be viewed as symptomatic returns of this repressed material in myriad ways and on a variety of registers.

24   For his part, journalist Farhad Manjoo (2009) despises both answering machines and voice mail, looking forward to the day when all messages are text based, eliminating the voice completely, along with all its ticks and frailty: "So don't spin me on how voice mail is somehow inherently warmer and more human than e-mail. Speaking into a dead phone has always seemed unnatural. That's why we stammer, ramble on, leave awkward pauses. I submit that whatever finally makes voice mail obsolete will make us all sound far more human—and a little more polished at that." The remarkable thing here is the assumption that writing—which of course antedates speech—is somehow more "natural" to our technocratic milieu.

25   With scientific terms like this, one wonders if NASA is sometimes deliberately courting blockbuster movie franchises.

26   In his book *Does God Play Dice?*, Ian Stewart (2002, 182) notes, "I can't decide whether I think this particular cosmic gesture is a heartwarming manifestation of the indomitable human spirit, a dangerous betrayal of our galactic coordinates to a potential enemy, or a pointless conceit." No doubt Derrida would also have something interesting to say about this exceptional case of archive fever.

27   In point of fact, the Voyager Gold Record is gold-plated copper, with a sample of the isotope uranium-238 on the cover. It was designed to play at sixteen and two-thirds revolutions per minute. See Carl Sagan's (1978) *Murmurs of Earth*.

28   In an instance that should convert any obdurate holdouts against copyright reform, EMI refused to allow the inclusion of "Here Comes the Sun" by the Beatles, despite wholehearted enthusiasm from the Fab Four themselves.

29   It has become an ironic piece of folk knowledge that despite NASA's attempts to make the Pioneer plaque semiotically rich, with the maximum amount of information in the minimum amount of space, most human scientists could not decode the content (boding badly for alien interpretation). Both Ernst Gombrich (1994, 150) and Edward Tufte (http://www.edwardtufte.com/tufte/space) have criticized the semiotic presumptions of this project.

30   The humbling premise of *Star Trek IV: The Voyage Home* (1986) may be worth noting here: that intelligent probes from deep space visit earth not to communicate with humans but to find out why their regular transmissions of whale songs have suddenly ceased.

4. THE WAR ON TERRA

1   The standard cinematic reference for this ecological crash is Godfrey Reggio's *Koyaanisqatsi: Life out of Balance* (1982).

2   See Andrew Robinson's (2007) book *The Story of Writing*.

3   Here it is prudent to remember that "in Enlightenment times, the relationships between animals, plants, and minerals was figured as 'the economy of Nature.'" See Timothy Morton's (2007) *Ecology without Nature* (103).

4   See Steven Leblanc and Katherine Register's (2003) *Constant Battles: The Myth of the Peaceful, Noble Savage*, which argues that none of the

indigenous poster people for environmentalism—Native Americans, Australian Aborigines, etc.—were ever "in harmony with nature" in the romantic sense.

5   A technobucolic alternative to the apocalyptic loss of Nature is provided by Richard Brautigan (1989, 127) in his poem that looks forward to a "cybernetic ecology . . . all watched over by machines of loving grace."

6   Speaking from personal experience, there is certainly a bitter pathos to be had streaming Birdsong Radio through one's laptop in the middle of Manhattan, car alarms blazing outside the window. On the other hand, as I write, printed notices in my building are attempting to galvanize tenants to lobby management to "remove the robin which sings incessantly outside, day and night."

7   As the narrator writes in Robert Musil's (1999a, 31) short story "Grigia," "one must not believe that Nature is anything but highly unnatural: she is earthy, edgy, poisonous, and inhuman at all points where man does not impose his will upon her."

8   Nature, for Morton (2007, 14–15), is also akin to "the subject"—"a being who searches through the entire universe for its reflection, only to find none."

9   Morton (2007, 51) quotes Latour, who states, "Political philosophy . . . finds itself confronted with the obligation to *internalize* the environment that it had viewed up to now as another world." What is more, Latour's notion of "quasi-objects" (asbestos, radioactivity, dioxins, etc.) has undermined the classical difference between humanity and nature.

10 Differences in human impact are only matters of degree at this point—in fact, "the catastrophe . . . *has already taken place*" (28).

11 For Morton, "deep ecologists" are simply reverse humanists, whose fantasy of pristine nature, untouched by human hands, plays into the same dangerous fantasy of those who seek to exploit its riches. Thus he advocates a position that gives no privilege whatsoever to the human—either as hero or as villain. Deep ecology, he argues, is *not deep enough*.

12 One unacknowledged inspiration for such a project may be *solastalgia,* a syndrome identified by the environmental philosopher Glenn Albrecht, in which humans feel great mourning for, and existentially estranged from, the loss of contact with animals and natural surroundings (Manaugh 2009, 137). No doubt Morton would see the invention of such a syndrome as yet another melancholic–romantic symptom that itself compounds the alienation in the first place.

13 According to the U.S. Census Bureau, the world's population in 2030

is expected to be double that of only fifty years earlier. See http://www.
census.gov/ipc/www/idb/worldpopinfo.php.

14   See Alister Doyle (2007). For the current publicly available data in the
"Catalogue of Life," Youatt points us to http://www.sp2000.org/ and
http://www.allspecies.org/.

15   Anthropologist Hugh Raffles (2002, 40–41) reminds us that "the se-
ductions of classification should not be denied." For a beautiful work
on "the obstinacies of non-humans" (171), as well as "the fullness and
multiplicity of nature as . . . a domain with complex agency" (8), see his
book *In Amazonia* (Raffles 2002).

16   The previous paragraphs notwithstanding, I have deliberately avoided
the phrase *biopolitical* in the following pages as I believe discussions
around this term have become somewhat overdetermined in the wake
of Agamben's (1998) book *Homo Sacer*. This is not to devalue the important work currently emerging around biopolitics, of which Youatt's
is a fine example. However, the term has itself unfortunately become a
hegemonic one against which other—non-Foucauldian—approaches
to "life" or "politics" are measured, subsumed, and/or rejected.

17   For commentators of the John Gray school of cultural pessimism, humanity's ultimate act of misplaced arrogance may be to believe firmly
in its own capacity to reverse the catastrophic effects of its lifestyle.

18   One particularly bold-faced example of greenwashing was in evidence
during the 2006 ECO:nomics conference, sponsored by the *Wall Street
Journal* and organized to help businesses share information on creating and leveraging so-called environmental capital. See http://www.
globenewswire.com/newsroom/news.html?d=128315.

19   Slavoj Žižek, "Ecology: A New Opium for the Masses," paper presented
at the Tilton Gallery, November 8, 2007. See http://www.lacan.com/
blog/.

20   Most theoretical appropriations of the potlatch avoid the residual exchange underlying the ceremony. Thus it is not simply a destruction of
property—as modern-day anarchists would have it—but an economic
contract with the community: the exchange of earthly goods for social
recognition.

21   The difference gestured to here is between, say, a feudal arrangement and
the yields afforded by new speculative financial instruments. It is not to
romanticize the former over the latter, via the currency of familiarity and
a global understanding, but to point to the aggressively antidemocratic
forces ushered in under the mantle of liberal–democratic institutions.

22   Interview with Russia Today television, May 20, 2009, http://rt.com/usa/news/us-banks-bailout-is-robbery-in-progress-naomi-klein/.

23   David Price (1995, 301–2), of Cornell University, writes, "The human species may be seen as having evolved in the service of entropy, and it cannot be expected to outlast the dense accumulations of energy that have helped define its niche. Human beings like to believe they are in control of their destiny, but when the history of life on Earth is seen in perspective, the evolution of *Homo sapiens* is merely a transient episode that acts to redress the planet's energy balance."

24   Whereas Joseph A. Tainter (1996, 73) writes, "The alternative is the 'soft landing' that many people hope for—a voluntary change to solar energy and green fuels, energy-conserving technologies, and less overall consumption. This is a utopian alternative that . . . will come about only if severe, prolonged hardship in industrial nations makes it attractive, and if economic growth and consumerism can be removed from the realm of ideology." See also http://www.beyondpeak.com/.

25   Current energy alternatives on the table are hydrogen, ethanol, solar, nuclear, etc. However, none of these can pack anything near the power of oil. See David MacKay's (2009) *Sustainable Energy: Without the Hot Air* (http://www.withouthotair.com/). Those readers wondering about the energy required for *non*-manual labor in today's post-Fordist workplace may be interested in the quantities expended during the average business meeting. Ben Kafka (2008–9, 7–8) refers us to the fact that "sitting-meetings, general, and/or with talking involved" consume 1.5 METs—a unit representing the ratio of working metabolic rate to a resting metabolic rate—whereas conducting an orchestra consumes 2.5 METs.

26   The landmark study analyzing the "human element" harnessed by, and to some sense *created* by, the Industrial Revolution is Anson Rabinbach's (1992) *The Human Motor: Energy, Fatigue, and the Origins of Modernity*.

27   The wars in the Persian Gulf are as much about securing import supplies of petroleum as the exporting of democracy. Indeed, the title of the film *There Will Be Blood* (2007) seems to be a bleak realist retort to the naive antiwar slogan "No Blood for Oil." See also Werner Herzog's *Lessons of Darkness* (1992) for a sobering visual aria to the political economies of scale between human industry and natural resources.

28   In his incomparable book *Cyclonopedia: Complicity with Anonymous Materials*, Reza Negarestani (2008) provides a crypto-Deleuzian—rather than Freudian—reading of oil, exploring its schizo-ontological

"blobjectivity," somewhere between animal and mineral, with a prime-evil, even occult life force of its own, feeding the most modern geopolitical situations. This is what he calls the "'Thingness' of oil, its subterranean cohesion as a singular anorganic body with its own agendas" (20). Negarestani's book is as intriguingly opaque as its subject matter.

29   Ian Pindar and Paul Sutton discuss Doyle's story in their introduction to Félix Guattari's (2000) *The Three Ecologies*. I am quoting from the e-text, available online at http://www.classic-literature.co.uk/scottish-authors/arthur-conan-doyle/when-the-world-screamed/.

30   See "The Job Nobody Wanted," in Rachel Maines's *The Technology of Orgasm* (1998).

31   See Peter Ward's (2009) *The Medea Hypothesis*, in which the question raised in the subtitle—*Is Life on Earth Ultimately Self-Destructive?*—is answered with an emphatic yes. See also Steven Shaviro's (2009) interesting blog response to this book, "Against Self-Organization."

32   Lovelock believes that a human population of two billion is the maximum in the absence of fossil fuels, and given the earth's overall energy budget in such a scenario. Some extremists, however, see no reason to be concerned, such as the Voluntary Human Extinction Movement, whose guiding philosophy states, "Phasing out the human race by voluntarily ceasing to breed will allow Earth's biosphere to return to good health. Crowded conditions and resource shortages will improve as we become less dense." See http://www.vhemt.org/.

33   Žižek makes an interesting Lacanian slip when quoting biologist Lynn Margulis (1998, 119), who wrote in the *Symbiotic Planet* that "Gaia, a tough bitch, is not at all threatened by humans." In his version, the phrase is rendered "Gaia is a *dirty* bitch." I shall leave speculation regarding the precise significance of this adjectival switch to others, but note the continuing eroticization of the earth itself.

34   Stoekl (2007, 133) adds, "Nature is to be pristine exactly to the extent that that untouched state furthers man's permanence and comfort on Earth. The quantified, mechanized destruction of the Earth becomes the quantified, mechanized preservation of the Earth."

35   Physician Pierre Winter (and friend of Le Corbusier) is cited as claiming that "human being is nothing but a transformer of solar energy; life is only the circulation of this energy; light is one of our fundamental nutrients [*aliments*]" (quoted in Stoekl 2007, 228). The difference between humans and other animals is split in slightly different ways by Stoekl, depending on the angle of analysis. For the most part, however,

the distinction rests on a surprisingly traditional orientation, in which humanity's exceptionalism derives from consciousness or self-consciousness: "[Animals], unlike us, are still in profound communication with an order not of avaricious concentration but of open energy flows, an order where densities of energy break out rather than lend themselves to use" (178).

36   Indeed, Ballard's fictional universe is increasingly being cited as an accurate road map for the dystopian tone and unexpected interrelationships of the postindustrial present. To pluck one example from recent newswire chatter, neatly illustrating the symbiotic relationship between economy and ecology, we read how mass housing foreclosures have created mosquito swarms arising from abandoned suburban swimming pools. See http://www.thebigmoney.com/articles/video/2009/09/10/how-foreclosures-breed-mosquitoes.

37   Indeed, there is an easy way to rain on Bataille's sun-drenched parade, and that is to quote the figures relating to the energy produced by solar panels: not nearly as impressive as his visions of abundant cosmic surplus suggest. On the other hand, it is not that Bataille is incorrect about the enormous "excess" of solar energy produced by the sun and reaching the earth, but the human capacity to capture it languishes in the very low percentiles. The very urge to quantify as such, however, offends the Bataillean approach to this prodigious giver of life and death, to which counting units of sunbeams is as offensive as looking a gift horse in the mouth.

38   Stoekl (2007, 184) also sees the manifestations of these ideas in urban bicycle culture, especially as crystallized in the often confrontational "critical mass" events around the world. These gatherings are an active alternative to a hegemonic car culture: "The automobile—the self-movement of technology—becomes, by metonymy, the empty signifier at the summit of fossil fuel modernity."

39   Morton (2007, 109) echoes Stoekl here: "Since it looks like capitalism is about to use an ecological rhetoric of scarcity to justify future developments, it is vital that we recognize that there are serious problems with imagining an ecological view based on limits, even at the level of abstraction. . . . And we need to notice that scarcity and limitation are not the only ecological concepts on the block. What if the problem were in fact one of a badly distributed and reified *surplus*?"

40   Stoekl's (2008, 146–47) example of orgiastic recycling is Agnès Varda's fascinating documentary *The Gleaners and I* (2000): "[The gleaned

object] is not a means to an end, but an end; the end is its force, its power of suggestion, its erotic, totemic sway, its social (de)centrality."

41 One of the few industries immune to material scarcity is that of the apocalyptic prophet, resulting in a constant glut of visions of excess, disorientation, and retribution from which to choose. Indeed, the I-told-you-so temptations of survivalism often provide their own *jouissance*: the pleasure gleaned in foreseeing the end.

42 Stiegler thus operates on an implicit neo-Freudian hierarchy, in which animal behavior is regulated by instinct alone, whereas human behavior is the result of a tripartite conflict between instinct, drive, and libido (ordered from lowest to highest, and where *drive* mediates between the two other terms). To give a cartoonish example: the arm of a gambler, mesmerized by the jackpot machine and its promised payload, pulls the lever because of *drive*. If he remembers to eat when he is hungry, then this decision is based on the pangs of *instinct*. If, however, he decides finally to forsake the casino for a life-affirming experience with his fellow beings, then the *libido* has—at least for that moment—triumphed. However, it is an open question if the animal test subjects—obliged by scientists to press buttons, solve puzzles, and recognize symbols to receive instinctual rewards (food, most commonly)—are functioning according to drive, in Freud's sense, and if so, whether this means they are nudging closer to the right-hand side of the animal–human continuum. In such a scenario, animal libido is not out of the question, despite the paucity of people willing to entertain its existence or emergence as a genuine possibility.

43 Most of the texts written by Stiegler on which I am relying for this chapter are working papers posted on his Web site, http://www.arsindustrialis. org/. These are not dated and have no page numbers. As a result, in the following pages, I will cite different articles according to the following code: "The Disaffected Individual in the Process of Psychic and Collective Disindividuation" (DI), "Within the Limits of Capitalism, Economizing Means Taking Care" (WLC), "Constitution and Individuation" (CI), "Desire and Knowledge: The Dead Seize the Living" (DK), "Take Care *(Prendre Soin)*" (TC) , "Our Ailing Educational Institutions: The Global Mnemotechnical System" (AE).

44 Stiegler's conception of a "postlibidinal subject" would thus include all humans, to only notional different degrees. Žižek, by contrast, would only place extreme cases (posttraumatics, Holocaust survivors, Alzheimer's patients, etc.) in such a category. "You cannot play the game of

transference," Žižek claims, "with the living dead." For Stiegler, however, we are all zombies in terms of the libido, at this point.

45   Hence the universally recognized *jouissance* that can accompany the act of consuming, i.e., "shopaholism" as a sublimated form of sex mania (or vice versa). On a similar note, an anonymous author for *N+1* magazine analyzes the intimate link between phallocentric, onanistic arousal and no-collar labor conditions: "To the painful postindustrial syndromes of carpal tunnel, repetitive stress injury, and chronic eyestrain is added Masturbator's Thumb. This is confusing. The work machine is also a porn machine; the porn machine is also a work machine. Work enters everything. And therefore porn becomes, in its way, a revenge. . . . Masturbation . . . is the workers' sabotage!" See http://www.nplusonemag.com/porn-machine.

46   For an unforgettably wrenching depiction of the ways in which a particular ecosystem symbiotically spawns a toxic economy, see Huber Sauper's film *Darwin's Nightmare* (2004). Another extremely disturbing mesh between libidinal and market economies has been recently brought to the world's (fleeting) attention by feminist activist Eve Ensler, who explains that Congolese militias routinely "use rape to enforce discipline among a slave workforce that mines columbite-tantalite ore, a common raw material for many [modern technological] devices." Ensler states, "We create those atrocities through our consumption." See the video interview at http://www.boingboing.net/2009/05/28/rape-camps-lurk-in-t.html.

47   Another piece of newsreel propaganda, from a decade earlier, promotes petroleum products by showing an attractive young woman at her dressing table. In a common motif from the time, we are asked to "imagine a world without oil" so that items are taken away one by one, including her dress, revealing her undergarments. At this point, the disappointed narrator says, "Science can go no further." The focusing of libidinal energies into a jovial voyeurism, a key refrain of contemporary life, makes the contract between these two economies explicit.

48   Capitalism and cars were indeed a match made in heaven, given that they are both figures of incessant circulation. Today's commercials for credit cards often stress the pleasure to be had from making seamless purchases, seemingly unashamed of their depictions of daily life as nothing more than a *ballet mécanique* of transactions. J. G. Ballard's (1973) genius in his novel *Crash* was to show how, under such disaffecting conditions, the libido attaches to moments of crisis, accident, or congestion.

49 Freud famously stated that money cannot buy happiness because money is not an infantile wish (and only the fulfillment of an infantile wish will bring a true sense of happiness). But this argument does not anticipate the perverse metapleasure—or pleasure stemming from denial—of adult desires, nor does it acknowledge that money buys the *simulation* of infantile wishes, which in this epoch is the very definition of happiness.

50 Ethologists are often more willing to acknowledge the existence of culture among animals, least controversially in the case of chimpanzees. See Helen Briggs's (2005) rather cautiously titled *BBC News* article "Chimpanzee Culture 'Confirmed,'" which discusses a recent study by a research team from the University of St. Andrews as well as Emory University's National Primate Research Center. The learned trait of "tail-walking" is also seen as a form of cultural transmission in dolphins, according to Richard Black (2008). No doubt the growing scientific record will add many more examples to this list.

51 It is certainly illustrative, in terms of this new fusion between the modes of the production and the modes of memorization, that the bulk of media work is now performed in that strange limbo known as postproduction: a space haunted by neo-Marxist specters and well described in the work of Hardt and Negri (2000).

52 Stiegler's grand narrative is extremely presumptuous about how changes are "experienced" by a rather general and abstract subject of history. It simply ignores that many people may have found such a fall into new social relations and technologies—beyond the algorithms of kinship and inflexible affinities—invigorating, even joyful. As we shall see, Jean-François Lyotard will go too far in the other direction, claiming that the working class "enjoyed" their exploitation and cultural disorientation.

53 In his terminology, Stiegler seems to use *desire* as a synonym for *libido* and thus as an antonym for *drive*. To minimize confusion, however—given the popular use of the word *desire* in a commercial context—I simply contrast *libido* and *drive* throughout the following discussion. Nevertheless, it is worth noting that desire can be either desirable or undesirable (as it were), depending on the situation, the object, and the source.

54 Stiegler also points out that "the speculator is typically the person who pays no attention to the objects of his speculation, and who takes no care of them either" (WLC). Elsewhere, he calls speculation a "mimetic madness" (Stiegler 2009, 70), implying that a speculator is haunting Europe.

55   Against the prevailing, enervating, fatalistic sense that "things have always been this way," it is important to recall that "it was only in 1972 that the word *consumerism* made its appearance in the United States" (WLC).

56   In an episode of the animated comedy series *Drawn Together* (2004), a Pikachu-like creature secretes a hallucinogenic drug whenever it is disappointed. On discovery, the other characters become intent on raising the creature's hopes, only to crush them soon after, at which point they lick its fur and begin tripping. This, in a nutshell, is the desublimative modus operandi of hypercapitalism.

57   "We," in this case, is a very privileged subset of humans: those who reap the benefits of the mass exploitation and slavery of the third world, now geographically located as much in the Northern and Western hemispheres as elsewhere. It must be noted, however, that this demographic—the infamous middle class—is "a luxury capitalism can no longer afford" (Gray 2007, 161).

58   According to Jodi Dean's (2009b) Lacanian schema, "desire and drive each designate a way that the subject relates to enjoyment. Desire is always a desire to desire, a desire that can never be filled, a desire for a jouissance that can never be attained. In contrast, drive attains jouissance in the repetitive process of not reaching it. Failure (or the thwarting of the aim) provides its own sort of success. If desire is like the path of an arrow, drive is like the course of the boomerang. . . . Drive is loss as a force or the force loss exerts on the field of desire."

59   Surely it is significant—in unconscious recognition of the dialectic between subject and object, self and other, singularity and the generic— that we personalize our coffee cup in the workplace but would feel very strange if our wine glass were unique at the dinner table.

60   Stiegler (2009, 76–77) writes that "individuation is not individualization. Individualization is the result of individuation. This is the manner in which the diverse in general unifies itself asymptotically in an indivisible way. I *tend* to become indivisible—but I never get there. . . . A process of individuation is that which *structurally cannot* be completed . . . unless it *carries on through a process of transmission*, through which this *I* that individuates itself, and which has come to the end of its individuation—it is dead—may eventually become a source for a new process of individuation for its descendents" (2009, 76–77). In a nutshell, to attempt to "know oneself" is only ever a way to know a specific concentration

of others who came before the self. You may enjoy the singularity of a snowflake, but you are still made out of snow.

61   It is worth noting that the lament concerning what is now referred to as ADD predates the technologies that are usually blamed for the syndrome, as witnessed in Alexis de Tocqueville's (2003, 709) remark—made in the mid-nineteenth century—that "the habit of inattention has to be regarded as the great defect of the democratic character." Note also that de Tocqueville is also a Frenchman tut-tutting his cousins in the New World.

62   One example of the lack of shame in our current age—plucked from the media flux almost at random—is a recent commercial for Ladders. com, a Web site specializing in employment opportunities for "100K plus talent." This television spot features child-sized Godzillas comically failing to terrorize city dwellers, until the genuine article arrives and begins laying waste to the streets. The message is clear: the higher your earning potential, the more destruction you wreak on the polis. And yet this is something to boast about and exploit.

63   This is not so much Whitney Houston's "Greatest Love of All," which confuses the ego and ego-ideal to celebrate a mistakenly complete subjectivity, but rather relies on Lacan's mirror-stage, in which the possibility of loving oneself is initiated by the scopic recognition-event of an ontological alienation from oneself. That is to say, loving oneself depends on recognizing the alterity immanent to one's fractured relationship with oneself, which only then can be absorbed as the principle for relating to the alterity of others. See "The Destruction of Primordial Narcissism" in Stiegler's (2009) *Acting Out*.

64   In his eloquent article "The Cinematic Condition of the Politico-Philosophical Future," Dan Ross (2007) gives the example of William Powell and Fred Astaire as "masters of the technique of living" and "possessors of *savoir-vivre*" for the generation engaging with this most influential mnemotechnology of the early twentieth century. During the Great Depression, film rushes in to fill the vacuum of quotidian know-how created by capitalist specialization and by its subsequent overvaluation in the stock market. The movie palaces are ambivalent spaces, on one hand providing role models to help people navigate the new urban world of emergent globalization, but on the other alienating people further by commodifying, reifying, and canalizing their attention according to the profitable imperatives of the Spectacle. In keeping with Stiegler's Edenic

subtext, Ross notes that the postwar generations, largely switching from classical cinema to TV, have since experienced a fall: "The movement from the *fictional* characters portrayed by William Powell to the 'reality' programming of *Big Brother* may, paradoxically, constitute a net loss of reality, its impoverishment."

65   Indeed, there is enough intellectual affinity between Marcuse and Stiegler for one contemporary scholar to complain to me that it is possible to date the latter's ideas to the exact month, like rings in a tree trunk—that month being April 1968. Moreover, I do not mean to sound snide when I point out that much of Stiegler's work is a rewriting of Marcuse for our own time, for the latter has been unjustly neglected as a relic of the Summer of Love. To return to his original writings is to see the sophistication with which he understood the ideological paradoxes of the culture industries and thus laid the groundwork for concepts such as psychic vs. collective individuation (Marcuse 1974, 56); the repressive and false notion of the autonomous individual (57, 97); the insidious influence of the electronic media in relation to the family (97); the belief in true, hijacked knowledge (104); the desire to refind a primordial or primary narcissism (166–69); the importance of nonrepressive sublimation (5), and so on. It is also significant that Marcuse was quoting Simondon at length decades ago, something Stiegler is wont to do today. But whereas Marcuse is working within the triangle of Marx, Freud, and Adorno—and was well aware of the importance of technics (85)—Stiegler provides a more intense and nuanced reading of such.

66   All subsequent Marcuse quotes are from *Eros and Civilization* (1974), unless otherwise noted.

67   Interestingly, Marcuse avoids any reference to capitalism in his critique, preferring more abstract terms, such as the *period of total mobilization,* to denote historical forces that ascend and descend in different epochs. Plato, for instance, is blamed for being the first to introduce "the repressive definition of Eros into the household of Western culture" (210–11).

68   This is to conflate Marcuse and a figure like Wilhelm Reich into the same spokesman for the intellectually driven sexual revolution. However, for Marcuse, Reich neglects "the historical dynamic of the sex instincts" so that no distinction was made—especially in his notion of orgone energy—between repressive and nonrepressive sublimation. Thus "a sweeping primitivism becomes prevalent" (239). For a contemporary and intellectually savvy psychedelic treatment of Reich's life and work, see Dusan Makavejev's *W.R.: Mysteries of the Organism* (1971). For a

much more recent reappraisal of the Sexpol discourse and time period, see Owen Hatherley's (2009) chapter "Revolutionary Orgasm Problems" in *Militant Modernism*.

69 Marcuse makes the rather fascinating point that before so-called sexual liberation, "the full force of civilized morality was mobilized against the use of the body as mere object, means, instrument of pleasure; such reification was tabooed and remained the ill-reputed privilege of whores, degenerates, and perverts" (200–1). The hypocrisy here is clear: whereas it is OK to use people as mere means for labor, it is not OK to use them for pleasure (one of the few compensations or distractions for labor). However, were we equipped with the will to engineer a *non*-repressive reality principle, then "reification would be reduced as the division of labor became reoriented on the gratification of freely developing individual needs; whereas in the libidinal relations, the taboo on the reification of the body" would be lessened. "No longer used as a full-time instrument of labor, the body would be resexualized" (200–1). That is to say, an index of our true erotic freedom is the degree to which we are sexually objectified and objectifying, in direct inverse ratio to the subjective frame of quotidian life. In work we are but an end, but in bed we are mutual means.

70 One wonders about the prurient voyeurism underwriting such "investigations," especially when they are focused exclusively on women (as if men do not have sexual daydreams while at work).

71 Marcuse talks across himself when it comes to this distinction between nature and culture, as if it is only pertinent during lovemaking. For elsewhere in the same book, he writes, "Glorification of the natural is part of the ideology which protects an unnatural society in its struggle against liberation" (Marcuse 2002, 242), giving the defamation of birth control as a key example.

72 In the vocabulary of the later Freud, *sexuality* denotes the "specialized," partial drive, whereas *Eros* embodies the entire organism.

73 Marcuse's latent humanism comes to the fore when he writes, "Pleasure contains an element of self-determination which is the token of human triumph over blind necessity" (227).

74 Another resonance effect between Stoekl and Marcuse occurs when the latter writes that "liberation from affluent society does not mean return to healthy and robust poverty, moral cleanliness, simplicity. On the contrary, the elimination of profitable waste would increase the social wealth available for distribution" (Marcuse 2002, 247).

75   In point of fact, Marcuse is well aware of the complicitous, compensatory, and anestheticizing potentials of art, as witnessed in the following insight: "The dual function of art: both to oppose and to reconcile; both to indict and to acquit; both to recall the repressed and repress it again—'purified.' People can elevate themselves with the classics: they read and see and hear their own archetypes rebel, triumph, give up, or perish. And since all this is aesthetically formed, they can enjoy it—and forget it" (145). Art is thus the "handmaiden" of the repressive apparatus, beautifying business and misery rather than destroying the same (Marcuse 2002, 243–44).

76   Marcuse (2002, 129) states that the role of truth to save reality from destruction is "the essentially human project." Indeed, *human* is the only term he refuses to parse critically, the blind spot on which his otherwise illuminating critique depends.

77   While the American metropolis is still considered ground zero of hyperalienation, we may consider Dubai as the true capital of the libidinal crash. For evidence leading to this alternative, see John Hari's (2009) nightmarish article for *The Independent*, "The Dark Side of Dubai," in which we learn of European expats (and ex-executives) living in parking lots after their passports were seized by officials and of immigrant laborers working as a veritable slave force in some of the harshest conditions (speaking ecologically and economically) on earth.

78   See Soderbergh's discussion of his film at the Tribeca Film Festival in 2009 at http://gothamist.com/2009/04/30/soderbergh_sasha_grey_explain_the_g.php.

79   Marx wrote that "prostitution is only the specific expression of the general prostitution of the labourer" (quoted in Lyotard 1993, 136).

80   Lyotard (1993, 185) teases out the parallels within the shrink–whore complex, stating that like the prostitute, the analyst "neutralizes the other's *jouissance*" by instantiating it "on the zero of exchangeability, and this due to payment." Yet analysis is even more compromised by political economy than prostitution "since it wants to extract the affect itself, and place it on the circle of exchangeabilities" (186). It is in statements such as this, however, that we see how difficult it is, even for Lyotard, to escape the political–libidinal distinction.

81   It is unlikely that Stephen Soderbergh was inspired by Deleuze and Guattari for this name of "personology," which they mention with contempt in *A Thousand Plateaus* (Deleuze and Guattari 1987, 264). Nevertheless,

the resonance machine this word creates between the two texts is both suggestive and intriguing.

82   Stiegler makes an implicit distinction between that myopic vanity that we—along with Christopher Lasch (1991)—tend to call "narcissism" from the essential, properly erotic "primordial" kind, which he believes is so lacking today. This leads Stiegler to state that "Lasch takes the wrong path by using a conception of narcissism which takes into account only a part of the emerging pathology, although the submerged part is none other than the psychological apparatus itself in its totality. Far from exacerbating narcissism, the capitalist libidinal economy of the twentieth century has destroyed narcissism—and that's why psychotic pathologies are more common now than the neuroticism that was the principal study of the Freudian clinic" (CI). Moreover, "narcissism is the precondition of all dreams and all psyche" (CI). Likewise, Morton (2007, 184) notes that "if, as Derrida observes, there are only different forms of narcissism, rather than narcissism and something else, the true escape from narcissism would be a dive further into it, and an extension of it . . . to include as many other beings as possible." Clearly we need two different words to denote these two different types of self-relation or autospeculation. But as long as *narcissism* is a popular and pejorative term, Stiegler's or Bersani's or Derrida's reappropriation of the term will only have currency in restricted academic circles, which is why I continue to attack *narcissism* in toto throughout this book, in an attempt to keep the Other as constitutive of psychic individuation. In other words, though someone like André Green (2001) may make valuable and nuanced distinctions between types of narcissism—in a study such as *Life Narcissism, Death Narcissism*—the front line of the public debate is drawn and fought by books such as *The Narcissism Epidemic: Living in the Age of Entitlement*, by Jean Twenge and Keith Campbell (2009).

83   Nicholas Roeg's disquieting film *Performance* (1970) is still a fascinating exploration of the conflicts and tensions that arise when public personas spend too much time in private spaces.

84   See my chapter "Working Ass in the Age of Bio-Mechanical Reproduction" in *Love and Other Technologies* (Pettman 2006).

85   Stoekl might say, however, that this generational disconnect itself leads to the spontaneous ingenuity of orgiastic recycling, as with DJs or renegade jewellers. Behind every prophet of doom, there is a *bricoleur*-heretic grinning among the ruins.

262 NOTES TO CHAPTER 4

86 In Marcuse's words, "hate encounters smiling colleagues, busy competi-
     tors, obedient officials, helpful social workers who are all doing their
     duty and who are all innocent victims. Thus repulsed, aggression is again
     introjected" (99)—until the nervous system becomes so choked up with
     introjection that it leads to violent projection and displacement.
87 If various news reports and sensationalist documentaries are anything
     to go by, then humans are not the only animal to become psychotic
     when faced with cultural and environmental distress. Take, for instance,
     National Geographic's *Elephant Rage,* which resurrects the ghost of
     Topsy by focusing on recent violent attacks on humans in West Bengal.
     The promotional material for the show states, "Villagers awake to the
     terrifying spectacle of rampaging elephants wrecking their home. They
     flee in panic grabbing family members who stumble into the chaotic
     darkness. But in many cases, as the dust settles, families discover that
     not everyone made it out alive." See http://ngccommunity.nationalgeo-
     graphic.com/ngcblogs/explorer/2006/06/elephant-rage.html. See also
     the incredible statistics—more than 539 humans killed, and several
     rhinoceroses "raped," by elephants in India in five years—in Charles
     Siebert's (2006) piece "Are We Driving Elephants Crazy?"
88 The medical profession only exacerbates the situation by finding so-
     phisticated (not to mention lucrative) Band-Aid solutions to a problem
     beyond the mechanics of physiology: "Ritalin . . . [is] a chemical strait-
     jacket, that is, a technology of pharmaceutical control, which both opens
     a new market, and avoids the question of sociopathology, which is here
     the only genuine question" (DI).
89 We should acknowledge the glum pleasure to be had even reading such
     bleak diagnoses, as if the libido's last spasm is coaxed at the cost of being
     told one has cancer. *Finally! A brush with the real!* (Indeed, the down-
     cast music throughout *A Crude Awakening*—and most environmental
     movies—suggests that we are in the bittersweet process of losing a lover,
     oedipal or otherwise.)
90 As Laura Hudson (2008, 104) describes the situation, referring to von
     Uexküll, by way of Agamben, "it is under capitalism that spectacle
     and private experience replace the search for historical meaning. We
     become captivated, like animals, by the spectacles of consumer culture;
     no longer actively seeking meaning for our lives, we passively await the
     stimulation of our man-made disinhibitors."
91 Elsewhere Stiegler (2009, 68) refers to "the American machine for the
     liquidation of the *we.*" Morton (2007, 165), for his part, agrees, being

moved to proclaim that "the United States has pioneered experiments in just how much ignorance people can tolerate."

92   In her response to a paper delivered by Stiegler at New York University in 2009, Avital Ronnell essentially asked how his reading of the situation changes if there is no such thing as knowledge per se? To put it bluntly, what if we are all equally stupid? On this point, see Mike Judge's frighteningly proleptic film *Idiocracy* (2006).

93   There are glimmers of hope in Stiegler to escape the predicament he so grimly portrays, as when he calls for "demassifying the diffusion of information" (Stiegler 2009, 75) or gestures toward the "unheard-of possibility for the reconstitution of the long circuits of transindividuation" (WLC) or his fusion of Derrida's Pharmakon and Heidegger's "danger that saves," without going into detail. At one point, he notes, "As poor and disappointing as the social–digital networks appear to us, most of the time, they bring together, henceforth, hundreds of millions of psychical individuals in a processes of collective individuation that can sometimes be evaluated as rich and inventive" (WLC). Yet we must remember that "all technologies of attention can be captured and reversed to deform such attention" (WLC).

94   One coping mechanism for this knowledge in the hypersurveillance society is to think of oneself as just "a drop in the ocean." The sheer quantity of data is a form of protection, ensuring a certain amount of anonymity, at least until the authorities decide to target you specifically (at which time, a detailed profile can be assembled). This perverse empowerment-through-quasi-anonymity is an uncanny corollary to the democratic citizen, who is ascribed one vote out of millions. Only in the scenario first described, homeopathic participation is experienced negatively: "They won't notice me, as long as my click trail doesn't raise any red-flags." The fear is of existing to a degree that is noticeable. (As the Chinese say, "the nail that sticks out is the nail that gets hammered down.") In other words, we have come a long way from the days of "the squeaky wheel gets the grease."

95   As Albert Camus (1984, 11) puts it in *The Rebel*, "man is the only creature who refuses to be what he is."

96   Technics, according to Stiegler (1998, 17), is the pursuit of life by means other than life. As Ross (2007) puts it, "something happens at the origin of the human, an event which, while part of the history of life, is also the discontinuous beginning of another history, a *technical* history."

97   See Viegas (2009). For Stiegler (2009, 67), the great ape represents "an

outer limit" of prosthetic memory but ultimately cannot be included alongside that lonely creature in which the "apprenticeship of the individual" can be transmitted to the species.

98   Cf. Bradley (2006, 96).

99   Stiegler writes, "We who feel ourselves being distanced from our own, feel ourselves irresistibly condemned to live and think like pigs" (DI), thereby showing his hand in terms of prioritizing human life over nonhuman life (as well as assuming he has access to the thoughts of the latter).

100 This term is taken from the following quote: "We therefore might ask ourselves what continuing means of escape the zoological flux will have at its disposal—for complete dehumanization would eventually become prejudicial to the efficacy of the social machine, and it must therefore be kept in a sufficiently 'sapient' state" (Stiegler 2009, 57).

101 From this important perspective, Alain Badiou (2002) is also guilty of human exceptionalism, albeit of an exceedingly sophisticated kind. In the chapter "Does Man Exist?" found in his book *Ethics*, Badiou comes up with his own twist on the definition of the anthropological machine by stating that "man is *the being who is capable of recognizing himself as a victim*." To be sure, argues Badiou, man has an "animal substructure" and is both mortal and predatory, like other animals. However, "neither of these attributes can distinguish humanity within the world of the living," for man is unique through the refusal to be merely victimized, like, say, a horse. Man (yes, capital *M*) thus "distinguishes himself within the varied and rapacious flux of life" through his refusal to be merely *for-death*. Humanity is thus "*something other than a mortal being*"—an immortal, in fact, who "runs counter to the temptation of wanting-to-be-an-animal." Thus, like Heidegger and Nietzsche and before, Man is a potentiality that may or may not be realized, but when it is, transcends the biological base. He is a value-added animal, as it were, or at least is the only creature capable of being so. And on those (rather commonplace) occasions when he does not rise to the ethical occasion, he is merely a "'biped without feathers,' whose charms are not obvious" (10–12). On this last we can agree, but the preceding logic is based on a persistent human error.

102 For Bradley (2006, 96), all anthropological systems are contingent, which is to say, *violent*.

103 See the second half of Pixar's *WALL-E* (2008), which literalizes this metaphor of consumer-induced obesity comas.

104 Available at http://www.generation-online.org/p/fp_bifo5.htm.

105 The village green market is certainly making a big comeback, even where giant malls seemed to have wiped them out.

106 Dean (2009a).

107 There is a tension, then, in Stiegler's solution to the crisis, for he goes to great lengths to stress the "originary technicity" of humans and thus human encounters. And yet, while insisting that there is no humanity without technology, he does not simply reduce the former to the latter. There is an existential surplus or difference at play. Thus Stiegler's call for more attentive relations relies on a relative self-extrication from attention-sapping technologies but not a full, imaginary return to some unmediated human authenticity.

108 From such a standpoint, McLuhan's notion of "media ecology" does not sound quite so quaint as it did before the mainstreaming of green issues.

109 In contrast to Marcuse's depiction of the situation, Morton (2007, 68) believes that "we posit nature retroactively. Narcissus is only aware of his beloved Echo through the repetition of his words."

110 Adorno, Horkheimer, and Marcuse all follow Hegel's lead here in depicting Nature as "wanting in its own existence" (Marcuse 2002, 241): an assumption at once the apex and foundation of modern anthropocentrism. As Marcuse explains, "the historical transformation of Nature by Man is, as the overcoming of this negativity [i.e., lack], the liberation of Nature. Or, in Hegel's words (as quoted in Marcuse 2002, 241), "Nature is in its essence non-natural."

111 Regarding the *dispositif*, Agamben's (2009) recent book *What Is an Apparatus?* unpacks a specific affinity between this "decisive technical term in the strategy of Foucault's thought" (1) and the "theological genealogy of economy" (8). Indeed, Agamben's increasing technophobia comes to the fore in this text, whereby he admits to despising mobile phones, even hoping to punish or imprison those who cannot stop using them. Such a violent reaction stems from his belief that such apparatuses are the terrain on which the struggle between the governors and the governed occurs, insofar as the *dispositif* is "literally anything that has in some way the capacity to capture, orient, determine, intercept, model, control, or secure the gestures, behaviors, opinions, or discourses of living beings" (14). Agamben seems less and less willing to acknowledge the "contamination" of such technologies as constitutive but rather sees them as an ontological encroachment on the possibility of enjoying being "insofar

as it is being" (17). In this he aligns himself with Stiegler and other pessimists of the Frankfurt School stripe, all of whom sound like Luddites compared to the alternative critical angle forged by protechnological, but antineoliberal, theorists such as Geert Lovink, McKenzie Wark, Alex Galloway, and Eugene Thacker.

112   Ironically, and revealingly, journalist Lucy Wadham (2009) explains the somewhat surprising success of arch-neoliberal president Sarkozy in France in traditional psychosocial terms: "that it was the collective desire of the French people to be represented by a dominant and libidinous male, rather than a dominant and matriarchal female." Stiegler would no doubt be cast by Wadham as an example of the "hypocritical *gauche caviar*," whose call for a new compassionate collectivity repels the new generation, seduced by the rhetoric of individuality but in fact enslaved by the herd mentality.

113   Lyotard (1993, 175) writes, "The negotiation of investments on the pulsional body-band *produces* the negotiating subject. This latter *is not* the negotiator, but the unstable result of an interminable negotiation. *Neg-otium*: end of the leisurely fluidity of the influxes." This statement creates an interesting resonance with Stiegler's use of the term *otium* in WLC.

114   See my first book, *After the Orgy* (Pettman 2002).

115   Bersani's notion of "impersonal intimacy," discussed in chapter 2, offers a less "inhuman" critique of the subject—one that allows for a certain amount of poetic agency of the self, albeit under the dictates of archetypal forces.

116   Regarding such fantasies, Walter Benjamin (2006, 104–5) writes, "According to Fourier, cooperative labor would increase efficiency to such an extent that four moons would illuminate the sky at night, the polar ice caps would recede, seawater would no longer taste salty, and beasts of prey would do man's bidding. All this illustrates a kind of labor which, far from exploiting nature, would help her give birth to the creations that now lie dormant in her womb."

117   The litmus test for whether this regulating principle is in effect is very straightforward: "as soon as there is *someone* . . . one is already in the great Zero" (Lyotard 1993, 22–23; emphasis added).

118   In his slim volume *On Dreams*, Freud (2001) laments his psychic subjection to the regulating principle of what Lyotard calls the "great Zero." Specifically, he is saddened by the emotional expenditure he feels is necessary to receive any kind of attention in return. "I have never had

anything for nothing" (14), Freud writes, itself a "stinging thought." On no less than three separate occasions, in a very short treatise, does he make note of this frustratingly asymmetrical state of affairs, in which he has "always paid dearly for whatever kindness others have shown" (6), to the extent where "I should for once like to experience affection for which I should not have to pay . . . an affection that should entail no outlay" (32). Thus the great discoverer of libidinal economy consciously struggles to escape its omnipotent force and logic, like a hedge-fund manager of the emotions. Not only is there no free lunch, but neither is there free love—save for exceptional (fantasy) cases such as Barry Manilow's "Mandy" ("you came and you gave without taking").

119 For Morton (2007, 212; emphasis added), "the discovery of the beautiful soul as *the* form of ecological consumerism is the most important concept" in his own book.

120 In one of his last published pieces, Baudrillard (2010, 72–73) explicitly linked the cultural and economic crisis of contemporary life with looming environmental catastrophe: "Everything inclines us to think that this accumulation, this over-production, this proliferation of meaning constitutes (a little like the accumulation of greenhouse gases) a virtual threat for the species (and for the planet), since it is gradually destroying, through experimentation, that domain of the inviolable that serves us, as it were, as an ozone layer and protects us from the worst—from the lethal irradiation and obliteration of our symbolic space. Should we not, then, work precisely in the opposite direction, to extend the domain of the inviolable? To restrain the production of meaning the way they are trying to restrain the production of greenhouse gases, reinforce that constellation of the mystery and that intangible barrier that serves as a screen against the welter of information, interaction and universal exchange. This countervailing work exists—it is the work of thought. *Not* the analytic work of an understanding of causes, of the dissection of an object-world, *not* the work of a critical, enlightened thought, but another form of understanding or intelligence, which is the intelligence of the mystery."

121 Hence one of Deleuze and Guattari's key questions: "Why does desire desire its own repression?" (quoted in Guattari 2000, 88).

122 At times, Lyotard (1993, 87–88) seems to fall back on the libido–drive distinction, as when he notes that "the images offered to the potential consumer do not have as their function the stimulation of his phantasmatic forces *[puissances],* but the stimulation of his propensity to buy

the choc-ice or the refrigerator; they do not claim to make him spend his libido, but his money." For his part, Baudrillard (1990, 109–10) was also anticipating the notion of "ecological libido," which he described as "a product specific to our epoch, spread out everywhere in homeopathic and homeostatic doses. . . . Floating, it can be drained, diverted, magnetized from one niche to another, according to the flow. It corresponds ideally to an order of manipulation."

123 One of Morton's (2007, 87) observations is relevant here, namely, that "the notion of the disco or house DJ is that of an anonymous worker in a 'sound factory,' generating libidinal pulses in a space of dancing, producing ambience, in the same way as fairgrounds provide machines for enjoyment rather than work. Work your body."

124 See the short, animated corporate propaganda film *Destination Earth* (1956), available at http://www.archive.org/details/Destinat1956.

125 BP's Deepwater Horizon oil disaster occurred just as the present book was going into production, as if to literalize the arguments of the main theorists composing this chapter. As I write this endnote, crude oil continues to gush out of the compromised wellhead sixty-two days after the initial accident, with estimates of the flow and impact rising exponentially every hour and no solution in sight. It is as if Conan Doyle's Professor Challenger had decided to deliberately cooperate with James Arnold Ross Jr. and Hugh Hefner to illustrate the blind and relentless postlibidinal drive behind the increasingly penetrating search for oil: a drive that cannot be shut off, much as we collectively will it so. (Indeed, a "sex for oil" scandal concerning mining companies, license givers, and putative government watchdogs only made real headlines in the aftermath of the disaster rather than in 2008, when it was first uncovered by the press.) The gusher in the Gulf of Mexico was repeatedly referred to as a wound inflicted by us hubristic humans on an already battered Mother Earth, and it was indeed difficult to resist the temptation to conflate oil with blood as we watch the subaquatic hemorrhage on live webcam. There, in ominously silent pixels, we witnessed the horrifying "return of the compressed": a severed geological jugular that, for months, stubbornly resisted any technical tourniquet we could devise.

126 For a rather preposterous perspective on the latest financial crisis, see George Akerlof and Robert Shiller's (2009) *Animal Spirits: How Human Psychology Drives the Economy, and Why It Matters for Global Capitalism.* Were this book actually engaged in examining and redefining the key terms that make up its title, it would no doubt be a fascinating

addition to the nebulous bibliography of species-being. However, the powerful forces of the publishing market have ensured that it is in fact a neo-Keynesian-Darwinian caricature of cultural commentary.

127 It is statements such as this that lead Madan Sarup (1993), among others, to label Lyotard a neoconservative. However, there is a world of difference between someone like Lyotard and someone like Dick Cheney, even if some of their statements seem to overlap ideologically (as with the surreal affinities between radical feminists and fundamentalist Christians over pornography). Politics is thus exposed as a far more fraught and complex terrain than simply the one-dimensional line linking Left and Right.

128 Everyone thus becomes her own accountant, leading to Lyotard's (1993, 176) rhetorical question, "is there any *jouissance* outside this keeping of accounts, beyond this instantiation on the zero?"

129 Marcuse (2002, 250) hoped that "the non-functioning of television and the allied media might . . . begin to achieve what the inherent contradictions of capitalism did not achieve—the disintegration of the system." Clearly, in the age of time-shifted reality TV, this nonfunction (or rather *dys*-function) is an asset for the system and further erodes Marx's belief that the snake will eat its own tail. See Neil Postman's (2006) curmudgeonly classic *Amusing Ourselves to Death*.

130 I.e., the internalization of ideologies harmful to those who perpetuate them, e.g., voting against one's own financial interests for the sake of "security" (as only one instance of a potentially infinite list).

131 France's Minitel bulletin board is often cited as the proto-Internet and was in operation during the time of writing. However, given Guattari's emphasis on both the media and the ecological, the absence of any reference to McLuhan's media ecology is quite surprising.

132 The crucial question is whether capitalism can be convinced to become symbiotic rather than parasitic. For his part, Guattari (2000, 64) believes that "it is less and less legitimate that only a profit-based market should regulate financial and prestige-based rewards for human social activities, for there is a range of other value systems that ought to be considered, including social and aesthetic 'profitability' and the values of desire."

133 Echoing Marcuse at times, Guattari (2000, 69) vocally supports "group Eros," noting also that "individuals must become both more united and increasingly different." In contrast to Lyotard, then, Guattari argues for the possibility of a collectively coherent political stance because if one is not taken, "social ecology will ultimately always be dominated by

reactionary nationalist enterprises" (64). Amusingly, the example he gives of the latter is "men like Donald Trump," who "are permitted to proliferate freely, like another species of algae, taking over entire districts of New York City." (We also learn the disturbing fact that Andy Warhol felt compelled to write that "Donald Trump is real good-looking" in his diary [85].)

134   The moral of *Terminator 4: Salvation* is supposedly that "the strength of the human heart" is what separates men and women from machines. Yet the unexpected existence of a cybernetic organism—with metallic exo-skeleton, human organs, and "dual nervous system"—complicates this distinction. The movie predictably loses its nerve in the denouement, when this human-sympathizing cyborg is obliged to sacrifice himself, and his strong heart, for the sake of a fully fledged human (despite the massive military advantage of keeping him alive for the sake of the resistance). It seems that the human element is not so easily identified after all and that physiological resemblance does not necessarily translate to metaphoric relevance.

Also, an anecdote. One of my students, clearly frustrated by my treasonous attitude toward my own species, asked me point-blank if I would join the resistance against the machines if the situation from the Terminator franchise presented itself. My response was to draw attention to the human reliance on all sorts of machines as part of the resistance in those films, from cars to weaponry to communications systems. The war depicted is not against hardware per se but against an unjust extinction command. I would therefore like to think I have the courage (not to mention the charisma) to mimic John Conner if loved ones were threatened. But loved ones may not necessarily be only friends and family, but perhaps a dog or an artwork or a laptop. Moreover, these films displace actual historical conditions onto the vectors of anonymous anthropogenic power channels. For just as most abuse or violence is inflicted by those ostensibly close to us, we are far more likely to be terrorized by inhumane humans—technologically enhanced—than by our future Roomba overlords.

135   It is unclear how Guattari's (2000, 58) deployment of "the human" in this text relates to the Body-without-Organs, "traversed by a powerful, nonorganic vitality." Indeed, he seems to presume a kind of antihuman nature quality of species-being when he states that "violence and negativity are the products of complex subjective assemblages; they are not intrinsically inscribed in the essence of the human species, but are

constructed and maintained by multiple assemblages of enunciation."

136 This quote is found in the notes and originally appeared in Guattari's (1995) book *Chaosmosis*.

137 It is important not to get too optimistic (i.e., naive) about scaling down into organic microcommunities, or what the French call "the negative growth movement." The Invisible Committee's truly terrifying account of the burgeoning bioeconomy exposes the complicities, hypocrisies, and privileges often underlying "the steely smile of the new green capitalism" (Invisible Committee 2009, 76). In their home-truth treatise, *The Coming Insurrection*, the committee states that "the environment will be the pivot of the 21st century political economy" (76) and that "ecology isn't simply the logic of a total economy; it's the new morality of capital" (78). That is to say, "we have to consume a little less *to be able to keep consuming*. We have to produce organically *to keep producing*. We have to control ourselves *to go on controlling*" (78). Echoing Stoekl's warnings concerning the puritanical subtext of frugality, asceticism, and sustainability, the committee claims that "the planetary hyper-bourgeoisie wouldn't be able to make its normal lifestyle seem respectable if its latest whims weren't so scrupulously 'respectful of the environment.' Without ecology, nothing would have enough authority to gag every objection to the exorbitant progress of control" (79). Composting, recycling, etc., are figured as the homeopathic assuaging of guilt and little more. The paradox of environmentalism is thus exposed: "Under the pretext of saving the planet from desolation it merely saves the causes of its desolation" (81). This should not mean, however, that we should abandon any alternative conception to the horrors of agribusiness. But we should do so under the aegis of global systemic change and not as self-righteous local stop-gap measures that leave the controlling mechanisms essentially intact.

138 Witness the words of "Jimmy," an amateur one-man band and YouTube sensation in Russia: "All I want now is a synthesizer. If I had a Yamaha, I could do more. The bucket doesn't let me show my true worth."

139 Morton (2007) warns against the kind of thinking that seeks to downplay the differences between humans and animals, calling it "inverted speciesism." An impressively detailed attempt to see both points of distinction and overlap—from a predominantly phenomenological standpoint—can be found in Glen Mazis's (2008) book *Humans, Animals, Machines: Blurring Boundaries*.

CONCLUSION

1   For an entertaining study on learning from mistakes, see the wonder-fully titled (but somewhat too neatly cognitivist) book *Bozo Sapiens: Why to Err Is Human,* by Michael and Ellen Kaplan (2009).

2   Descartes would disagree, stating idealistically that humanity "acquires the habit of not erring . . . since this compromises the greatest and prin-cipal perfection of man" (quoted in Mazlish 1993, 21).

3   Freud's full quote is as follows: "America is a mistake. A tremendous mis-take, it is true, but a mistake nonetheless" (quoted in Damisch 2001, 133).

4   E.g., Derrida's (2008, 76) "semiotic machine"—"of artificial intelligence, of cybernetics and zoo- and bio-engineering, of the *genic* in general, etc."

5   In the animated comedy *Futurama,* Bender, the obnoxious robot, as-sumes the existence of his own "robo-humanity." For his part, Richard Dawkins (1989, 270–71) asks, "what on earth do you think you are, if not a robot, albeit a very complicated one?"

6   According to the English Research Institute's journal *Deleuze Studies,* "haecceity is the quality of 'this-ness' in a 'thing-in-itself.' Haecceities are intensive states experienced by the automatic or autoerotic movements of machinic desire rather than by the psychoanalytical subject. The use of colour, the timbre of a voice or the rhythm of a movement are haec-ceities not reducible to symbolic meaning." Available at http://www.eri. mmu.ac.uk/deleuze/on-deleuze-key_concepts.php (accessed July 2008).

7   This term—also deployed by Deleuze—counters the misleading notion that the subject is in-dividual, that is, "one in substance or essence; forming an indivisible entity; indivisible" *(Oxford English Dictionary).* In truth, the self is supremely separable: into conflicting thoughts, dif-ferent imperatives, competing desires, and distinct temporalities.

8   "More humanity per pixel," boasted Annenberg's Space for Photography in 2009.

9   The most eye-rolling recent example being Lee Siegel's (2008) *Against the Machine: Being Human in the Age of the Electronic Mob.*

10   Speaking of the radio as a device that turns participants into listeners, Adorno and Horkheimer lament that "no machinery of rejoinder has been devised" (quoted in During 1999, 33).

11   The discount carrier Ryanair recently announced a feasibility study around the possibility of standing-only flights, thereby almost literal-izing the notion of "cattle class."

12   I thank Ken Wark for this concept and also Geoff Manaugh's BLDG Blog (http://bldgblog.blogspot.com/), which excels in antisentimental, chronologically posthuman scenes and scenarios. These are a refreshing contrast to the melancholic–proleptic nostalgia of TV shows such as *Life After People* (2008).

13   Rather than the "posthuman," which smuggles in a dubious chronology, we might talk instead of the "*extra*-human," as a way of keeping the elusive element, without necessarily ascribing it to any specific form of being. But we should not forget that there is an ongoing salvage operation for humanism proper, conducted by those who seek to rescue our species-being—or at least the *potential* of our species-being—from its corrupted and/or naive modes. Terry Eagleton (2009, n.p.) calls this operation "tragic humanism," which "shares liberal humanism's vision of the free flourishing of humanity, but holds that attaining it is possible only by confronting the very worst. The only affirmation of humanity ultimately worth having," he continues, "is one that, like the disillusioned post-Restoration Milton, seriously wonders whether humanity is worth saving in the first place, and understands Swift's king of Brobdingnag with his vision of the human species as an odious race of vermin. Tragic humanism, whether in its socialist, Christian, or psychoanalytic varieties, holds that only by a process of self-dispossession and radical remaking can humanity come into its own. There are no guarantees that such a transfigured future will ever be born. But it might arrive a little earlier if liberal dogmatists, doctrinaire flag-wavers for Progress, and Islamophobic intellectuals got out of its way."

14   Extending this point, Manuel de Landa (1991, 6) writes, "While at one time only biological phenomena were considered to be relevant for a study of evolution, now inert matter has been found to be capable of generating structures that may be subjected to natural selection. It is as if we have discovered a form of 'non-organic life.'"

15   Anticipating the subsequent discussion, Graham Harman (2002, 37) notes that "both hammers and Dasein are involved in the sheer execution of their respective realities; however different these realities may be from one another, both unleash their forces amidst the world. . . . Regardless of the trivial fact that hammers do not seem to die, gossip, or have a conscience, it must be acknowledged that even inanimate objects require an *existential* consideration of their own."

16   Such an inclusive conception of tool-being is anticipated by Schiller's remarkable statement: "In the Aesthetic State everything—even the tool

which serves—is a free citizen, having equal rights with the noblest; and the mind, which would force the patient mass beneath the yoke of its purpose, must here first obtain its assent" (quoted in Arendt 2007, xxiv). The difference for Harman is that we need not wait for any teleological stage of human history to arrive for such a thing to occur: it does so—always already—whether we decree it or not.

17   Another speculative realist on the rise is Quentin Meillassoux (2008), whose book *After Finitude* resonates sympathetically with much of Harman's work. Meillassoux takes particular issue, however, with what he calls "correlationism": the virtually unchallenged post-Kantian philosophical tradition that "consists in disqualifying the claim that it is possible to consider the realms of subjectivity and objectivity independently of one another" (5). Insisting on the impossibility of accessing external reality, without the mediation of consciousness or language, is—for Meillassoux—to be trapped in "the correlationist circle." It is to be blinded by the prejudice that we cannot think any reality outside of, or independent from, thought. As a result, "all we ever engage with is what is given-to-thought, never an entity subsisting by itself" (36). Thus "contemporary philosophers have lost the *great outdoors,* the *absolute* outside of pre-critical thinkers: that outside which was not relative to us, and which was given as indifferent to its own givenness to be what it is, existing in itself regardless of whether we are thinking of it or not" (7). The swift popularity of this school of thought, represented by Harman and Meillassoux, among others, is partially due to its refusal to place the cognitive or phenomenological, or even ontological, human at the center of the universe. It fosters a radical leveling of phenomena. Some critics, however, believe that it leaves nothing so much in its wake than a poetic list of unconnected objects: a jettisoning of not only the bathwater and the baby but the bathtub itself. The alternative worlds it reveals and unravels are too complex to address in any sustained fashion in this book. I do intend, however, to navigate my way through these ideas and their implications for anthropocentrism in a forthcoming project. In the meantime, the stakes of this philosophical swerve itself, as well as the internal debates it has raised, are published in *The Speculative Turn: Continental Materialism and Realism,* a collection edited by Harman, Bryant, and Srnicek (2010).

18   In a notable passage, Harman (2002, 63) writes, "In everyday life, we tend to conceive of the world as a relatively stable landscape that we ourselves can personally reorganize as thinking, acting, transcending

animals. This encourages the faulty ontological inference that the world's ecstatic structure results from a sort of human mental–physical kinesis, a subjective *Bewegtheit* [motility/emotion] that resolutely goes to work in a theater made up of bland solid blocks. But although the ecstatic environment is indeed conditioned by our own projections, it is still the ecstasis *of the things*: it is still the machine itself that either functions quietly or falls into ruin."

19   In *The Coming Community,* Agamben (1993, 18–19) states, "Decisive here is the idea of an *inessential* commonality, a solidarity that in no way concerns an essence. *Taking-place, the communication of singularities in the attribute of extension, does not unite them in essence, but scatters them in existence.*" For Bataille's notion of "the community of those who have nothing in common," see "Joy in the Face of Death" in *The College of Sociology* (Bataille 1998) as well as Alphonso Lingis's (1994) book, which employs this phrase as its title.

20   An interesting place to begin exploring vegetal machines would be the Swiss-based Federal Ethics Committee on Non-human Biotechnology. Their report, titled "Moral Consideration of Plants for Their Own Sake"—based on the testimony of lawyers, philosophers, geneticists, and theologians—calls for the "dignity" of all life-forms to be taken into consideration as we move into a biotechnological brave new world. The resulting Gene Technology Act aims to establish and respect "an ethical perspective in relation to plants." See http://www.ekah.admin.ch/en/index.html.

21   Recent science newswire reports announced that particles of "inorganic dust" form helical structures and go through "lifelike" changes, interacting, bonding, and bifurcating in analogous ways to biological molecules. What is more, "these complex, self-organized plasma structures exhibit all the necessary properties to qualify them as candidates for inorganic living matter. . . . They are autonomous, they reproduce and they evolve." See the press release available at http://www.eurekalert.org/pub_releases/2007-08/iop-mb081007.php (accessed November 2007).

22   Elsewhere, Baudrillard (1990, 33) writes, "It's as if the species had had enough of its own definition and had thrown itself into an organic delirium."

23   Which would make a certain sense, given Arendt's (1998, 272) claim that "Kant was the last philosopher who was also a kind of astronomer." She also has much to say about "the astounding human capacity to think in terms of the universe while remaining on the earth" (264).

24   See Peter Kreeft, "The Pillars of Unbelief—Kant," http://www.peterkreeft.
     com/topics-more/pillars_kant.htm. In a more recent version of this
     story, Harry Elmer Barnes claims that "astronomically speaking, man
     is almost totally insignificant," to which George Albert Coe responded,
     "Astronomically speaking, man is the astronomer." See Moore (1957, 65).

25   Despite his scientific training, Uexküll has a mystical, almost messianic
     understanding of the logic underpinning and connecting all these her-
     metically sealed environments: "The role which nature plays as the
     object of different scientists' worlds is highly contradictory. Should one
     attempt to combine her objective qualities, chaos would ensue. And
     yet all these diverse *Umwelten* are harbored and borne by the One that
     remains forever barred to all *Umwelten*. Behind all the worlds created
     by Him, there lies concealed, eternally beyond the reach of knowledge,
     the subject—Nature" (von Uexküll 1959, 80).

26   Other than humans, these include all the great apes (chimps, bonobos,
     gorillas, orangutans), bottle-nosed dolphins, elephants, and European
     magpies. See Best's (2009) "Minding the Animals: Ethology and the
     Obsolescence of Left Humanism"; de Veer et al.'s (2003) "An 8-Year
     Longitudinal Study of Mirror Self-Recognition in Chimpanzees *(Pan
     troglodytes)*"; Marten and Psarakos's (1994) "Evidence of Self-Awareness
     in the Bottlenose Dolphin *(Tursiops truncatus)*"; Plotnik, de Waal, and
     Reiss's (2006) "Self-Recognition in an Asian Elephant"; and Prior, Schwarz,
     and Güntürkün's (2008) "Mirror-Induced Behavior in the Magpie *(Pica
     pica)*: Evidence of Self-Recognition."

27   Pierre Teilhard de Chardin (1975, 181) once wrote, "When for the first
     time in a living creature instinct perceived itself in its own mirror, the
     whole world took a pace forward."

28   Derrida (2008, 132) discusses Lacan and "animal mimetism" in relation
     to "the image and 'seeing oneself looking.'" Indeed, he almost approaches
     Harman when he talks of "being seen looking even by a can of sardines
     that doesn't see me."

29   Glen Mazis (2008, 257; emphasis added) closes his sustained meditation
     on the blurred boundaries between the three points of the cybernetic
     triangle with an observation that retains some of the mechanics of the
     anthropological machine, while going beyond its species centrism: "Hu-
     mans, animals, and machines, in their being kin and in being different
     simultaneously, give the planet an opportunity to find itself *mirrored*
     in differing kinds of enactments and differing sorts of *registrations* of
     its wonder." This is not an anthropological machine, then, nor even a

zoological one, but a more inclusive kind of "cosmological machine." Previous to this conclusion, Mazis almost succumbs to the astronomic double gesture, as when he talks of humanity's unique excellence being its capacity to "witness" the wonder of the world (and beyond). However, his marriage of phenomenology and ecospirituality manages to keep a certain symmetry at work between all the elements involved, much like a kinder, gentler version of Harman.

30   The first time we find this proverb in its colloquial form is in Leonardo da Vinci's (2008, 105) notebooks: "The eye which is the window of the soul is the chief organ whereby the understanding can have the most complete and magnificent view of the infinite works of nature." The phrase can be traced back, however, to the New Testament: "The light of the body is the eye: if therefore thine eye be single, thy whole body shall be full of light. But if thine eye be evil, thy whole body shall be full of darkness. If therefore the light that is in thee be darkness, how great is that darkness!" (Matthew 6:22–23). Indeed, Cicero came close to the familiar saying when he stated, "*Ut imago est animi voltus sic indices oculi*" ("The face is a picture of the mind as the eyes are its interpreter").

31   Lacan (2004, 3) begins his famous piece on the mirror stage by differentiating between human children and chimpanzees, positing a complex interplay between recognition, reflection, "illuminative mimicry," and "the expression of situational apperception." "This act," he asserts, is distinct from "the case of the monkey," in which "the image has been mastered and found empty." Thanks to Cynthia Lugo for encouraging me to look at this canonical text with fresh eyes.

Bibliography

Adorno, Theodor W. 2005. *Minima Moralia: Reflections on a Damaged Life.* New York: Verso.

Agamben, Giorgio. 1993. *The Coming Community.* Minneapolis: University of Minnesota Press.

———. 1998. *Homo Sacer: Sovereign Power and Bare Life.* Stanford, Calif.: Stanford University Press.

———. 2000. *Means without End: Notes on Politics.* Minneapolis: University of Minnesota Press.

———. 2004. *The Open: Man and Animal.* Stanford, Calif.: Stanford University Press.

———. 2007. *Profanations.* New York: Zone Books.

———. 2009. *What Is an Apparatus? and Other Essays.* Stanford, Calif.: Stanford University Press.

Akerlof, George A., and Robert J. Shiller. 2009. *Animal Spirits: How Human Psychology Drives the Economy, and Why It Matters for Global Capitalism.* Princeton, N.J.: Princeton University Press.

Alleyne, Richard. 2008. "YouTube: Overnight Success Has Sparked a Backlash." *The Telegraph,* July 31.

Arendt, Hannah. 1998. *The Human Condition.* Chicago: University of Chicago Press.

———. 2007. *Reflections on Literature and Culture.* Stanford, Calif.: Stanford University Press.

Badiou, Alain. 2002. *Ethics: An Essay on the Understanding of Evil.* New York: Verso.

Baker, J. A. 2005. *The Peregrine.* New York: New York Review Books Classics.

Baker, Steve. 2000. *The Postmodern Animal*. London: Reaktion.

Bataille, Georges. 1988. *The College of Sociology (1937–39)*. Trans. Denis Hollier. Minneapolis: University of Minnesota Press.

———. 1993. *The Accursed Share: An Essay on General Economy*. New York: Zone Books.

Baudrillard, Jean. 1987. *Forget Foucault*. New York: Semiotext(e).

———. 1990. *Fatal Strategies*. New York: Semiotext(e).

———. 1993. *Symbolic Exchange and Death*. London: Sage.

———. 2010. *Ventriloquous Evil*. Trans. Chris Turner. London: Seagull Press.

Ballard, J. G. 1973. *Crash*. New York: Picador, Farrar, Straus, and Giroux.

Benjamin, Walter. 2006. *Selected Writings, Volume 3: 1935–1938*. Cambridge, Mass.: Belknap Press.

Bentham, Jeremy. 1907. *An Introduction to the Principles of Morals and Legislation*. London: Oxford at the Clarendon Press.

Berger, John. 1980. "Why Look at Animals?" In *About Looking*. New York: Pantheon.

Bersani, Leo. 1986. *The Freudian Body: Psychoanalysis and Art*. New York: Columbia University Press.

Bersani, Leo, and Adam Phillips. 2008. *Intimacies*. Chicago: University of Chicago Press.

Best, Stephen. 2009. "Minding the Animals: Ethology and the Obsolescence of Left Humanism." *American Chronicle*, May 17. http://www.american-chronicle.com/articles/view/102661.

Bieder, Robert E. 2005. *Bear*. London: Reaktion.

Black, Richard. 2008. "Wild Dolphins Tail-Walk on Water." *BBC News Online*, August 19. http://news.bbc.co.uk/2/hi/science/nature/7570097.stm.

Bloom, Harold. 1998. *Shakespeare: The Invention of the Human*. New York: Riverhead.

Bourke, Anthony, and John Rendall. 2009. *A Lion Called Christian: The True Story of the Remarkable Bond between Two Friends and a Lion*. New York: Broadway.

Bradley, Arthur. 2006. "Originary Technicity? Technology and Anthropology." In *Technicity*, ed. Arthur Bradley and Louis Armand. Prague: Litteraria Pragensia.

Brautigan, Richard. 1989. *Troutfishing in America—The Pill versus the Springhill Mine Disaster—In Watermelon Sugar*. Boston: Mariner Books.

Briggs, Helen. 2005. "Chimpanzee Culture 'Confirmed,'" *BBC News Online*, August 22. http://news.bbc.co.uk/2/hi/science/nature/4166756.stm.

Broch, Hermann. 1995. *The Death of Virgil*. New York: Vintage Books.

Buber, Martin. 1996. *I and Thou.* Trans. Walter Kaufman. New York: Touchstone.

Caillois, Roger. 2003. "The Praying Mantis: From Biology to Psychoanalysis." In *The Edge of Surrealism: A Roger Caillois Reader,* trans. and ed. Claudine Frank. Durham, N.C.: Duke University Press.

Camus, Albert. 1984. *The Rebel: An Essay on Man in Revolt.* Trans. Anthony Bower. New York: Alfred A. Knopf.

Cassidy, Rebecca. 2009. "Zoosex and Other Relationships with Animals." In *Transgressive Sex: Subversion and Control in Erotic Encounters,* ed. Donnan Hastings and Fiona Magowan. Oxford: Berghahn Books.

Cavell, Stanley, Cora Diamond, John McDowell, Ian Hacking, and Cary Wolfe. 2008. *Philosophy and Animal Life.* New York: Columbia University Press.

Chamberlain, Lesley. 1996. *Nietzsche in Turin: The End of the Future.* London: Quartet Books.

Chris, Cynthia. 2006. *Watching Wildlife.* Minneapolis: University of Minnesota Press.

Clemens, Justin, and Dominic Pettman. 2004. *Avoiding the Subject: Media, Culture, and the Object.* Amsterdam, Netherlands: Amsterdam University Press.

Collins, Francis S. 2006. *The Language of God: A Scientist Presents Evidence for Belief.* New York: Free Press.

Collodi, Carlo. 2008. *Pinocchio.* New York: New York Review Books Classics.

Commercial Advertiser. 1903. "Bad Elephant Killed. Topsy Meets Quick and Painless Death at Coney Island." January 5.

Connolly, Kate. 2007. "Court to Rule If Chimp Has Human Rights." *The Observer,* April 1. http://www.guardian.co.uk/world/2007/apr/01/austria.animalwelfare.

Damisch, Hubert. 2001. *Skyline: The Narcissistic City.* Stanford, Calif.: Stanford University Press.

da Vinci, Leonardo. 2008. *Notebooks.* Ed. Theresa Wells. Oxford: Oxford University Press.

Dawkins, Richard. 1989. *The Selfish Gene.* Oxford: Oxford University Press.

Dean, Jodi. 2009a. *Democracy and Other Neo-liberal Fantasies: Communicative Capitalism and Left Politics.* Durham, N.C.: Duke University Press.

———. 2009b. "The Real Internet." Paper presented to the Faculty of Philosophy, Erasmus University, June 22.

Deibert, Ronald J. 1997. *Parchment, Printing, and Hypermedia: Communication in World Order Transformation.* New York: Columbia University Press.

de la Mettrie, Julien O. 1996. *Machine Man and Other Writings*. Cambridge: Cambridge University Press.

de Landa, Manuel. 1991. *War in the Age of Intelligent Machines*. New York: Zone Books.

Deleuze, Gilles, and Félix Guattari. 1986. *Kafka: Toward a Minor Literature*. Minneapolis: University of Minnesota Press.

———. 1987. *A Thousand Plateaus: Capitalism and Schizophrenia*. Minneapolis: University of Minnesota Press.

Derrida, Jacques. 1994. *Specters of Marx: The State of the Debt, the Work of Mourning, and the New International*. New York: Routledge.

———. 2008. *The Animal That Therefore I Am*. New York: Fordham University Press.

Descartes, René. 2006. *A Discourse on the Method of Correctly Conducting One's Reason and Seeking Truth in the Sciences*. Oxford: Oxford University Press.

de Tocqueville, Alexis. 2003. *Democracy in America: and Two Essays on America*. London: Penguin.

de Veer, Monique, Gordon G. Gallup Jr., Laura A. Theall, Ruud van den Bos, and Daniel J. Povinelli. 2003. "An 8-Year Longitudinal Study of Mirror Self-Recognition in Chimpanzees *(Pan troglodytes)*." *Neuropsychologia* 41, no. 2: 229–34.

Diamond, Jared. 2006. *The Third Chimpanzee: The Evolution and Future of the Human Animal*. New York: Harper Perennial.

Dick, Philip K. 1996. *Do Androids Dream of Electric Sheep?* New York: Ballantine Books.

Doane, Mary A. 1997. "Screening Time." In *Language Machines: Technologies of Literary and Cultural Production,* ed. Jeffrey Masten, Peter Stallybrass, and Nancy J. Vickers. New York: Routledge.

Dolar, Mladen. 2006. *A Voice and Nothing More*. Cambridge, Mass.: MIT Press.

Donnan, Hastings, and Fiona Magowan. 2009. *Transgressive Sex: Subversion and Control in Erotic Encounters*. New York: Berghahn Books.

Dorré, Gina M. 2006. *Victorian Fiction and the Cult of the Horse*. Surrey, U.K.: Ashgate.

Doyle, Alister. 2007. "UN Urges World to Slow Extinction: 3 Each Hour." Reuters, May 23. http://www.planetark.org/dailynewsstory.cfm/newsid/42067/story.htm.

Doyle, Arthur C. 1928. "When the World Screamed." Online: Classic Literature Library. http://www.classic-literature.co.uk/scottish-authors/arthur-conan-doyle/when-the-world-screamed/.

Doyle, Jack, and Environmental Health Fund. 2004. *Trespass against Us: Dow Chemical and the Toxic Century*. Monroe, Maine: Common Courage Press.

Dumont, Louis. 1974. *Homo Hierarchicus: The Caste System and Its Implications*. Chicago: University of Chicago Press.

During, Simon, ed. 1999. *The Cultural Studies Reader*. 2nd ed. London: Routledge.

Eagleton, Terry. 2009. "Culture and Barbarism: Metaphysics in a Time of Terror." *Commonweal* 136, no. 6. http://commonwealmagazine.org/culture-barbarism-0.

Ernst, Wolfgang. 2005. "Resonance of the Siren Songs." Lecture, Bard Hall, New York, April 8. http://www.e2-nyc.org/pics/TADs/TAD10/TAD%252010%2520Ernst.pdf (accessed February 2007).

Estés, Clarissa P. 1992. *Women Who Run with the Wolves: Myths and Stories of the Wild Woman Archetype*. New York: Ballantine Books.

Evans, E. P. 1998. *The Criminal Prosecution and Capital Punishment of Animals*. Union, N.J.: Lawbook Exchange.

Foucault, Michel. 1973. *The Order of Things: An Archaeology of the Human Sciences*. New York: Vintage.

———. 1995. *Discipline and Punish: The Birth of the Prison*. New York: Vintage Books.

Frayn, Michael. 2006. *The Human Touch: Our Part in the Creation of a Universe*. London: Faber and Faber.

Freud, Sigmund. 1950. *Totem and Taboo: Some Points of Agreement between the Mental Lives of Savages and Neurotics*. London: Routledge and Paul.

———. 1955. *Moses and Monotheism*. New York: Vintage Books.

———. 1989. *Civilization and Its Discontents*. New York: W. W. Norton.

———. 2001. *On Dreams*. New York: Dover.

Galloway, Alexander R., and Eugene Thacker. 2007. *The Exploit: A Theory of Networks*. Minneapolis: University of Minnesota Press.

Garnsey, Peter. 1999. "Forbidden Foods." In *Food and Society in Classical Antiquity*. Cambridge: Cambridge University Press.

Genta, G. 2007. *Lonely Minds in the Universe*. New York: Copernicus Books.

Geras, Norman. 1983. *Marx and Human Nature: Refutation of a Legend*. London: Verso.

Goethe, Johann Wolfgang von. 1998. *Maxims and Reflections*. London: Penguin Classics.

Goldsby, Jacqueline D. 2006. *A Spectacular Secret: Lynching in American Life and Literature*. Chicago: University of Chicago Press.

Gombrich, E. H. 1994. *The Image and the Eye: Further Studies in the Psychology of Pictorial Representation.* London: Phaidon.

Goodman, Lenn Evan. 1978. Introduction to *The Case of the Animals versus Man before the King of the Jinn: A Tenth-century Ecological Fable of the Pure Brethren of Basra.* By Basra Ikhwān al-Ṣafāʾ. Boston: Twayne.

Grandin, Temple. 2009. *Animals Make Us Human: Creating the Best Life for Animals.* New York: Houghton Mifflin Harcourt.

Grandin, Temple, and Catherine Johnson. 2005. *Animals in Translation: Using the Mysteries of Autism to Decode Animal Behavior.* New York: Scribner.

Gray, John. 2007. *Straw Dogs: Thoughts on Humans and Other Animals.* New York: Farrar, Straus, and Giroux.

Green, André. 2001. *Life Narcissism, Death Narcissism.* London: Free Association Books.

Guattari, Félix. 1995. *Chaosmosis: An Ethico-Aesthetic Paradigm.* Sydney, Australia: Power Institute.

———. 2000. *The Three Ecologies.* London: Athlone Press.

Haraway, Donna J. 1991. *Simians, Cyborgs, and Women: The Reinvention of Nature.* New York: Routledge.

———. 2008. *When Species Meet.* Minneapolis: University of Minnesota Press.

Hardt, Michael, and Antonio Negri. 2000. *Empire.* Cambridge, Mass.: Harvard University Press.

Hari, John. 2009. "The Dark Side of Dubai." *The Independent,* April 7. http://www.independent.co.uk/opinion/commentators/johann-hari/the-dark-side-of-dubai-1664368.html.

Harman, Graham. 2002. *Tool-Being: Heidegger and the Metaphyics of Objects.* Chicago: Open Court.

Harman, Graham, Levi Bryant, and Nick Srnicek, eds. 2010. *The Speculative Turn: Continental Materialism and Realism.* Melbourne, Australia: Re.Press.

Harper, Jennifer. 2008. "Biggest New Year's Tradition: The Kiss." *Washington Times,* December 31. http://www.washingtontimes.com/news/2008/dec/31/biggest-new-years-tradition-the-kiss/.

Hatherley, Owen. 2009. *Militant Modernism.* Kalamazoo, Mich.: Zero.

Hauser, M. D., N. Chomsky, and W. T. Fitch. 2002. "The Faculty of Language: What Is It, Who Has It, and How Did It Evolve?" *Science* 298: 1569–79.

Hazlitt, William. 1889. "On Wit and Humor." In *Essays of William Hazlitt.* London: Walter Scott.

Heidegger, Martin. 1977. "The Age of the World Picture." In *The Question*

Concerning Technology, and Other Essays. New York: Harper and Row.

Heise, Ursula K. 2003. "From Extinction to Electronics: Dead Frogs, Live Dinosaurs, and Electric Sheep." In *Zoontologies: The Question of the Animal,* ed. Cary Wolfe. Minneapolis: University of Minnesota Press.

Hsu, Feng-hsiung. 2002. *Behind Deep Blue: Building the Computer That Defeated the World Chess Champion.* Princeton, N.J.: Princeton University Press.

Hudson, Laura. 2008. "The Political Animal: Species-Being and Bare Life." *Mediations* 23, no. 2: 88–117.

Ikhwān al-Ṣafāʾ, Basra. 1978. *The Case of the Animals versus Man before the King of the Jinn: A Tenth-century Ecological Fable of the Pure Brethren of Basra.* Boston: Twayne.

Invisible Committee. 2009. *The Coming Insurrection.* Los Angeles, Calif.: Semiotext(e).

Johnson, Marguerite, and Terry Ryan. 2005. *Sexuality in Greek and Roman Society and Literature: A Sourcebook.* New York: Routledge.

Jones, David. 2009. "Hermes Breeds Own Crocs to Meet Bag Demands." Reuters, June 8. http://www.reuters.com/article/GlobalLuxury09/idUSTRE5573QI20090608.

Kafka, Ben. 2008–9. "Ingestion: Power Hungry." *Cabinet* 32: 7–8.

Kampowski, Stephen. 2008. *Arendt, Augustine, and the New Beginning.* Grand Rapids, MI: William B. Eerdmans.

Kaplan, Michael, and Ellen Kaplan. 2009. *Bozo Sapiens: Why to Err Is Human.* New York: Bloomsbury.

Kastner, Jeffrey. 2001. "Animals on Trial." *Cabinet Online,* no. 4. http://www.cabinetmagazine.org/issues/4/animalsontrial.php.

Keats, John, and Hyder E. Rollins. 1958. *The Letters of John Keats.* Cambridge, Mass.: Harvard University Press.

Khalip, Jacques. 2006. "Virtual Conduct: Disinterested Agency in Hazlitt and Keats." *ELH* 73, no. 4: 885–912.

Kittler, Friedrich. 1999. *Gramophone, Film, Typewriter.* Stanford, Calif.: Stanford University Press.

———. 2001. *Discourse Networks: 1800/1900.* Stanford, Calif.: Stanford University Press.

Klein, Naomi. 2007. *The Shock Doctrine: The Rise of Disaster Capitalism.* New York: Metropolitan Books/Henry Holt.

Kurosawa, Akira. 1983. "Some Random Notes on Filmmaking." In *Something Like an Autobiography.* New York: Vintage.

Lacan, Jacques. 2004. "The Mirror Stage as Formative of the *I* Function." In

Écrits: A Selection. New York: W. W. Norton.

Lasch, Christopher. 1991. *The Culture of Narcissism: American Life in an Age of Diminishing Expectations.* New York: W. W. Norton.

Latour, Bruno. 1993. *We Have Never Been Modern.* Cambridge, Mass.: Harvard University Press.

———. 2004. "A Collective of Humans and Nonhumans." In *Readings in the Philosophy of Technology,* ed. David Kaplan. Lanham, Md.: Rowman and Littlefield.

Lautréamont, Comte de. 1994. *Maldoror and the Complete Works of the Comte de Lautréamont.* Cambridge: Exact Change.

Leblanc, Steven, and Katherine Register. 2003. *Constant Battles: The Myth of the Peaceful, Noble Savage.* New York: St. Martin's Press.

Levin, Thomas. 1995. "Before the Beep: A Short History of Voice Mail." In *Technophobia: Essays in Sound 2.* http://www.sysx.org/soundsite/csa/eis2content/essays/p59_beep.html.

Levinas, Emmanuel. 1990. "The Name of a Dog, or Natural Rights." In *Difficult Freedom.* Baltimore: Johns Hopkins University Press.

Lingis, Alphonso. 1994. *The Community of Those Who Have Nothing in Common.* Bloomington: Indiana University Press.

Lovelock, J. E. 1990. "Hands up for the Gaia Hypothesis." *Nature* 244, no. 6262: 100–2.

Luhmann, Niklas. 1990. *Essays on Self-Reference.* New York: Columbia University Press.

Lyotard, Jean-François. 1993. *Libidinal Economy.* Bloomington: Indiana University Press.

MacKay, David. 2009. *Sustainable Energy: Without the Hot Air.* Cambridge: UIT Cambridge. http://www.withouthotair.com/.

Maines, Rachel P. 1998. *The Technology of Orgasm: "Hysteria," the Vibrator, and Women's Sexual Satisfaction.* Baltimore: Johns Hopkins University Press.

Manaugh, Geoff. 2009. *BLDG Blog.* San Francisco: Chronicle.

Manjoo, Farhad. 2009. "You Have No New Messages—Ever." *Slate,* May 8. http://www.slate.com/id/2217998/.

Marcuse, Herbert. 1974. *Eros and Civilization: A Philosophical Enquiry into Freud.* Boston: Beacon Press.

———. 2002. *One-Dimensional Man: Studies in the Ideology of Advanced Industrial Society.* London: Routledge.

Margulis, Lynn. 1998. *Symbiotic Planet: A New Look at Evolution.* New York: Basic Books.

Marten, Kenneth, and Suchi Psarakos. 1994. "Evidence of Self-Awareness

---

in the Bottlenose Dolphin *(Tursiops truncatus)."* In *Self-Awareness in Animals and Humans: Developmental Perspectives,* ed. Sue Taylor Parker, Robert W. Mitchell, and Maria Boccia. Cambridge: Cambridge University Press.

Martial. 1993. *Epigrams.* 3 vols. Loeb Classical Library. Cambridge, Mass.: Harvard University Press.

Marx, Karl. 1970. *The German Ideology.* New York: International.

———. 1986. *Karl Marx: A Reader.* Ed. Jon Elster. Cambridge: Cambridge University Press.

———. 1988. *Economic and Philosophic Manuscripts of 1844.* Buffalo, N.Y.: Prometheus Books.

———. 1992. *Capital: A Critique of Political Economy.* London: Penguin and New Left Review.

———. 2002. *Marx on Religion.* Ed. John Raines. Philadelphia: Temple University Press.

———. 2008. *The Poverty of Philosophy.* New York: Cosimo Classics.

Mason, Peter. 1997. *The Brown Dog Affair.* London: Two Sevens.

Maturana, Humberto R., and Francisco Varela. 1980. *Autopoiesis and Cognition: The Realization of the Living.* Dordrecht, Netherlands: D. Reidel.

Mazis, Glen A. 2008. *Humans, Animals, Machines: Blurring Boundaries.* Albany: State University of New York Press.

Mazlish, Bruce. 1993. *The Fourth Discontinuity: The Co-evolution of Humans and Machines.* New Haven, Conn.: Yale University Press.

McConnell, Louise. 2003. *Exit, Pursued by a Bear: Shakespeare's Characters, Plays, Poems, History, and Stagecraft.* London: Bloomsbury.

Mcfarlane, Robert. 2005. Introduction to *The Peregrine.* Edited by J. A. Baker. New York: New York Review Books Classics.

Meillassoux, Quentin. 2008. *After Finitude: An Essay on the Necessity of Contingency.* Trans. Ray Brassier. London: Continuum.

Miller, Jacques-Alain. 2009. "You Are the Woman of the Other, and I Desire You." Trans. Jorge Jauregui. http://www.lacan.com/essays/?page_id=331.

Milton, John. 1996. *Dynamics of Small Neural Populations.* Providence, R.I.: American Mathematical Society.

Moore, James B. 1957. "Why Young Ministers Are Leaving the Church." *Harper's,* July.

Morris, Desmond. 1967. *The Naked Ape: A Zoologist's Study of the Human Animal.* New York: McGraw-Hill.

Morton, Timothy. 2007. *Ecology without Nature: Rethinking Environmental*

Aesthetics. Cambridge, Mass.: Harvard University Press.

Musil, Robert. 1999a. "Grigia." In *Five Women.* Boston: D. R. Godine.

———. 1999b. "The Temptations of Veronica." In *Five Women.* Boston: D. R. Godine.

Nabokov, Vladimir, and Alfred Appel Jr. 1991. *The Annotated Lolita.* New York: Vintage Books.

Nardo, Don. 2008. *Tycho Brahe: Pioneer of Astronomy.* Mankato, Minn.: Compass Point Books.

Negarestani, Reza. 2008. *Cyclonopedia: Complicity with Anonymous Materials.* Melbourne, Australia: Re.Press.

Nietzsche, Friedrich. 1967. *The Genealogy of Morals.* New York: Random House.

Parker-Pope, Tara. 2008. "The Brain of a Bully." *New York Times,* November 12. http://well.blogs.nytimes.com/2008/11/12/the-brain-of-a-bully/.

Pearson, Emma. 2003. "Fish Porn Casts Sexy Lure." *The Age,* June 13. http://www.theage.com.au/articles/2003/06/12/1055220705939.html.

Perel, Esther. 2007. *Mating in Captivity: Unlocking Erotic Intelligence.* New York: Harper.

Pessoa, Fernando. 2003. *The Book of Disquiet.* London: Penguin Classics.

Pettman, Dominic. 2002. *After the Orgy: Toward a Politics of Exhaustion.* Albany: State University of New York Press.

———. 2006. *Love and Other Technologies: Retrofitting Eros for the Information Age.* New York: Fordham University Press.

Plotnik, Joshua M., Frans de Waal, and Diana Reiss. 2006. "Self-Recognition in an Asian Elephant." *Proceedings of the National Academy of Sciences of the United States of America* 103, no. 45: 17053–57.

Postman, Neil. 2006. *Amusing Ourselves to Death: Public Discourse in the Age of Show Business.* New York: Penguin.

Price, David. 1995. "Energy and Human Evolution." *Population and Environment* 16, no. 4: 301–19.

Prior, Helmut, Ariane Schwarz, and Onur Güntürkün. 2008. "Mirror-Induced Behavior in the Magpie *(Pica pica):* Evidence of Self-Recognition." *PLoS Biology* 6, no. 8: 1642–50.

Rabinbach, Anson. 1992. *The Human Motor: Energy, Fatigue, and the Origins of Modernity.* Berkeley: University of California Press.

Raffles, Hugh. 2002. *In Amazonia: A Natural History.* Princeton, N.J.: Princeton University Press.

———. 2007. "The Language of Bees." *Cabinet Online,* no. 25. http://www.cabinetmagazine.org/issues/25/raffles.php.

———. 2010. *Insectopedia*. New York: Pantheon.

Rilke, Rainer M. 1939. *Duino Elegies*. Berkeley: New York: W. W. Norton.

Robinson, Andrew. 2007. *The Story of Writing*. London: Thames and Hudson.

Rosen, Jody. 2008. "The Best Music of 2008 Was the Oldest." *Slate*, December 22. http://www.slate.com/id/2206848/entry/2207289/.

Ross, Daniel. 2006. "Democracy, Authority, Narcissism: From Agamben to Stiegler." *Contretemps* 6. http://www.usyd.edu.au/contretemps/6January2006/ross.pdf.

———. 2007. "The Cinematic Condition of the Politico-Philosophical Future." *Scan: Journal of Media Arts and Culture* 4, no. 2. http://scan.net.au/scan/journal/display.php?journal_id=99.

Roth, Daniel. 2009. "Do Humanlike Machines Deserve Human Rights?" *Wired* 17, no. 2. http://www.wired.com/culture/culturereviews/magazine/17–02/st_essay (accessed February 2009).

Ryder, Richard D. 2000. *Animal Revolution: Changing Attitudes toward Speciesism*. New York: Berg.

Sagan, Carl. 1978. *Murmurs of Earth: The Voyager Interstellar Record*. New York: Random House.

Salen, William. 2007. "Chess Bump: The Triumphant Teamwork of Humans and Computers." *Slate*, May 11. http://www.slate.com/id/2166000?nav=tap3.

Santner, Eric L. 2006. *On Creaturely Life: Rilke, Benjamin, Sebald*. Chicago: University of Chicago Press.

Sarup, Madan. 1993. *An Introductory Guide to Post-structuralism and Postmodernism*. New York: Harvester Wheatsheaf.

Scarry, Elaine. 1985. *The Body in Pain: The Making and Unmaking of the World*. New York: Oxford University Press.

Scribner, Charles Siebert. 2009. *The Wauchula Woods Accord: Toward a New Understanding of Animals*. New York: Scribner.

Shaviro, Steven. 2009. "Against Self-Organization." *The Pinocchio Theory*, May 26. http://www.shaviro.com/Blog/?p=756.

Siebert, Charles. 2006. "Are We Driving Elephants Crazy?" *New York Times Magazine* 6: 44.

Siegel, Lee. 2008. *Against the Machine: Being Human in the Age of the Electronic Mob*. New York: Spiegel and Grau.

Singer, Peter. 2001. "Heavy Petting." *Nerve*, March 1. http://www.nerve.com/opinions/singer/heavypetting/.

Sloterdijk, Peter. 2005. "Kynicism and Legality." Lecture, Cardozo School of Law, April 18.

Standage, Tom. 2003. *The Turk: The Life and Times of the Famous Eighteenth-*

century Chess-Playing Machine. New York: Berkley Books.

Steiner, Gary. 2005. *Anthropocentrism and Its Discontents: The Moral Status of Animals in the History of Western Philosophy.* Pittsburgh, Pa.: University of Pittsburgh Press.

Stewart, Ian. 2002. *Does God Play Dice? The New Mathematics of Chaos.* Malden, Mass.: Blackwell.

Stiegler, Bernard. 1998. *Technics and Time.* Stanford, Calif.: Stanford University Press.

———. 2009. *Acting Out.* Stanford, Calif.: Stanford University Press.

———. n.d. "Constitution and Individuation." *Ars Industrialis.* http://www.arsindustrialis.org/node/2927.

———. n.d. "Desire and Knowledge: The Dead Seize the Living." *Ars Industrialis.* http://www.arsindustrialis.org/desire-and-knowledge-dead-seize-living.

———. n.d. "The Disaffected Individual in the Process of Psychic and Collective Individuation." *Ars Industrialis.* http://www.arsindustrialis.org/disaffected-individual-process-psychic-and-collective-disindividuation.

———. n.d. "Our Ailing Educational Institutions: The Global Mnemotechnical System." *Culture Machine.* http://www.culturemachine.net/index.php/cm/article/viewArticle/258/243.

———. n.d. "Take Care *(Prendre Soin)*." *Ars Industrialis.* http://www.arsindustrialis.org/node/2925.

———. n.d. "Within the Limits of Capitalism, Economizing Means Taking Care." *Ars Industrialis.* http://www.arsindustrialis.org/node/2922.

Stoekl, Allan. 2007. *Bataille's Peak: Energy, Religion, and Postsustainability.* Minneapolis: University of Minnesota Press.

Tainter, Joseph A. 1996. "Complexity, Problem Solving, and Sustainable Societies." In *Getting Down to Earth: Practical Applications of Ecological Economics,* ed. Robert Costanza, Olman Segura Bonilla, Juan Martinez Alier, and International Society for Ecological Economics. Washington, D.C.: Island Press.

Teilhard de Chardin, Pierre. 1975. *The Phenomenon of Man.* New York: Harper Perennial.

Tolstoy, Leo. 2006. *Anna Karenina.* New York: Penguin Classics.

Twain, Mark. 1919. *What Is Man? and Other Essays.* London: Chatto and Windus.

Twenge, Jean, and Keith Campbell. 2009. *The Narcissism Epidemic: Living in the Age of Entitlement.* New York: Free Press.

Viegas, Jennifer. 2009. "Chimp-Made Toolkit Most Complex Ever Found." *Discovery Channel News,* June 2. http://dsc.discovery.com/news/2009/06/02/chimpanzee-tool-kit.html.

von Uexküll, Jakob. 1959. "A Stroll through the Worlds of Animals and Men: A Picture Book of Invisible Worlds." In *Instinctive Behavior: A Development of a Modern Concept,* ed. Claire H. Schiller. New York: International Universities Press.

Wadham, Lucy. 2009. "Sarko the Sex Dwarf." *Prospect,* June. http://www.prospect-magazine.co.uk/article_details.php?id=10820.

Walker, Matt. 2007. *Fish That Fake Orgasms: And Other Zoological Curiosities.* New York: St. Martin's Press.

———. 2008. "'Sex Pest' Seal Attacks Penguin." *BBC News Online,* May 2. http://news.bbc.co.uk/2/hi/science/nature/7379554.stm.

Ward, Peter. 2009. *The Medea Hypothesis: Is Life on Earth Ultimately Self-Destructive?* Cambridge, Mass.: MIT Press.

Wiener, Norbert. 1988. *The Human Use of Human Beings: Cybernetics and Society.* New York: Da Capo Press.

Williams, Alex. 2009. "Planet Earth Rocks (or Even Waltzes). You Pick." *New York Times,* April 19. http://www.nytimes.com/2009/04/19/fashion/19planet.html?hpw.

Wills, David. 2008. *Dorsality: Thinking Back through Technology and Politics.* Minneapolis: University of Minnesota Press.

Wilson, Edward O. 1998. *Consilience: The Unity of Knowledge.* New York: Knopf.

Youatt, Rafi. 2008. "Counting Species: Biopower and the Global Biodiversity Census." *Environmental Values* 17, no. 3: 393–417.

Žižek, Slavoj. 1997. *The Plague of Fantasies.* London: Verso.

Zuckerman, Andrew. 2007. *Creatures.* San Francisco: Chronicle Books.

Filmography / Videography

Alien. Dir. Ridley Scott. Brandywine Productions, 1979.

American Furry. Dir. Marianne Shaneen. Rabbit Hole Films, 2009.

Animal Love. Dir. Ulrich Seidl. Lotus Film, 1995.

Artificial Intelligence: AI. Dir. Steven Spielberg. Warner Bros., 2001.

Barbarella. Dir. Roger Vadim. Dino de Laurentis Cinematografica, 1968.

The Beast. Dir. Walerian Borowczyk. Argos Films, 1975.

Beautiful World. Dir. Mieke Gerritzen and Geert Lovink. All Media Productions, 2006.

Blade Runner. Dir. Ridley Scott. The Ladd Company and Warner Bros., 1982.

Brief Encounter. Dir. David Lean. Cineguild, 1945.

Cannibal Holocaust. Dir. Ruggero Deodato. F. D. Cinematografica, 1980.

The Century of the Self. Dir. Adam Curtis. BBC, 2002.

The Crowd. Dir. King Vidor. MGM, 1928.

A Crude Awakening: The Oil Crash. Dir. Basil Gelpke, Ray McCormack, and Reto Caduff. Lava Productions, 2006.

Darwin's Nightmare. Dir. Hubert Sauper. Mille et Une Productions, 2004.

David Hockney: Secret Knowledge. Dir. Randall Wright. BBC, 2002.

Desk Set. Dir. Walter Lang. Twentieth Century Fox, 1957.

Drawn Together. Dir. Dave Jeser. Comedy Central, 2004.

Ecstasy. Dir. Gustav Machatý. Elektafilm, 1933.

Electrocuting an Elephant. Dir. Thomas Edison, Arthur Kennedy, and Harold P. Brown. Edison Manufacturing Company, 1903.

Encounters at the End of the World. Dir. Werner Herzog. Discovery Films, 2007.

E.T.: The Extra-Terrestrial. Dir. Steven Spielberg. Universal Pictures, 1982.

Fast, Cheap, and Out of Control. Dir. Erol Morris. American Playhouse, 1997.

Flight of the Conchords. Dir. Jemaine Clement and Bret McKenzie. HBO, 2007–9.

The Girlfriend Experience. Dir. Steven Soderbergh. 2929 Productions, 2009.

The Gleaners and I. Dir. Agnès Varda. Ciné Tamaris, 2000.

Green Porno. Dir. Isabella Rossellini. Sundance Channel, 2008.

Grizzly Man. Dir. Werner Herzog. Discovery Films, 2005.

Heaven's Gate. Dir. Michael Cimino. Partisan Productions, 1980.

Idiocracy. Dir. Mike Judge. Twentieth Century Fox, 2006.

Immoral Women. Dir. Walerian Borowczyk. Argos Films, 1979.

The Ister. Dir. David Barison and Daniel Ross. Black Box Sound and Image, 2004.

Koko: A Talking Gorilla. Dir. Barbet Schroeder. Institut National de l'Audio-visuel, 1978.

Koyaanisqatsi. Dir. Godfrey Reggio. Santa Fe Institute for Regional Education, 1982.

L'avventura. Dir. Michelangelo Antonioni. Cino del Duca, Produzioni Cinematografiche Europee (PCE), and Societé Cinématographique Lyre, 1960.

Lessons of Darkness. Dir. Werner Herzog. Canal+, 1992.

The Letter. Dir. William Wyler. Warner Bros., 1940.

Life after People. Dir. David de Vries. Flight 33 Productions, 2008.

Mechanical Love. Dir. Phie Ambo. Tju-Bang Film, 2007.

My Kid Could Paint That. Dir. Amir Bar-Lev. A&E IndieFilms, 2007.

Ninotchka. Dir. Ernst Lubitsch. MGM, 1939.

No Maps for These Territories. Dir. Mark Neals. Mark Neale Productions, 2000.

Performance. Dir. Nicolas Roeg. Goodtimes Enterprises, 1970.

The Pervert's Guide to Cinema. Dir. Sophie Fiennes. Amoeba Films and Lone Star Productions, 2006.

Project Grizzly. Dir. Peter Lynch. National Film Board of Canada, 1996.

Revenge of the Nerds. Dir. Jeff Kanew. Interscope, 1984.

Southern Comfort. Dir. Kate Davis. Q-Ball Productions, 2001.

Speed. Dir. Jan de Bont. Twentieth Century Fox, 1994.

Star Trek IV: The Voyage Home. Dir. Leonard Nimoy. Paramount Pictures, 1986.

Stay (aka Sleeping Dogs). Dir. Bobcat Goldthwaite. HareBrained Pictures, 2006.

Terminator 2: Judgment Day. Dir. Cameron James. Carolco Pictures, 1991.

Terminator 4: Salvation. Dir. McG. The Halcyon Company, 2009.

There Will Be Blood. Dir. Paul T. Anderson. Ghoulardi, 2007.

WALL-E. Dir. Andrew Stanton. Pixar, 2008.

Waltz with Bashir. Dir. Ari Folman. Bridgit Folman Film Gang, 2008.

Winged Migration. Dir. Jacques Perrin. Bac Films, 2001.

Zoo. Dir. Robinson Devor. ThinkFilm and Cook Ding, 2007.

Index

in, 21, 23; functional meshing
of machines, 205; Haraway's
focus on animals in, 87;
instability of properties for
points of, 7; technics in, 99; as
trinity of human, animal, and
machine, 5–7, 216nn10–11
"Cyborg Manifesto" (Haraway),
87, 88
Cyclonopedia (Negarestani), 137,
250n28

Damacy, Katamari, 201
Damisch, Hubert, 51–52
Darwinism, Gray on, 27–28
Dasein (being-toward-death), 98
Dawkins, Richard, 126, 272n5
*Daybreak: Thoughts on the
Prejudices of Morality*
(Nietzsche), 59
de Landa, Manuel, 273n14
de Tocqueville, Alexis, 257n61
Dean, Jodi, 173, 256n58
death drive, 78
Deep Blue (chess-playing
computer), 22, 219n33
Deepwater Horizon oil disaster,
268n125
Deleuze, Gilles: affection for pet
cat, 91; on animals without
faces, 90; on becoming-animal,
48–49, 50; on desiring machine,
158; on pets, 72, 225n23; on
species as moralism, 56–57; *A
Thousand Plateaus* (Deleuze
and Guattari), 260n81
Derrida, Jacques: on the animal,
93–94; on animal as automatic
responder, 113; on animal
narcissism, 106; *The Animal
That Therefore I Am*, 85; on
avoiding traps of human

exceptionalism, 87; on filming
of elephant execution, 61; on
human–animal relationship,
56; mirror effect in sexual
behavior, 107; on Nietzsche's
empathy toward horse, 225n3;
on other-induced shame of
nakedness, 91–92, 103, 116,
243n11; on realist paintings,
236n65; *Specters of Marx*, 123;
on Western/Middle Eastern
attitude toward animals, 228n20
Descartes, René: on animal as
automatic responder, 113,
242nn4–6; denial of suffering
by animals, 61, 112–13;
Discourse on Method, 111,
112–13; on human error, 242n2,
272n2
desires: authenticity of, 183;
created by capital, 183–85,
267n122; destruction by
libidinal economy, 168–69;
liquidation and replenishment
of, 154–55, 257n64; Lyotard on,
178, 179–80, 182–83, 266n113;
regulation of expenditure, 137
Desk Set (film), 215n4
desublimation and capitalism,
153–54, 256nn57–59
Devor, Robinson, 83
Dick, Philip K., 62
disappearance, act of, 207
disconnection, as zoophilia
motivation, 82
Discourse Networks: 1800/1900
(Kittler), 245n19
Discourse on Method (Descartes),
111
Discovery Channel, 1
dividuality, 197, 272n7
DNA: as genetic memory, 53;

(continued from page ii)

Dominic Pettman is associate professor of culture and media at The New School. His previous books include *After the Orgy: Toward a Politics of Exhaustion, Love and Other Technologies: Retrofitting Eros for the Information Age,* and the cowritten *Avoiding the Subject: Media, Culture, and the Object.*